Library of
Davidson College

Education
and
the Process of Change

Education and the Process of Change

Edited by

RATNA GHOSH and MATHEW ZACHARIAH

SAGE PUBLICATIONS
New Delhi/Newbury Park/London

Copyright © Ratna Ghosh and Mathew Zachariah, 1987

All rights reserved. No part of this book may be reproduced or utilised in any form or by any means, electronic or mechanical, including photocopying, recording or by any information storage or retrieval system, without permission in writing from the publisher.

First published in 1987 by

Sage Publications India Pvt Ltd
M 32 Greater Kailash Market I
New Delhi 110 048

Sage Publications Inc
211 West Hillcrest Drive
Newbury Park, California 91320

Sage Publications Ltd
28 Banner Street
London EC1Y 8QE

Published by Tejeshwar Singh for Sage Publications India Pvt Ltd, phototypeset at South End Typographics and printed at Chaman Offset Printers.

ISBN 0-8039-9527-X (US)

Contents

Acknowledgements   7

1. *Ratna Ghosh:* Introduction   9

STRUCTURAL CONSTRAINTS

2. *Krishna Kumar:* Reproduction or Change? Education and Elites in India   27
3. *Iqbal Narain:* Administration of Higher Education in India   42
4. *Poromesh Acharya:* Education: Politics and Social Structure   64
5. *Suma Chitnis:* Education and Social Stratification — An Illustration from a Metropolitan City   80

ECONOMIC, SCIENTIFIC AND TECHNOLOGICAL ISSUES

6. *A M Nalla Gounden:* Education and Economic Growth: Lessons from India   103
7. *Dinesh Mohan:* Science and Technology Policy in India: Implications for Quality of Education   125

STRATEGIES TO OVERCOME THE CONSTRAINTS

8. *Anrudh K Jain* and *Moni Nag:* Importance of Female Primary Education for Fertility Reduction in India   157
9. *Usha S Naidu:* Child Labour and Education in India— A Perspective   178
10. *Vina Mazumdar:* Education, Development and Women's Liberation: Contemporary Debates in India   198
11. *Rajesh Tandon:* Participatory Research, Educational Experience and the Empowerment of Adults   212

SOCIAL CHANGE FOR CULTURAL REVITALIZATION

12. *Joseph Di Bona* and *R P Singh:* Modernity of Tradition in Indian Education: The Revival of Indian Languages and Indigenous Systems of Education   225
13. *Arvind Sharma:* Religious Traditions in Modern Indian Educational Policy and Practice   245
14. *Mathew Zachariah:* Conclusion: Theses, Antitheses and Syntheses   270

About the contributors   298

Acknowledgements

The Editors sincerely thank the many people who contributed to the success of the Conference and to this publication. It is not possible to name everybody. However, in addition to those whose papers constitute this volume, we wish to list the following persons. Those who were discussants, namely, Philip Altbach (SUNY, Buffalo), Don Attwood (McGill University), May Jean Bowman (University of Chicago), Claude Deblois (Université Laval, Québec), Carolyn Elliot (Case Western Reserve University, Ohio), Jeff Jacob (University of Calgary), Gail Kelly (SUNY, Buffalo), Kari Levitt (McGill University), Madhuri Mathema (Stanford University), Paulos Milkias (Marionopolis College, Montreal), Baldev Nayar (McGill University), Pramud Parajuli (Stanford University), George Psacharopoulos (World Bank), Gunvant Shah (University of South Gujarat) and Katherine Young (McGill University). Also, the people who acted as chairpersons, namely, Joti Bhatnagar (Concordia University, Montreal), Glenn Cartwright (McGill University), Carole Christensen (McGill University), Margaret Gillett (McGill University), Madan Handa (Ontario Institute for Studies in Education, Toronto), George Kurian (University of Calgary), Robert Lawson (University of Calgary), Raj Pannu (University of Alberta, Edmonton), Francis Pinto (McGill University), Douglas Ray (University of Western

Ontario), Arthur Rubinoff (University of Toronto), Bir Sahni (Concordia University, Montreal); and members of the program committee, Ginette Lamontagne (McGill International), Phyllis Browne (Conference Secretary), Ramesh Singal (Conference Coordinator) Sarah Amato, Ann Douglas, Morris Dufour, Rashida Kashevjee, Nina Nichols, Pamela Pritchard, Duffy VanBolkam and Zhijian Lou, without whose help the Conference could not have been a success.

The Conference was made possible by the financial and administrative assistance received from several sources. We gratefully acknowledge the financial support received largely from the Canadian International Development Agency as well as from the Graduate Faculty of McGill University, the administrative support received from the Faculty of Education and the assistance of the Delhi Office of the Shastri Indo-Canadian Institute.

Others who graced the Conference with their presence were David Burke, Secretary-General, McGill University, Lewis Perinbam, Vice-President, Canadian International Development Agency, K.P. Fabian, Acting High Commissioner for India and David Smith, Dean of Education, McGill University.

Finally, we are grateful to James Wishart for his typing and editorial assistance

Ratna Ghosh
Mathew Zachariah

1

Introduction

Ratna Ghosh

This chapter is divided into three sections. The first section describes the Conference on which the papers in this volume are based. Section 2 provides a general overview of Indian education. The third section focuses on the broad issues dealt with in the papers. It is our hope that the dialogue generated in the Conference can be continued here.

1

'Education is that which liberates'. This Sanskrit adage was the theme of the Conference on 'Education and Social Change in India: Reinterpretations and New Directions,' held at McGill University in Montreal in June 1985. On achieving independence in 1947, India set an ambitious goal of liberating its population from ignorance and poverty. The organizers of this Conference aimed at taking a comprehensive look at the role education has played in the reconstruction and revitalization of Indian society over the past four decades.

An important reason for organizing this Conference was to rekindle interest in India as an area worthy of scholarly study in the social sciences, particularly in education. It is our view that the general field of education in India has not received the attention it deserves outside India in the past two decades partly because concerns in other Third World countries have overshadowed India.

We wanted to go beyond the usual issues (such as, the problems of elementary or secondary education) and emphasize others (such as, the relationship between education and fertility behaviour, child labour, and religion). We have also focused on the growing interest in indigenous education and participatory research in adult education. Both the participants and the topics were selected for the variety of theoretical and practical perspectives and the disciplines they represent. We hope graduate students will find this collection useful. All the major papers (except Di Bona and Sharma) were written for this Conference by scholars and practitioners who live and work in India, while all the discussants were from North America—Canadians and Americans—who have been teaching and doing research on the problems of education and development in India. This was done with the idea of having a cross-cultural dialogue. Concurrent sessions were avoided in order to promote full participation and the papers were distributed in advance, as far as possible, so as to generate stimulation and a high quality of discussion. Most of the papers presented here were revised in the light of the discussion sessions. The insightful comments of the discussants are incorporated in the concluding chapter.

2

India is a land with a bewildering variety of religions, languages and people. It is the seventh largest country in the world in terms of area, covering 3,287,263 square miles. It has the second highest population with 685,184,692 people according to the 1981 Census, of which about 354 million are males and 331 million are females. The birth rate is 33.3 while the death rate is 12.5 per 1,000 population. Life expectancy in 1976–77 was 50.8 years for males and 50.0 for females. With a soaring population (25 per cent increase between 1971 and 1981), it is one of the poorest countries in the world with a per capita income of $250 in 1981 (*World Almanac*, 1986).

The people of India belong to different religions. The majority are Hindus (82 per cent), Muslims account for 11.21 per cent of the population, whereas Christians (2.60 per cent), Sikhs (1.89 per cent), Buddhists (0.70 per cent), Jains (0.47 per cent) and others (0.41 per cent) comprise much smaller minorities (1971 Census). In 1981, 23.51 per cent of the total population comprised the Scheduled Castes (104 million) and the Scheduled Tribes (51 million). [Scheduled Castes and Scheduled Tribes are listed officially by the Indian government as deserving special protection and privileges enshrined in the Constitution.]

Although 1,652 languages and dialects are spoken in India (1961 Census), 15 languages have been specified in the Eighth Schedule of the Constitution as the recognized languages of India. Hindi is the official language but the continued use of English as a link language has been authorized by Parliament.

India became independent of British colonial rule in 1947. It is now a union of 22 states and nine union territories with a parliamentary form of government. It is a sovereign, socialist, secular, democratic republic. The Constitution, which came into force in January 1950, guarantees fundamental rights to all its citizens which are justiciable based on the belief that democracy cannot be established unless each individual is assured equality of status and opportunity, and freedom from discrimination. The Indian Constitution looks upon education as a directive principle of state policy which, though not justiciable, is fundamental in the governance of the country (Govt. of India, 1985a).

The Preamble of the Indian Constitution reflects the spirit of Article I of the UN Declaration of Human Rights, that 'all human beings are born free and equal in dignity and rights.' The cornerstones of the Constitution on which the new India was to be built were justice, liberty, equality, and fraternity as inalienable rights of each citizen. These basic values which underlie the new social order are not indigenous to Indian society. The traditional world-view which has been operative for nearly two millennia was one of rigid hierarchy and extreme inequity. Education was categorically exclusive and denied to the lower castes and women. On Independence, the nation looked upon education as a vehicle for the transmission of these new values. The Report of the Education Commission (1954–56) on which the national educational policy was based asserted that if the 'great ascent' to economic development 'is to be achieved without violent revolution (and even then it would still be necessary), there is one instrument and one instrument only that can be used: *Education* . . . it needs the education of the whole population in new ways of life, thought, and work.'

In 1947, India inherited a system with great educational disparities between males and females, upper and lower classes, economically advantaged and disadvantaged groups and urban and rural populations. The downward filtration policy of the colonial period—due to limited economic development, a feudal agricultural society, and a hierarchical society which lacked an egalitarian philosophy—prevented the spread of education. Further, the aim of the colonial administration was to train upper class males for government jobs and the educational system was cast in an elitist and male mould. Social handicaps (such as, *sati*, [the ritual suicide performed by a widow throwing herself on her husband's funeral pyre], child marriage, ban on widow remarriage and *purdah* [literally: veil; refers to a group of traditions that keep women segregated from certain social interactions]) prevented women from being educated. The practice of untouchability and discrimination based on caste prevented the spread of education among the lower castes. A history of isolation in the remote areas led to educational backwardness among the Scheduled Tribes.

After four decades of political independence and six development plans, where does India stand today?

Education has been the primary responsibility of state governments. Since 1976 it has become a concurrent subject and the joint responsibility of the central and state governments. The national policy on education (issued in the form of a government resolution in 1968) aimed at a variety of achievements. These included abolishing illiteracy and providing universal elementary education to children in the age group 6 to 14; providing equal opportunity to every individual to receive all the post-elementary education desired and for which one qualifies; providing equal and adequate opportunities to all citizens for continuing education and life-long learning and maintaining adequate standards. The central government has the responsibility of promoting the education of the weaker sections of the population, particularly the Scheduled Castes and Scheduled Tribes.

Most states have enacted legislation for compulsory education and a $10 + 2 + 3$ pattern of education has been adopted generally. This pattern means ten years of school education, plus two years in higher secondary, followed by three years in college for the Bachelor's degree. The idea was to transfer the intermediate stage (i.e., + 2) to school and make vocationalization of the higher secondary stage easier to suit national development needs. At the end of the Sixth Five-Year Plan (1985), primary education for ages 6 to 11 is free in all states, and for the age group 11 to 14 it is free in all states, except Orissa, Uttar Pradesh and West Bengal. In these states, only girls and members of the Scheduled Castes and Scheduled Tribes get free education. At the secondary stage, several states have free education for all children, and those who do not have free education for girls, Scheduled Castes and Scheduled Tribes.

Tremendous expansion has taken place since 1950 (see Table 1). The literacy rate has risen from 16.6 per cent in 1951 to 36.23 per cent in 1981. The number of educational institutions as well as that of teachers and students has grown rapidly. The number of universities has increased from 27 in 1950–51 to 137 at present. The outlay on education in the national Five-Year Plans has gone up from Rs. 15,300,000 in the First Five-Year Plan to Rs. 25,240,000 in the Sixth Plan. Yet, the availability of educational facilities does not ensure their utilization. The major reasons are socio-economic and cultural constraints, which result in educational constraints.

Although the percentage of literacy has risen by 20 per cent, the absolute number of illiterates has increased. Nearly 120 million people in the functional age group of 15 to 35 are still illiterate. The eradication of adult illiteracy of the functional age group of 15 to 35 in half-a-decade is unlikely.

Regional variations indicate a very wide range of literacy rates— from above 70 per cent literacy in Kerala to 24 per cent in Rajasthan. The gender gap continues to exist. In 1951, 7.9 per cent females were literate as compared to 25 per cent males. In 1981, only 24.8 per cent females were literate as compared to 47.7 per cent males. What is most alarming is that the literacy ratio by sex (number of women per 1,000 men) has barely increased (from 1,058 per 1,000 men in 1931 to 1,322 women per 1,000 men in 1981). Interestingly, states which have higher literacy rates show a greater difference between the literacy rates of men and women, while states with low literacy have less difference in the literacy rates of men and women. For example, the literacy-sex ratio in states like Kerala (1,428) and Maharashtra (1,482) show greater discrepancy than Rajasthan (1,278) and Uttar Pradesh (1,241) (Mazumdar, 1985).

Table 1: Achievements and Targets at Different Levels of Education, 1950–83

Enrolment Figures	1950–51	1978–79	1982–83
Number of Pupils in Class I to V (lakhs)*	191.5	689.6	770.4
Percentage thereof to Total Population in Age Group 6 to 11	42.6	81.6	87.2
Number of Pupils in Class VI to VIII (lakhs)	31.2	181.8	222.1
Percentage thereof to Total Population in Age Group 11 to 14	12.7	38.0	43.9
Number of Pupils in Class IX to XI/XII (lakhs)	12.2	84.1	118.2
Percentage thereof to Total Population in Age Group 14 to 17	5.3	18.8	24.6
Number of Pupils at the University Stage—Arts, Science, and Commerce (lakhs)	3.6	38.2	47.5
Percentage thereof to Total Population in Age Group 17 to 23	0.8	4.9	NA
Institutions			
Number of Primary/Junior Basic Schools	209,671	472,519	50,374
Number of Middle/Senior Basic Schools	13,596	112,801	123,423
Number of High/Higher Secondary Schools	7,288	6,874	52,279
Number of Arts, Science (including Research Institutions) and Commerce Colleges	542	8,698	8,011
Number of Universities†	27	125	137
Teachers			
Number of Teachers in High/Higher Secondary Schools	126,504	818,507	993,115
Number of Teachers in Universities, Arts and Science Colleges	18,648	249,399	NA

* 1 lakh = 100,000
† Includes those deemed to be universities and institutions of national importance
Source: *India Manual*, 1984.

Despite the high priority given to the Constitutional directive of universalization of elementary education (6 to 14 age group), the first target date of 1960 was undoubtedly too ambitious. Nor is the intended target of 1990 likely to see this accomplished. In India today, nearly 30 per cent of the 6 to 14 year-olds or 60 million children, do not go to school. The majority of children who do not enrol are from the socio-economically disadvantaged sections of the population, who for a variety of economic, social and cultural reasons either stay away or drop-out. Poverty is an important cause for not going to school and not wanting to attend school. Poor children work to supplement the family income. 90 per cent of working children are in the villages where poverty is widespread. Even when they do enrol, they are characterized by starting school at a later age, absenteeism, failure, and drop-out due to hunger, malnutrition, illness, and other well-known cognitive correlates of poverty which interfere with their learning and motivation. As a result, poor children cluster in inferior institutions, have less chance of going to the higher educational stage and fail to compete successfully for more prestigious fields of study.

Of the 77 per cent of the children who drop out, a large percentage are girls and those belonging to the Scheduled Castes and Scheduled Tribes. Drop-out rates are higher among girls than among boys and two-thirds of this wastage occurs in Class 1. Only about a quarter of all the girls enrolled in Class 1 complete primary school, and about a fifth reach Class 8. Girls constitute 80 per cent of the total non-enrolled children in the 6 to 14 age group. Their enrolment has been the main hurdle in the universalization of elementary education. Dimensions of traditional culture, religion, and class are linked to attitudes and decisions regarding the education of girls. Despite the most progressive and the wide variety of legislation to counter injustices faced by women, inequality in their education is still pervasive. Notwithstanding the far-reaching changes that have taken place in the position of women since Independence, disparities continue to exist in terms of access at different levels of education, their survival in the system, sex-differentiation in field and content and, finally, in economic outcome.

The gains have been largely in higher education and the benefits have been derived mostly by urban middle class women. Only about 3 per cent of the female population have University degrees and a small percentage of them are visible in positions of power and prestige. Undoubtedly, women's legislation has created a greater awareness of sex inequality but this has not yet resulted in widespread changes in a concrete way.

The number of Scheduled Caste and Scheduled Tribe pupils has gone up three-fold between 1950-76. Yet, the literacy rate was only 21.38 per cent among Scheduled Castes and 16.35 per cent among Scheduled Tribes in 1981. This is despite the fact that the Constitution prescribes special protective measures for the promotion of educational and economic interests of Scheduled Castes and Scheduled Tribes, and the Untouchability Offences Act (1956) makes the caste system illegal. The literacy rate among women in this group is far lower—10.93 per cent among Scheduled Castes and 8.04 per cent among Scheduled Tribes.

The dichotomy in Indian society is such that the commitment to equality itself has conflict built into it (Beteille, 1981) because the law takes the individual as the unit for rewards based on merit (e.g., education). On the other hand, the Constitution recognizes that equality did not exist in traditional Indian society because there was inherent discrimination in attributing merit to groups rather than to individuals. Therefore, certain socially and educationally *backward groups* (Scheduled Castes and Tribes) needed compensation in the form of protective discrimination. The paradox is that a person must establish his or her membership in a Scheduled Caste in order to escape the handicaps and benefit from protective discrimination. Moreover, the system continues to tolerate extreme injustices (such as, a vast majority of illiterates) while a minority benefit from a huge system of higher education. The promotion of equality of opportunity in modern India goes hand-in-hand with a continuing inequality in conditions which exacerbate problems.

The success of education in providing opportunities for social mobility is confined to the middle and upper castes in rural and urban areas. The success of a small number of persons belonging to the Scheduled Castes and Tribes in prestigious civil service jobs through reserved seats, as Kumar points out in this volume, indicates the recruitment of a small number from disadvantaged groups to elite positions. Due to legislation, the caste system has undergone considerable change. Rather than become diluted, there is an apparent increase in caste loyalties and interests which have political dimensions, with some restructuring of caste loyalties and identities. On the whole, however, Scheduled Castes and Scheduled Tribes continue to be the most oppressed groups.

The educational system remains elitist and urban-oriented. This is despite the fact that 93 per cent of the rural population now has access to schools. Mobility is sponsored through private schools into elite institutions of higher learning and positions of power and status in society. The University Grants Commission (UGC) promotes and coordinates University education. The growth rate of student enrolment in higher education has been phenomenal. The student population in higher education has risen to 31,300,000 in 1982–83. India has the largest University population in the world. The proportion of women enrolled at the collegiate level rose from 10 per cent in 1950–51 to 28 per cent in 1982–83. This is because class is an important determinant of educational opportunities for girls. The percentage of Scheduled Castes enrolment to total enrolment rose only slightly from 10.8 per cent in 1964–65 to 12.6 per cent in 1977–78.

However, in terms of fields of study, 40.6 per cent of the total enrolment in higher education is in the Arts stream (56.54 per cent are women). The number of women enrolled in science courses has risen sharply because of the preferential treatment given by the UGC in the 1960s and 1970s to science education in girls' colleges. Female enrolment (at nearly 40 per cent of the total science enrolment) is among the highest in the world. Yet the main problem of the educated is unemployment. In 1977–78, 45.94 per cent of the Arts graduates and 23.66 per cent of the Science graduates were unemployed. It is clear that the direction of expansion in higher education has not been related to the needs and capacity of national development. This expansion has unfortunately been accompanied by an erosion in standards within a system which is dictated by an unwieldy examination structure.

The problems of justice and equality (of opportunity, status, and rights) remain. In addition, the social evils of casteism, regionalism, dowry, and the overriding evil of poverty and its concomitants have been on the rise.

'The desired improvements have not materialized,' according to a policy perspective on the new educational policy, 'because neither the resources nor the measures for restructuring were commensurate with the imaginative and purposeful thrust of the education policy adopted in 1968' (Govt. of India, 1985b). The country now stands on the threshold of the twenty-first century. 'Besides the imperatives arising from the revolution which is taking place in the realm of technology, India is faced with the challenges of accelerated change.'

While India's political revolution may be said to have been adequate, its social revolution is incomplete. The failure to implement the values of a new egalitarian ideology through a national education policy has challenged the effectiveness of education and even resulted, paradoxically, in retarding social change. It is evident that social changes cannot be limited to a legal approach.

According to a Report of the Women NGO [Non-Governmental Organization] (National) Consultation (Delhi, April 1985):

> New values that need to be promoted for the peaceful coexistence of all people and reduction of social tensions and inequalities of all kinds, such as the values of secularism, equal rights of participation of all citizens and of social and economic justice at national and international levels, usually run counter to some of these deeply entrenched, cultural identities.

While an important aim of education is transmission of culture and India's rich heritage, the task of education for national development is to recognize and eliminate those traditional elements which form the basis of exploitation and inequality in society. Educational policy has not been firm in this regard.

This has promoted the formulation of a new education policy which was passed in Parliament in May 1985. The social and economic context for this policy is riddled with problems that have surfaced in regard to the role of education in national development. The marginalization of socially-handicapped groups (like women, Scheduled Castes and Scheduled Tribes) in socio-economic terms has actually accelerated since Independence. Despite goals of equality, there is a growing gender disparity in literacy and employment and an increasing devaluation of women as indicated by an escalation in dowry demands based on rising educational levels. There is a rise in casteism for political ends. The majority of the lower castes are, paradoxically, facing on the one hand, oppression in a caste structured society and, on the other, oppression from among a new elite in their own group who monopolize the benefits of protective discrimination. Greater education has led to 'Sanskritization,' a process which leads lower castes to emulate traditionally hierarchical and inegalitarian elite values (such as, patriarchy). Education has not promoted values of secularism, equality of rights and opportunity and social and economic justice. The structures of subordination in terms of class, caste, religion, and cultural values have been strengthened and contribute to furthering the powerlessness of oppressed groups.

3

In the papers that comprise this book, readers will note that several major themes arise. I shall state them in the form of questions.

Is formal education a sophisticated form of indoctrination on behalf of economic and political elites? Does it promote economic growth? Does it advance scientific thinking and technological literacy? Does education foster social progress or does it merely promote new forms of dependency? How does formal education accommodate or ignore the aspirations of religious, ethnic, and gender minorities? Must education necessarily alienate persons from linguistic, cultural, and religious roots? What role does it have in cultural revitalization? What role, if any, should education play in the urgent matter of reducing fertility rates and changing attitudes towards population growth? What role has education played in promoting or inhibiting women's liberation from ignorance, poverty and injustice? How does the widely prevalent practice of child labour in India affect universalization? How has rapid expansion, erosion of quality and political interference affected the contribution higher education can make in national development? What is India's experience in promoting participatory research and other innovative adult education programs?

The papers in this volume have been clustered around four themes—structural constraints; economic, scientific, and technological issues; strategies to overcome the constraints; and social change for cultural revitalization.

Four articles deal with socio-cultural and political constraints. Krishna Kumar describes the system of education in India which he says reproduces elites rather than produces necessary change. Mobility is sponsored through private schools into elite institutions and the system is legitimized by mass examinations and selection tests which perpetuate the myth of equal opportunity. The benefits of education for social mobility have been largely derived by the middle castes in rural areas. Kumar is disturbed by the trend of survivalism in society and education which he sees as regressive. He insists that the values of egalitarianism and secularism enshrined in the Constitution be reaffirmed.

Iqbal Narain's paper deals with the problems of University administration: the lack of acceptance of 'education' as a part of the University culture, the conflicts arising out of University and national politics, the overpowering influence of examinations, and the uniqueness of educational administration which requires an academic rather than a management perspective. Although education is the dependent variable in a complex socio-economic system, Narain concludes that hope for reform lies within, not outside, the system.

Poromesh Acharya examines the implications of the expansion of popular education in West Bengal (a largely agrarian society) in relation to the special social and political developments there. Here, the benefits of the rapid expansion of educational facilities have been reaped primarily by the upper strata of rural society. The conflict of interests of different strata in society has induced differential responses to education. Acharya ends by searching for an alternative to the present structure, which must be organized by the labour class for universal elementary education through profit-yielding productive labour.

Suma Chitnis explores the results of massive investments in the expansion of educational institutions in terms of bridging the gap between the privileged and disadvantaged sectors of the population. In examining the particular case of the metropolitan Bombay area, she concludes that education has not been successful in narrowing societal divisions, especially for Scheduled Castes.

The next two articles are on economic, scientific and technology policies as they relate to education. Nalla Gounden looks at investment in education, rates of return to education (which he finds are positive and even favourable for some levels), the role of education in economic growth, and income distribution, showing that education contributes to income variance. He concludes that there is a case for increasing service costs for certain types of higher education because the rate of return for them is significantly higher. He also points out that the difference between wages for the lowest as opposed to the highest levels of education is much too great and must be reduced.

Dinesh Mohan dwells on the fall in the quality of India's higher educational system. While acknowledging some achievements in science and technology education, he is highly critical of it in general, and of the quality of scientific research in particular. He advocates disengagement from the West and the rejection of Western models and standards. By drawing attention to the weaknesses of the system, he concludes that the present science and technology policies in India have resulted in a reduction in equity and quality. Mohan advocates certain changes in technology policies (like curtailing the import of technology in areas of strength) which he says will spur meaningful research and make education relevant for science and technology.

Four articles suggest strategies to overcome constraining factors in education in relation to fertility reduction, child labour, women and adults. The relationship between education and fertility has been a subject of much research. Anrudh Jain and Moni Nag discuss this important issue and examine education sector policies in India suggesting modifications from the fertility reduction perspective. By analyzing macro- and micro-level Indian data on education and fertility, the authors demonstrate that education does indeed reduce fertility. Strong arguments are presented for high priority to be given to the increase in female primary education by reducing their high repetition and drop-out rates. Jain and Nag point out that budget allocations do not always reflect the urgency of universal female primary education emphasized in development plans.

Child labour is an important reason for the failure of the universalization of elementary education in India. Usha Naidu looks at the context of child labour and the educational status of a heterogeneous group of more than 13 million working children. She reviews the services and educational programs presently available to them and highlights the constraints in their education. The author concludes that since economic conditions compel children to work, strategies (such as, flexibility in the formal educational structure) be formulated and implemented effectively for their education.

The issue of education improving women's status has been studied in many societies. Vina Mazumdar discusses the major debates in India on this issue. She asserts that despite the founding principle of gender equality in modern India, illiteracy among women is far from being eradicated. Further, the gender gap has generally widened in terms of access, although it reduces at higher levels. Nor has there been a change in social values and attitudes towards women. The author points to the urban middle class bias of policies and their consequent failure for the majority of women. Recent discussions for the development of a new educational policy on the issue of education and women shows a shift in emphasis from access to a demand for change in the nature, objectives, and organizational structure.

Adult education in Third World countries has been a topic of considerable research. Rajesh Tandon examines people's participation through non-formal education in promoting social change in India. He presents illustrations of participatory research as a process which promotes the capacity of adults to seek and utilize knowledge in their interest. Because this process involves the collective empowerment of people, says the author, it reiterates faith in the capacity of ordinary people to transform reality and to bring about development.

The last two chapters discuss social change and cultural revitalization. Joseph Di Bona and R.P. Singh discuss the language question in Indian education. The English speaking elite, who are educated in English-medium schools, dominate cultural life in India and are alienated from the majority of the people who learn Indian languages only. The three-language formula adopted in 1968 has not changed the importance of English-medium schools over the last four decades. The authors argue that indigenous education movements (such as, Gandhi's basic education scheme) failed because the emphasis on manual labour and self-reliance oppose the philosophy of urban English schools which dominate entry to the power structure. Di Bona and Singh end on an optimistic note that the growing trend in politics, in which indigenous elites are replacing the English speaking minority, may eventually spread to the business, government, and professional milieux.

The issue of religious education is discussed by Arvind Sharma. He surveys the historical and ideological evolution of the policy not to impart religious education in state-run schools but to allow it to be imparted in state-aided schools. Sharma concludes that an independent India should not divest itself from the responsibility of undertaking religious education. He advocates the teaching of comparative religion in state schools and that of specific religions in private schools so as to allow religious freedom while avoiding the problem of religious fanaticism.

The chapters in this book discuss the complex relations between education and the process we variously call social change, development and cultural revitalization. What they imply is that the process of education is determined by the very social, economic, political and cultural forces which it affects. As such, education is involved in a dialectical process whereby the major forces in development both influence and are influenced by each other and by the educational system. Moreover, the relationship between education and other systems in society is a dynamic one and in a process of continual change. The identification of these complex processes and relationships has implications for policy issues involving education and the achievement of national development goals.

References

BETEILLE, ANDRE. 1981. *The Backward Classes and the New Social Order*. Delhi: Oxford University Press.
GOVERNMENT OF INDIA. 1956. *Report of the Education Commission*. New Delhi: Ministry of Education.
———. 1985a. *India Manual*, 1984. New Delhi.
———. 1985b. *Challenge of Education—A Policy Perspective*. New Delhi: Ministry of Education.
MAZUMDAR, VINA. 1985. *Education and Women's Equality* (mimeo). New Delhi: Centre for Women's Development Studies.
World Almanac and Book of Facts. 1986. New York: Newspaper Enterprise Association Inc.

Structural Constraints

2

Reproduction or Change? Education and Elites in India

Krishna Kumar

This paper reviews the function of education in the circulation of elite roles in Indian society. Although the term 'elite' is used throughout the paper, this use does not imply that the paper is based on the perspective or ideology embedded in theories of elitism.[1] Rather, the 'circulation of elite roles' is seen as an important aspect of the Indian path of egalitarian social change outlined in the Constitution. In the context of education, this path is described in the Constitution in terms of equality of opportunity, a term which implies the opportunity to rise higher in a stratified society (Bottomore, 1964). The concept of equality of educational opportunity is also consistent with the economic individualism accepted in India's liberal democratic set-up, to the extent that competition is permitted and encouraged as a legitimate strategy for the betterment of one's fortune. Indeed, competitiveness is a salient feature of Indian education, and one way to measure the success of

---

The most well-known theorists of elitism are G. Mosca and V. Pareto. Two major commentaries on Indian society and its recent history from the viewpoint of elite formation are B.B. Misra's *The Indian Middle Classes*, London: OUP, 1961, and B.M. Bhatia's *History and Social Development*, New Delhi: Vikas, 1974. For a competent summary and commentary on elite theorists, see Bottomore (1964). For recent Indian developments in the context of elites, see *Seminar*, No. 299, July 1984.

the competitive ethic in education is to apply it in the context of elite roles.

This paper is divided into three sections. The first section discusses a basic dialectic that governs the relationship between education and social mobility, in general, and mobility to elite positions, in particular. The dialectic is identified in terms of 'early selection' and 'mass examination'. The second section examines the distribution of opportunities for elite status in the case of one elite role, namely, the administrative service. This section also discusses the limits within which education has contributed to social mobility. The last section considers some recent developments that point towards a crisis in the elite's identity. The paper ends with a discussion of the implications of this crisis for education.

Key Dialectic

'Early selection' and 'mass examination' are two important features of the Indian education system. These two features form a dialectic that helps us understand the relationship between education and society, particularly the potential of education to bring about changes in the distribution of power in society through the circulation of elite roles.

By 'early selection' is meant the placing of children when they are very young in different types of institutions. According to Turner (1961), early selection is a major characteristic of systems that permit ascent through 'sponsored' (as opposed to 'contest') mobility. Those children who are selected are placed in separate institutions and are prepared—in terms of skills, behavioural norms, and values—specifically for elite status in their later life. This process accurately reflects the functioning of a large and rapidly growing elite sector of education in India.

Foremost among the schools that distinguish their clientele early from the rest of the children are the so-called 'public' schools. Strictly speaking, the term applies to the 55 members of the All India Public Schools Conference.[2] These schools draw their distinctiveness from the spirit of British public schools, which they

---

[2] Despite their crucial role in the formation of elites, Indian public schools are a neglected area of social and educational research. Among the few studies that have been made are A. De Souza's *Indian Public Schools*, New Delhi: Sterling, 1974, and R.P. Singh, *The Indian Public School*, New Delhi: Sterling, 1972.

imitate and whose historical origins they share. Like their British counterparts, Indian public schools breathe the spirit of a bygone era of history and continue to uphold an unmistakable aura of Imperial days. Tawney's commentary on British public schools applies just as well to their Indian counterparts:

> The better among them owed much, and added much, to the practical energy, the admirable moral seriousness, the respect for the hard grind of the intellect, without fancies or frills, of Victorian England. All of them, including the best, were impoverished by the feebleness of the social spirit of the same England. All of them were the victims of its precipitous class divisions, its dreary cult of gentility, its inability to conceive of education as the symbol and spirit of a spiritual unity transcending differences of birth and wealth (1964, p. 55).

These features would broadly fit a large number of other institutions that are not 'public schools' in the strict sense of the term, but which follow the public school model in matters like early selection, emphasis on a moral code, and the use of English for peer-interaction. The majority of these quasi-public schools are run by private organizations. As Table 1 shows, 44 per cent of all primary schools and over 60 per cent of all secondary schools in India are private. They are run by a variety of interests, ranging from business concerns to religious and ethnic bodies. The Inter-State Board for Anglo-Indian Education and Saraswati Shiksha Parishad are two among the several ethnic organizations whose member-schools operate on the basis of religio-cultural norms along with early selection.

Table 1: Private Schooling in India

	Primary	Secondary/Higher Secondary
Aided Private Schools	201,982 (42.5%)	26,991 (57.3%)
Unaided Private Schools	7,558 (1.6%)	1,672 (3.5%)

Note: Figures in brackets show the proportion in percentage out of the total number of schools at each level.
Source: *Fourth All India Educational Survey*. National Council of Educational Research and Training, 1982.

Both aided and unaided private schools practise different degrees of exclusiveness. At one level is the exclusiveness that comes from charging a tuition fee. This significantly curbs the number of potential clients for the education offered by a school. In their study of private schooling in Delhi, Bhatia and Seth (1975) found that different types of private schools could be grouped in terms of the income of the pupils' parents. They concluded that the 'economic status of [the] parent is a significant determinant of school selection,' and this was true of both aided and unaided private schools. Another type of exclusiveness comes from the meritocratic selection of children aged between three-and-a-half and six years. At this age, 'merit' is judged in terms of etiquette and certain kinds of skills (such as, drawing or piecing together a puzzle). Private pre-schools have mushroomed in all metropolitan towns. They claim to impart such skills along with fluency in English, specifically to facilitate a child's success in meritocratic admission tests. Clearly, the items of merit whereby schools test applicants for admission mirror parental inputs and socio-economic class. Thus, selection by merit becomes indistinct from selection according to socio-economic background.

Private schools are not the only avenue fed by early selection strategies. Within the government's own school system, there are schools that cater to specific groups of parents. 'Sainik' schools, meant for children of military personnel, are members of the All India Public Schools Conference. 'Central' schools are meant for children of the central government's civil servants. These schools are prestigious and they operate with far superior resources than those available to schools run by the state government in the same town. 'Central' schools also follow a different curriculum and examination pattern. There are also schools for 'gifted' children of government employees, such as the Navyug School run by the New Delhi Municipal Committee.[3] Yet another kind of selection-based school within the government sector is the 'model' school which aims to act as a pace-setting institution.

All these different types of exclusive schools offer routes of 'sponsored mobility' to elite jobs. These routes pass through elite institutions at the higher education level—institutions such as the Indian Institutes of Technology, Institutes of Management, Central

---

[3] For a commentary on the understanding of society and progress involved in the opening of the Navyug School, see my *Raj, Samaj aur Shiksha* (State, Society and Education), New Delhi: Macmillan, 1978.

Universities, famous city colleges, and so on. Each of these routes includes screening on the basis of merit, and, with predictable regularity, the products of the private sector of schooling, along with the products of elite schools in the government sector, far outnumber the products of common schools. The National Science Talent Search Examination conducted by the National Council of Educational Research and Training (NCERT) every year throughout the country ends up selecting students from private schools for the majority of the scholarships available.[4]

The private sector is neither an aberration nor a relic of the past. It is accepted as a legitimate means of expanding and improving education. Its meritocratic ideology has answered the common demand that talent should be spotted early and harnessed with whatever means available. The private sector fits nicely in the contradiction that has characterized Indian educational thought and policy on the question of equality versus merit. With rare exceptions, writings and debates on the development of education have always emphasized the need to keep the door for competitive enterprise in education open. The dominant concern has been the maintenance of quality defined in terms of rigour in instruction and the availability of resources. Even the Education Commission (1964–66), which was more egalitarian than any other previous or subsequent body in its outlook, supported the need to develop in the government sector certain 'quality schools' and at least 'one good college in each district' on a meritocratic basis. That the 'good college' will be monopolized by the products of private schools did not concern the Commission. The only way to protect the 'good college' from the monopoly of the better off sections of society that the Commission could offer was the provision of scholarships for the deserving poor. How they would make it to the college level, competing with the beneficiaries of sponsored mobility offered by elite schools through early selection, was not discussed.

The main mechanism operating in the education system to counterbalance the strong emphasis on early selection is that of

---

[4] According to the data given by M. Karlekar in her essay 'Education and Inequality,' (in A. Beteille, ed., *Equality and Inequality: Theory and Practice*, New Delhi: OUP, 1983), 172 or over 70 per cent of the candidates who were successful at the National Science Talent Search Examination in 1976 were from private (including 'public') schools. Out of the 2,176 students of government schools who appeared in the examination, only 17 were successful.

mass examination. Different types of schools share this feature; they are all obliged to take part in either state-level or national examinations. True, a student from an exclusive 'public' school, another from a 'Central' school, and a third from a government school do not compete with each other at the same examination at the end of the higher secondary classes. The first student may take the Indian School Certificate Examination, the second the All India Higher Secondary Examination, and the third the provincial Board's examination. However, all three examinations are mass events, and they share certain core features (such as, the secrecy of the paper-setter and the evaluator, strict invigilation when examinees write their answers, and delayed declaration of results).

These features of the ritual of mass examination carry a symbolic message—that all individuals have an equal chance. Thus, while emphasis on early selection ensures special treatment to the children of those who can afford to make extra inputs, mass examination promises total parity among all candidates. Early selection and mass examination are two conflicting characteristics that together endorse the legitimacy of the education system. While private schools, featuring early selection, ensure that the elite sections of society have a means to provide privileged treatment to their children, mass examination, featuring strict secrecy and parity among examinees, keep the confidence and aspirations of the masses alive.

Historically, the system of mass examination has played an important role in the development of modern education. During the latter half of the nineteenth century, when the old education system—characterized by a loosely structured network of locally-governed schools—died and the new system, with its centralized control, took over, the institutionalization of examinations acted as a major factor in the transformation. As Shukla (1978) points out, the new system depended on written examination to evolve a bureaucratic governance of education. The function of the written, impersonal examination in the emerging education system was to keep the curriculum stable and confined to the prescribed syllabus and text-books. Mass examination provided to the nascent Indian middle class a sense of hope and belief in the fairness of the colonial order. In practical terms, the examination system required students to rehearse endlessly the skills required to enter the newly introduced channels of secure jobs in the service of the colonial government.

The ultimate test of these skills was the Indian Civil Service examination, now known as the Indian Administrative Service.

We can view the transformation of education brought about by the institutionalization of mass examination in terms of the aims of education. The model developed by Weber (1951) on the basis of his study of the ancient Chinese literati helps us understand the change that has taken place in India during the last one hundred years in our perception of the aim of education. Weber says:

> Historically, the two polar opposites in the field of educational ends are: to awaken charisma, that is, heroic qualities or magical gifts, and, to impart specialized expert training. The first type corresponds to the charismatic structure of domination; the latter type corresponds to the rational and the bureaucratic (modern) structure of domination (1951, p. 119).

Centralized examination not only helped to bring education under bureaucratic control; it also reshaped the perception in society of the purpose of education and the image of the educated man. Formerly, the purpose of education was commonly accepted in terms of character-building and spiritual awakening. In the new situation, education began to be perceived as a process of acquiring status and skills. Given the narrow sphere of the civil service within which colonial education could lead to employment, education became associated with the specific skills that civil service required. And the highest image of the educated man became that of the administrator. As administration was the only elite role to which education could be expected to lead, all examinations became preparatory to and therefore similar, in terms of requirements, to the competitive examination for civil service jobs.

Thus, the examination system has played an important role in linking education with competition for the achievement of status and power. Whereas the strategy of early selection practised by the private education system continues to offer safe routes towards status professions to the children of the elite, mass examination offers to the rest of society the assurance that status can also be achieved through competition. So, while early selection is a 'reproductionist'[5] force in

---

[5] The point that education usually reproduces the prevailing social and economic order is not new, yet the term 'reproduction' is currently associated with the research and theorization provided by P. Bourdieu and J. Passeron in their *Reproduction in Education: Society and Culture*, London: Sage, 1977.

Indian education, mass examination is a symbol of the possibility of change. Since the mass examination system is historically so closely linked with civil service, an appropriate context to assess its effectiveness as a means of change—in the sense of change in the composition of an elite role—is the civil service itself. Such an assessment is made in the next section as a starting point to review the relationship between education and social mobility, particularly mobility to elite roles.

Mobility and the Limits of Education

The recruitment for the highest civil service in the country, namely, the Indian Administrative Service (IAS), is a convenient case to study the rate at which the circulation of elite positions is taking place. It also offers a useful, though limited, sphere to assess the impact that competitive, mass examinations have had on the circulation of elite positions, in particular, and social mobility, in general, during the recent past.

The studies made by Subramaniam (1971) and Gopalakrishnan and Joshi (1973) show that the recruitment process for the IAS is to a considerable extent a reproductive one.[6] Both studies show that the children of those already in the civil service form the single largest component of the IAS recruits, and this has consistently been the case year after year. Subramaniam's study showed that the proportion of recruits whose parents were in the higher civil services was from one-fourth to nearly one-third during the sixteen years since Independence. If we combine the recruits whose parents were in the higher civil services with those whose parents were in other ranks, the proportion of this combined category (which Gopalakrishnan and Joshi's study identifies as 'government service parents') comes to 55.9 per cent of the total recruits in 1972. Compared to the 1961 figure of 43.6 per cent, the 1972 figure shows that the already large share of recruits whose parents are in government service (including the IAS itself) is increasing. One can conclude that the highest civil service circulates to a considerable extent within the

---

[6] It is unfortunate that there are no more recent studies than the two discussed here. However, the trends they identify may not have changed much.

families in which parents are already in government service. In the Indian Foreign Service, this circulation has been even more well-established. Subramaniam's study showed that 45.9 per cent of the recruits during 1947–56 and 42.1 per cent of the recruits during 1956–63 had fathers working in the 'higher civil services'.

We arrive at a similar conclusion if we look at the data concerning some other aspects of the recruits' background. Gopalakrishnan and Joshi found that the percentage of 'public' school products has usually been around 10. In the 1972 batch, 15 per cent of the recruits had attended 'public' schools throughout their educational careers and another 10 per cent had completed part of their education there. Thus, no less than one-fourth of the country's highest civil service consisted of products of 42 'public' schools (1974 data). If one adds to this the number of those produced by other types of exclusive schools (such as, convents, and unaided private schools) we should expect to find a much higher proportion. The studies mentioned here did not use such a combined category. However, while analyzing the college-level background of recruits, Subramaniam found that 56 per cent of the total number recruited during 1947–56, and 58 per cent of the ones recruited between 1957–63, were educated in about a dozen famous colleges (such as, St. Stephen's, New Delhi, Presidency College, Madras, St. Xavier's and Elphinstone Colleges, Bombay). These data show that the supply of elite civil servants is a 'reproductive' process inasmuch as a few educational institutions account for a sizeable proportion of the total number recruited. There is little reason to suspect that the situation has changed much since the two studies reported here were made.

These studies also show that the single major means of entry to the elite service, through which the downtrodden sections of society have been able to send their sons, has been the reservation system (which applies to the Scheduled Castes and Scheduled Tribes). It is mainly through this route that recruits from rural or agricultural backgrounds have been entering the IAS. Their inclusion in the service cannot be seen as evidence of the success of the open competition strategy. The 'success' of the strategy would mean that it has been able to break the monopoly of those holding a higher status in society. The only signs that indicate the start of such a process can be identified if one takes into account the caste background of the recruits. A trend towards the slow erosion of the monopoly of the traditionally dominant Brahmin castes was observed by Subramaniam, especially in states such as Tamil Nadu, Maharashtra, West Bengal, and Uttar Pradesh, as a result of the ascendence of landowning middle castes into positions of political dominance.

The rise of 'middle caste' leadership is now widely recognized as a major phenomenon in Indian politics and society. It is often cited as proof of change in social stratification. In states such as Maharashtra, Karnataka, and Uttar Pradesh, the middle castes have emerged as the new rural power who are acting as a major pressure group in the political and economic affairs of their region and, to a certain extent, of the country. Kamat's (1978) study of Maharashtra shows how the middle castes advanced their political and economic interests by using the available educational opportunities and by creating new opportunities for themselves. According to Kamat:

> In the old days education, particularly beyond mere literacy, was mostly confined to the advanced castes—e.g., the Brahmins, the Kayasthas, etc.—to whom therefore the village population naturally looked up as its leaders and spokesmen. Now the situation is entirely different. The rural elite consists primarily of the educated youth of the middle castes and landowning communities (p. 259).

The rural elite of modern Maharashtra have opened private institutions on the 'public' school model and professional colleges for medical and engineering education on a capitation fee basis. The study made by Sivakumar (1982) records a similar phenomenon of the ascendence of the middle castes, especially the Vokkaliga and Lingayat, in Karnataka. These castes have used higher education facilities to advance their interests in the social structure, in particular in the political system.

The success of education in providing opportunities for social mobility, then, is largely confined to the middle castes of rural society—castes that have gained political dominance under the adult franchise system and which got economically stronger by using the facilities provided by the government to increase the productivity of the landowners (Desai, 1984). These middle castes are among the ones recognized as 'backward' in several states; in other states they are grouping together to be recognized as backward.

As Beteille (1981) says: 'The prospects of material advancement through job reservations has led to a kind of competition for backwardness among castes at the middle levels of the hierarchy. This kind of competition creates a vested interest in backwardness, and it combines the worst features of a hierarchical and a free-market society' (p. 48). The middle castes now have a politically vocal elite to represent the interests of their largely poor and educationally deprived following. Whether the language of 'backwardness,' 'caste,' and 'reservation' will prove effective in the struggle to win a better deal for this group is yet to be seen.

The urge for special treatment that we see in different parts of the country among the middle castes is a symptom of the crisis that the vision of meritocracy faces. It would be quite wrong to attribute this crisis to the Scheduled Castes and the Scheduled Tribes to whom the Constitution had awarded a distinct status. The educational progress of the Scheduled Castes and Tribes has been miserably slow despite the modicum of 'sponsored mobility' that they have been offered.[7] If the middle castes were to learn about the advantages of sponsored mobility through reservation from the Scheduled Castes and Tribes, it would have been a long and usually uninspiring lesson indeed.[8] A far more effective lesson was available from the urban elite who never abandoned their right to exclusive schooling for their children while promising all the time an egalitarian social order.

By maintaining a separate system of schooling on the basis of early selection, the urban elite pre-empted the development of a truly mass education system. The system of holding mass examinations did act as a symbolic corrective to a certain extent, but it could not prove sufficiently effective in upholding the myth of open competition and equal opportunity. Early selection impeded the erosion of ascription-based differentiation and also the emergence of an achievement-based differentiation in school and society. The situation described by Parsons (1959) in which the school—as a social institution—differentiates pupils strictly according to achievement, never fully emerged in India because the contest among pupils was

---

[7] For a review of research on the issue, see my 'Educational Experience of the Scheduled Castes and Tribes,' *Economic and Political Weekly*, Vol. 18, Nos. 36/37, 3–10 Sept. 1983, pp. 1566–72.

[8] The jealousy of the few Scheduled Caste individuals who moved up with the help of reservations is a different matter.

curbed by the grouping of pupils in different types of institutions according to their socio-economic background.

Revivalism or Progress?

The strains we see in the social order today are related to the decay of the vision of society that sustained the educated elite during the freedom struggle of the earlier half of this century and the first two decades after Independence. The vision was based on certain value-choices, particularly equality and secularism. I have discussed how equality as a value-choice was rendered hollow by the elite themselves by the maintenance of early selection as a strategy for nurturing the meritorious. By choosing to stick to this strategy, the elite forfeited the opportunity to use education as a means to draw upon the talent and resources of the overwhelming majority of the population. Whether the elite were capable of such an achievement or not is beside the point; what is important is to notice that the elite eschewed the path they had themselves charted in the Constitution—that of mobilizing the resources and talents of all sections of society.

Secularism was another value-choice enshrined in the Constitution, and as the following discussion will show, the chances of a secular attitude flourishing were closely linked to the fate of the first value-choice, namely, equality. Secularism can be understood, according to Khundmiri (1968), as

> . . . that attitude of mind . . . which refuses to accept the division of humanity into religions or races or historical classes as final . . . . It is incompatible with any extreme anti-scientific, anti-intellectual and dogmatic standpoints so far as they affect the solutions of human problems on this earth. It believes that man has a duty to prove his own condition and make the human situation the ultimate arbiter in matters exclusively human (p. 90).

Writings on social change in India during the last hundred and fifty years are replete with references to the impact of such secular ideas on the Indian elite. Education is customarily described as the means whereby certain sections of Indian society came under the influence of secular ideas during the later colonial period. It is a very widely held assumption that the educated, Westernized elite were destined to steer Indian society away from its mythopoeic consciousness towards a secular world-view. Education was the chief instrument with which such steering was to be accomplished. That the elite could use education for this purpose was assumed, despite the realization that there was 'a certain amount of continuity between the traditional elite and the new or Westernized elite' (Srinivas, 1966).

Faith in the instrumentality of education for the development of a secular society has received a serious jolt since the beginning of this decade. This jolt has come from the expression of a demand for the orientation of education in the direction of 'Indian' values.[9] More specifically, the demand is that 'sooner rather than later we must recognize the need of duly adjusting our education to our past' (Sen, 1983). The demand, which applies both to the school and higher level of education, has not been made by a fringe section of professional educators or sectarian politicians. It has been voiced by the topmost offices in the line of education, such as, the Ministry of Education and the University Grants Commission. Also, the current demand needs to be distinguished from previous demands, which were voiced in similar terms. Whereas the earlier expressions of the need for value-orientation in education and the inculcation of religiosity referred to purely educational aims, the present expression of the demand for value-orientation refers to the aim of stopping the moral decay of the whole society itself. The slogan of moral education that one hears today has a distinct political flavour. It represents a fresh regrouping of lobbies within the strata of the educated elite. Moreover, the regrouping cuts across conventional party lines in politics.

The changed situation of today clearly shows that earlier assumptions regarding the contribution of education, during colonial and post-colonial periods, towards the formation of an elite holding secular and egalitarian values were simplistic and erroneous. To a certain extent, the error can be attributed to the fact that historians and other social scientists who wrote about education ignored the

---

[9] Most important among the documents expressing the demand for value-orientation is *Report of the Working Group to Review Teacher Training Programme (in the Light of the Need for Value-Orientation)*, New Delhi: Ministry of Education, 1983. For a collection of commentaries on the demand for value-orientation, see *Seminar*, No. 297, May 1984.

internal processes of education—such as, the curriculum, the norms and content of pedagogy, and the culture of educational institutions. Had they not relied solely on the sentiments expressed by a few among the educated elite, they might have noticed that education in India has never been particularly secular or secularizing. Observation and inquiry, which are directly related to a this-worldly, secular attitude, have been a low priority in the pedagogy of Indian schools and colleges. Also, patterns of authority and daily rituals observed in schools have prevented the growth of a secular culture of education.

The current expression of the revivalist viewpoint on education is linked with the deepening of economic inequalities and the desperation of the elite to project a radiant identity in the midst of crisis. The aggravation of rural inequality in the decade following the Green Revolution, large-scale migration of the landless villagers to cities, the slow growth of employment opportunities, and the urge among the urban rich to live at par with their counterparts in the West are among the factors that have sharpened the conflict of interests in society. In this climate, revivalism has gained new grounds. Its adherents argue that India cannot go any further with borrowed identities such as 'secularism' and 'rationalism.' Also, since inequalities and poverty are here to stay, these should not cloud the emergence of a strong, self-confident identity for the nation as a whole. Such arguments, and the hidden assumptions on which these arguments are based, have great appeal not only for the urban rich but also for the urban middle class and the dominant, landowning sections of the middle castes in rural society. Moreover, the rise of fundamentalism in other countries facing problems similar to India's has found a resonance among the Indian elite across their ideological range. Reference to the ancient glory of India and the promise that it can be resurrected have obvious political value in the present situation. Education, more than any other sphere of cultural activity, is being looked upon as an agency for this resurrection.

The revivalist orientation of education will undoubtedly strengthen the 'reproductionist' tendency of the system and will weaken the energy for change. It is likely that the strategy of early selection will continue to be applied increasingly widely as a means to identify potential merit at an early age. On the other hand, 'value-orientation' will make the harnessing of merit in the chosen student indistinct from indoctrination into a mythologized value system related to ancient India. Thus, education will further aggravate the malady it is supposed to cure. The only real solution is to orient education—both in terms of the structures of selection and the structures of knowledge—to the value-choices enshrined in the Constitution. Pedagogy that is consistent with secularism (such as, learning by inquiry and reasoning) cannot develop within the framework pieced together by the propagandists of 'value-orientation'. On the other hand, the overall merit-pool of society, already stagnant and highly inbred, cannot be enlarged and revitalized unless early selection in all forms is outlawed and fought when it is practised illegally.

References

BETEILLE, A. 1981. *The Backward Classes and the New Social Order*. Delhi: OUP.
BHATIA, C.M. and V.K. SETH. 1975. 'Hierarchy in the System of Schools: Political Economy of Education.' *Sociological Bulletin*, Vol. 24, No. 1, pp. 13–28.
BOTTOMORE, T.B. 1964. *Elites and Society*. Harmondsworth: Penguin.
DESAI, A.R. 1984. *India's Path of Development*. Bombay: Popular.
GOPALAKRISHNAN, M. and R.S.K. JOSHI. 1973. 'Social Background of Regular Recruits to the IAS in a Quarter of Century from 1948 to 1972.' *Journal of the Lal Bahadur Shastri National Academy of Administration*, Vol. 28, No. 4, pp. 554–94.
KAMAT, A.R. 1978. 'Education and Social Change,' in A.B. Shah, ed., *The Social Context of Education*. Bombay: Allied.
KHUNDMIRI, S.A. 1968. 'Secularism, Religion and Education,' in V.K. Sinha, ed., *Secularism in India*. Bombay: Lalvani.
PARSONS, T. 1959. 'The School Class as a Social System.' *Harvard Educational Review*, Vol. 29, No. 4, pp. 297–318.
SEN, I. 1983. 'Education and Traditional Values in India.' *The Education Quarterly*, Vol. 35, No. 1, pp. 1–8.
SHUKLA S. 1978. 'Education, Economy and Social Structure in British India.' *Varanasi National Journal of Education*, Vol. 1, Nos. 1 & 2, pp. 112–25, 70–80.
SIVAKUMAR, C. 1982. *Education, Social Inequality, and Social Change in Karnataka*. Delhi: Hindustan Publishing.
SRINIVAS M.N. 1966. *Social Change in Modern India*. Berkeley: University of California Press.
SUBRAMANIAM, V. 1971. *Social Background of India's Administrators*. New Delhi: Publications Division.
TAWNEY, R.H. 1964. *The Radical Tradition*. London: George Allen & Unwin.
TURNER, R.H. 1961. 'Modes of Social Ascent through Education. Sponsored and Contest Mobility,' in A.H. Halsey, J. Floud, and C.A. Anderson, eds., *Education, Economy and Society*. Glencoe, Ill.: The Free Press.
WEBER, MAX. 1951. *The Religion of China: Confucianism and Taoism*. Glencoe, Ill.: The Free Press.

3

Administration of Higher Education in India

Iqbal Narain

This paper does not offer a description, or even a statistical appraisal, but a qualitative insider's evaluation of the administration of higher education in India. Such an attempt is naturally open to infiltration of the author's own bias, despite all his efforts to the contrary. Another handicap relates to the need to delimit the scope of the paper, which can, again, allow personal prejudice to prevail.

Administration is an all-pervasive concept. Educational administration, being no exception, therefore, covers in vertical terms the entire gamut of the educational system—from school to the university stage—with in-built organic linkages. Horizontally, the university system has to operate simultaneously with professional schools (some of which are a part of the university system as well) and research institutes. These, in turn, add to the dilemmas and problems of university administration in India, by way of a backlash or spill-over effects. However, this paper is only confined to a discussion of the administration of university education *per se*. Here, too, the focus is largely on the internal administration of universities. This should not be taken to mean that university administration in India is merely a case of self-management from within. It is common knowledge that union and state governments as well as central and state level University Grants Commissions (UGC) and other professional bodies (like the Bar Council of India, Medical Council of India and the Indian Council of Agricultural Research) impinge on the working of universities both in positive and negative terms. In fact, more often than not, the problems of coordination among these institutions affect the working of universities. Even courts intervene—sometimes to the embarrassment of the administration within universities. The influences thus generated cannot be entirely ignored, yet it should be repeated that this paper at best deals with them in passing.

The Approach

So far we have only discussed how the scope of this paper has been delimited. A word on the approach to the study of university administration in India will be appropriate here. It is to be noted that educational administration, in general, and particularly university administration, cannot be studied in isolation from the dynamics—in fact, the pulls and pressures—of polity, economy and society in the country. A systemic view is, therefore, necessary for the study of university administration in India (as also, perhaps, elsewhere) which, for all practical purposes, is just a sub-system operating within the confines of a larger societal system—nothing more or less. In fact, the university system in India often finds itself in the unenviable position of being a dependent variable, with the polity, economy and society acting as independent variables. Thus, the university sub-system tends to become a replica of mini-India with such endemic phenomena as political and party interference, the politics of scarcity, caste, class, communal, regional and linguistic loyalties getting the better of academic goals and purposes. This should, however, not be taken to mean that university administration in India uniformly typifies a situation of chaos; the fact is, generally speaking, that it has more islands of excellence than pockets of chaos and the rest exhibits simply a situation of placid normalcy.

The Existing Scenario

Before examining university administration more closely and critically, let us have a brief overview of the major types of universities in that country as well as the objectives of university education in India.

MAJOR TYPES OF UNIVERSITIES

The major types of universities in India can be identified as follows:

(*i*) central and state universities;[1]
(*ii*) residential, affiliating, and residential-cum-affiliating universities;[2]
(*iii*) deemed and full-fledged universities;[3]

---

[1] There are nine central universities in the country which are completely financed by the central government through the UGC. These are Aligarh Muslim University (Aligarh), Banaras Hindu University (Varanasi), Delhi University (Delhi), Indira Gandhi National Open University (Delhi), Hyderabad University (Hyderabad), Jawaharlal Nehru University (Delhi), North Eastern Hill University (Shillong), Pondicherry University (Pondicherry) and Visva-Bharati (Santiniketan). The rest (121) are state universities which are financed by state governments, unless they are private ones. Of course, the union government here also gives plan grants through the UGC, provided the state governments agree to take over the financial liability after the five-year plan period is over. (The data given here and elsewhere in this respect are as of 1 January 1986.)

[2] Residential universities, 35 in number, cater to their own students within a specified area, most of whom are supposed to live as residents on the campus itself. They do not generally affiliate colleges for the award of degrees. There are also non-affiliating but not necessarily residential universities. Seven belong to this category. In contrast, there are 75 affiliating universities which are largely degree-awarding universities and thereby cater to the needs of a large number of affiliated colleges. However, a third variant is now becoming popular, where an affiliating university also has a residential teaching wing of its own. These can be identified as residential-cum-affiliating universities, which are 13 in number.

[3] Deemed universities (17) are those which have shown enough potential to become a university and have as such been recognized by the UGC as potential ones. These are on the road to becoming universities, subject to certain conditions being fulfilled by them. There is another category of institutions of national importance which are also deemed as universities. These in all are ten, as follows:

centrally aided 8
private and state aided 2

(iv) graduate universities and graduate-cum-undergraduate universities;[4]
(v) professional universities and professional-cum-general universities;[5]
(vi) open and eligibility-based universities;[6]
(vii) private and state-aided universities;[7] and
(viii) women's and mixed universities.[8]

GOALS OF UNIVERSITY EDUCATION

The goals of university education cut across the major types of universities identified in the foregoing. The UGC expects each university to pursue three objectives—research, teaching and extension.[9] While research and teaching can be described as age-old objectives of university education, extension is a relatively new goal. This is linked with efforts to take universities

---

Of these, nine are professional and one general. Full-fledged universities, as the name suggests, are those which have already acquired the status of a university. These are 130 in number.

[4] Graduate universities are those which, by and large, run just M.A., M.Phil and Ph.D. classes, though there are some degree and diploma courses also. Jawaharlal Nehru University is an example.

[5] Among the professional universities, one can talk of universities like Pant Nagar which only cater to agriculture and as such relate to a single profession. As far as professional-cum-general universities are concerned, one can refer to such institutions as Banaras Hindu University, which have both professional and non-professional courses under one roof. While the number of professional-cum-general universities in the country is 106, professional universities are (a) agricultural—22; (b) Ayurvedic—1; and (c) technological—1.

[6] Open universities, in contrast to eligibility-based universities, are not always tied down to persons having a prior degree, as a pre-condition for eligibility for the next course. Courses here can also be taken up in parts. There is one open university in Andhra Pradesh and a national open university has recently been established in Delhi.

[7] Unlike the US, there are very few private universities in the country which are owned or largely financed by private sources. The Birla Institute, Pilani, can be cited as an example. The others are supported financially either by the union government or the state government or both.

[8] Women's universities, like S.N.D.T. University, Bombay, only cater to women students. Mixed universities cater to both boys and girls. There are three women's universities, while the remaining 127 are mixed.

[9] See *Policy on Higher Education*, New Delhi: University Grants Commission, 1978.

out of their four walls to society, on the one hand, and to give a vocational orientation to university education, on the other, though the vocational slant is largely directed at the school level. It is also true that universities are somewhat half-hearted and slow in adapting themselves to this new goal which, however, is acquiring an assured place for itself as the country begins to consider education as not just a social welfare activity but an investment in nation-building and development as well.

The system is expected to generate new knowledge in all fields within the reach of the human mind. In addition, it has to evolve principles, methodologies and guidelines for the application of knowledge for benefiting society. It is also expected to provide knowledge and skills for solving the problems of development. It must also enable the students to develop an understanding and a perspective of the physical and social environment. Research and development and extension, therefore, have to be accepted as essential ingredients of the educational process.[10]

It should be mentioned here that the purpose of this essay is not to discuss the problems of university administration according to its major types and goals but, by and large, to raise and discuss issues that cut across them. Of course, there are administrative problems which are specific to different types and goals but they do not constitute the main thrust of this paper.

Towards a Characterization

Let us now characterize university administration in India in terms of common denominators to whatever extent possible, even on the basis of assumptions and hypotheses.

First, the university administration in India offers an *asymmetrical* view as far as its smooth functioning is concerned. There are

---

[10] Govt. of India, *Challenge of Education—A Policy Perspective*, New Delhi: Ministry of Education, August 1985, pp. 68–69. To meet this challenge, the government of India has already adopted a national policy around which an action plan is in the making at present. For details see Govt. of India, *National Policy on Education, 1986*, New Delhi: Ministry of Human Resource Development, Department of Education, 1986.

differences both *among* universities and *within* universities. For example, a commonly held notion is that universities in south India are more peaceful than universities in the north, the former, in turn, presenting fewer law and order problems than the latter. The notion is yet to be empirically tested. Still, by way of explanation, it has been argued that university campuses in the south are less politicized than those in the north. It, therefore, follows hypothetically that the smooth running and management of universities is a function of the relative non-politicization of their campuses.

Similarly, it has been noted that in the professional-cum-general universities, there is less trouble and consequently fewer management problems in centres pursuing professional courses than in places offering, for example, humanities or social sciences. By way of explanation, it has been suggested that professional courses usually have assured career prospects which, in turn, imbue among the students a greater seriousness of purpose about education than what students of humanities or social sciences would have. As such they are less prone to holding the university to ransom. Thus it can be hypothesized that seriousness of purpose about education among the students is a function of assured career prospects.

These two hypotheses require further testing on a broader all-India canvas at different points of time and in various life situations, despite the obvious exceptions to both these hypotheses that come to mind.

Second, the basic issue is whether educational administration, or rather, university administration, is akin to administration in general or is qualitatively different from it. The answer to this question would depend on the reply to another query—whether a teacher is more suited than a civil servant to head educational administration. This is a difficult question to answer. The view which is usually taken these days is that the problems of educational administration are just law and order problems and these are best left to civil servants. This view is, however, too simplistic and stems from the fact that the university community usually refuses to be governed by an academician. A civil servant may at best deliver the goods from a short-term point of view. It is to be remembered, however, that educational administration, particularly university administration, differs from general administration in its development-oriented academic perspective, sensitivity, volatile character and, above all, in the need for a humane, flexible and yet firm approach to management. All this, in turn, requires an academic with a flair for administration to head an educational organization (with a self-disciplined and academically-oriented faculty), who belongs to the world of education and knows that a solely mechanistic law-and-order approach may keep an educational institution going but would deprive it of its right to develop naturally. However, there are exceptions among civil servants who could meet this requirement, where academics may be found wanting. But exceptions need not always prove the rule.

Third, it can hardly be denied that, more often than not, there is a wide gap between the formal and the actual, between the ideal type of educational or university administration described earlier and its empirical reality. By and large, it would not be wrong to say that the case of academic administration in India has gone by default. It has been a case of politics of survival at every level—a stereotype of law-and-order administration for which also the university administration has to depend in good measure on the district authorities. It is a situation more of maintaining the *status quo* than of furthering academic development, let alone of achieving change through education. In fact, the Vice-Chancellor and other authorities hardly have any time for the latter, though they could still make a difference if they are prepared to quit than to yield to irrational pressures. The general university scene in India with, of course, some exceptions can best be described with reference to a despatch in *The Times of India*:

> 'Our tragedy is that we are trying to find a substitute for learning in education and courage in administration.' This observation, made by an eminent educationist nearly a decade ago, still holds good in a far greater measure in respect of Lucknow University today than ever before.
>
> Hardly a week passes without some unsavoury incidents bursting on the academic scene. These involve the alleged issue of fake marksheets, leakage of question papers, irregularities in admissions, casteism in appointments and promotions, false claims by rival groups of teachers or administrators and proliferation of self-styled leaders of students, teachers and employees— all threatening agitation on one excuse or another.[11]

[11] *The Times of India*, 10 May 1985.

Finally, another fact is that examinations have tended to become the be-all and end-all of university administration in India, which are always on trial on this front with a handful of students trying to get the examinations postponed as much as possible and the authorities trying to hold them as scheduled. Some universities are found conducting examinations throughout the year—sometimes, main examinations (and, quite often, those of earlier years); at other times, the supplementary examination; sometimes an improvement examination, if not a second one, with the struggle to postpone examinations continuing all through. Almost any university in Uttar Pradesh could easily illustrate this point. It is not surprising that one of the criteria for evaluating the success of a Vice-Chancellor in the government and public eye has naturally become whether or not he can hold the examinations on time. They are not concerned about whether the courses have been properly finished prior to the holding of examinations, let alone the quality of teaching, whether there has been adequate secrecy about examination papers, or whether there were any cases of cheating or mass copying in the examination hall or not, and so on. This is a sad state of affairs and may become a situation of siege for the Vice-Chancellor. He usually knows that university administration, as one of the key instruments in the quest for academic excellence (which, in turn, is a positive input in the process of social change), is much broader in scope than merely holding examinations on time. He may want to gain new horizons on the basis of this valid assumption, yet he is held back because he is continually bogged down by the single-minded effort to hold the examinations as scheduled. To quote a government document on the subject which adds explanatory dimensions to the argument developed here:

> No description of the contemporary educational scenario can be complete without a reference to the examination system since it decides, not only the fate of students, but also the content, orientation as well as the quality of education at all levels. Apart from evaluating examinees on the basis of rote learning and memorising, their annual periodicity creates an environment in which students tend to while away their time for most part of the year and gear themselves to work for the last three or four months. For obvious reasons, lack of continuity in application results in the building up of unbearable pressures at the end of

the year which find expression in boycott of examinations, leakage of question papers, mass copying, payment of bribes to evaluators and other unethical practices. Consequently, degrees and grades do not generally command credibility as a whole with the public as well as employers in the public and private sectors and the whole process of higher education has become warped, disoriented, and dysfunctional, producing a large number of unemployable young men and women.[12]

It would be worthwhile to ask in this context whether delinking jobs from degrees would help the situation. In a manner of speaking, this has already been done because an employer usually treats a university degree as merely a base for eligibility and holds a separate test for actual recruitment. However, beyond this, one has to take the suggestion with a pinch of salt; otherwise, whatever objectivity is possible in selections based on degree-linked appointments in terms of qualitative criteria for eligibility and evaluation may also be lost in the wake of scarcity of jobs which has its natural corollary in the manipulative politics of patronage.

It is interesting to note that the attitude of the public has been, by and large, of unconcern towards the issue; those who have mentioned it have been rather divided in their response. The National Institute of Educational Planning and Administration (NIEPA) has analysed nearly 1,000 letters regarding the new education policy addressed to the Prime Minister, the Union Education Ministry and the Education Secretary to the Government of India received between January and May 1985.

In the letters under study, and among the multitude of issues touched by the respondents, delinking is the least frequently mentioned issue: 42 responses relate to delinking as against 447 in the case of content and curriculum. But there is something very unique about this both in terms of diametrically opposite

---

[12] *Challenge of Education—A Policy Perspective, op. cit.*, p. 9. For a penetrating analysis, see Amrik Singh, *Common Sense about Examinations*, Delhi: Oxford University Press, 1984. One may particularly recall an observation from his Preface:

> During the last few decades we have put all the emphasis on testing and how to improve it and make it more valid and reliable, but very little has been said or done in regard to teaching and learning. In consequence, we have neither been able to ensure good learning nor good teaching (p. 7).

views expressed as well as the complexity of the issue indicated by the respondents.[13]

The same survey further elaborates:

> There is broadly a three-fold division of the viewpoints relating to delinking. The first favours delinking by highlighting all its positive features. The second group consists of those who, while advocating delinking are also against it in certain cases, like engineering, medicine and other professional and technical fields. The third group comprises those who are questioning the very assumption on which the plea is made, besides explicating the serious implications it will have both in the educational as well as in the employment sectors.[14]

The Government of India seems to have opted for the view of the second group, as its latest policy document shows.

External Variables

As already indicated, university administration is not just a case of self-management from within. There are various natural influences of society (such as, stratification), of polity (in terms of interference, mainly due to patronage), and of economy (in the context, say, of manipulation of appointments because of their limited number). Other external but not necessarily non-interventionist variables relate to both government, semi-autonomous and autonomous bodies.

First, both the central and state governments, quite often tend to regard the office of the Vice-Chancellor as a political office and would like the incumbent to promote their partisan interests.

> The problem lies in the traditions of public life that we have developed wherein the pre-eminence and omnipotence of political authority in all walks of life is encouraged and fostered. Where institutions depend upon governmental support it is considered

---

[13] *Towards Restructuring Indian Education: Citizens' Perception* (mimeo), New Delhi: NIEPA, 1985, p. 52.
[14] *Ibid.*, p. 67.

natural that the government should have all the residual power and ultimate control over them. A democratic polity in which state-aided yet statutorily autonomous institutions in different walks of life—education, culture, sports, social welfare or mass-communication—can function with true independence has yet to strike roots in our public life.[15]

The government is not to be entirely blamed here. University and college employees, more often than not, are so faction-ridden and politicized that they report to the government, every now and then, that everything is rotten in their institution and that government intervention alone can set the house in order. Thus, the government often enters educational institutions at the invitation of those who are supposed to be guardians of their autonomy and self-management. Both types of cases have been noted. The situation is confounded when one buttresses the other.

Similarly, the union government has not always been doing all it can under its concurrent jurisdiction concerning education and has failed to bring about uniformity even where it has been found to be necessary. We could refer in this context to the story of the 10 + 2 + 3 system of education. The consequent situation of chaos is best described in the words of Malcolm S. Adiseshiah:

> At the Higher Secondary stage, there are several problems. First, as a recent study *Higher Secondary Education* (Pune: Indian Institute of Education, 1984) shows, there is utter chaos in the ... country at the + 2 stage. Five states—Punjab, Haryana, M.P., Rajasthan and U.P.—have still not adopted the 10 + 2 + 3 system. Vocationalization of the + 2 stage has not been adopted by most states; in one state which has a student enrolment of 180,000 at this stage, only 7,200 students, less than 4 per cent, are in the vocational stream, and that is the general position in most stages ... the location of + 2 stages varies widely; in a few states it is part of the school system and is called Higher Secondary, in others it is called junior college, either attached to degree colleges or established independently, in one the 11th year was attached to school and the 12th year to college, and in still others it is

---

[15] M.S. Gore, 'Universities and the Government,' *University News*, Vol. 24, No. 4, 23 January 1986, pp. 5–6.

called pre-degree and is part of the college affiliated to university.[16]

Concluding the argument, he observes:

> This wide-ranging variation is one of the reasons why the double purpose of this 2 year stage of education has not been understood or accepted by students, parents, teachers, state governments and society generally, and this is also the reason for the confusion in the curricular offerings of this stage of education. (Double purpose refers to the academic and vocational streams.)[17]

One can well imagine the situation when, in a state like Uttar Pradesh, all the state universities opt for the 10 + 2 + 2 system and a central university (like the Banaras Hindu University) goes in for the 10 + 2 + 3 stream, the latter option, in turn, becoming an administrative challenge for the institution to retain against both internal and external pressures. The non-enforcement of the three-language formula is another instance of non-action in the concurrent jurisdiction. Such examples are many.

Second, the role of the UGC can be a crucial variable in the functioning of the administrative system within universities. This may be so in different ways, some of which are listed here:

(*i*) The UGC Chairman or his/her nominee is usually associated with choosing a panel of Vice-Chancellors for a given university. This can help to build a panel of competent people in an impartial, non-partisan and non-sectarian manner. If the UGC succeeds in doing so, half the battle is won.

(*ii*) The UGC can act as a bridge between state universities and state governments, which are rather niggardly in their financial support to universities. Consequently, they cannot avail of UGC support in the wake of the five-year plans as well, as state governments do not readily take up the liability once the plan period is over. This role on the part of the UGC is even more necessary since state governments are not easily persuaded to take up the responsibility for programmes of excellence which the UGC initiates. So universities lag behind even when they

---

[16] Malcolm S. Adiseshiah, *Malaviya Memorial Lectures, 1984*, Varanasi: Banaras Hindu University, p. 19.

[17] *Ibid.*, p. 16.

have talent. One may recall here what M.S. Gore, Vice-Chancellor of Bombay University, has to say in this respect, which sums up the experience of all state universities: 'Delayed finalization of the plans, delayed acceptance by the state and the consequent short-falls in university utilization of plan allocations has become an indirect device of "economizing" on development expenditure.'[18] This has repercussions on the office of the Vice-Chancellor who

> has to function on the basis of a fast-dwindling prestige, since he is constantly at the doorstep of government officials for money to keep the university going and, on the other hand, he has to compromise at every step to get his way in bodies whose members are not accountable for the impact of their decisions on the working of the university.[19]

(*iii*) The UGC has to go beyond its fund-disbursing role and take up audit in terms of quality control in regard to the functioning of universities. The UGC has now adopted the role of quality controller within the confines of the concept of university autonomy, but it still has to go a long way in this regard. If pursuit of excellence is the objective both of the university system and the UGC, the former would only be re-inforcing the latter by quality control, which should not be regarded as an invasion of university autonomy. One may recall here what the report of the Conference of Vice-Chancellors, convened on 21–22 May 1984, had to say in this respect:

> The creation of the UGC itself has brought the issue of 'academic freedom' of universities to the fore. The Commission's responsibility is to coordinate and maintain standards of education, examination and research for which, among other things, the Commission can prescribe minimum qualifications for the appointment of teachers and it can lay down minimum standards for the award of any degree by any university—but through their Acts. The universities believe, or at least some in the universities believe, that these are exclusively the responsibilities of the universities. It has to be

---

[18] M.S. Gore, *op. cit.*, p. 3.
[19] See *Challenge of Education, op. cit.*, p. 50.

clarified that the Commission's statutory powers in this respect are over-riding. National standards would not exist and chaos would prevail if each university, entirely on its own, decided upon the duration of courses, standard of facilities, performance, etc. Sharing of facilities, coordination of teaching or research and maintenance of standards would only benefit all universities and the nation as a whole. The relationship of the universities with the UGC should find a suitable mention in the Acts of the universities. In fact, in every state there should be a committee of inter-university consultation and coordination, particularly in research.[20]

(iv) There have also been cases of lack of coordination between/among:

(a) The UGC, Education Ministry and Ministry of Finance;
(b) The UGC and other autonomous organizations, like the Bar Council, Indian Council of Agricultural Research, Bio-Technology Board; and
(c) The UGC and state governments.

These, in turn, have administrative implications for the operation and management of the university system. Some examples would illustrate the point. For example, the delay in the approval of the recommendations of the Cadre Review Committee of the UGC has been due to lack of coordination between the UGC, the Ministry of Education and the Ministry of Finance, which, in turn, could create unrest among the employees in the central university campuses. This is also true of the recommendations of the UGC about bringing the pay scales of the Registrar, Deputy Registrar and Assistant Registrar at par with those of professors, readers and lecturers, respectively. Again, the Bar Council can prescribe a five-year integrated course for law without prior clearance from the UGC (which would not provide the additional financial and human resource inputs required for implementing this recommendation by the universities). The Deans of law faculties can pressurize the Vice-Chancellors of their respective universities, who would find

---

[20] *Conference of Vice-Chancellors*, convened by the Ministry of Education and Culture and University Grants Commission (21–22 May 1984); *Proceedings*, New Delhi: University Grants Commission, 1984, pp. 41–42.

themselves helpless due to the deadlock between the UGC and the Bar Council.

Further, the Indian Council of Agricultural Research can insist that scientists working on the various research schemes over a period of time should be absorbed in the university's regular cadre in the capacity of lecturers, readers and professors, to which the UGC would not readily agree. This, in turn, would create unrest among scientists working on research projects and adversely affect not only their performance and efficiency, but also funding by the Council for schemes of agricultural research. Again, the Bio-Technology Board can choose departments in some universities to start study and research in this new area. However, the implementation of the scheme would be delayed because of the lack of co-ordination between the UGC and the Board.[21] Finally, as stated earlier though in a different context, the UGC would like state universities to negotiate with their respective governments. The UGC does not usually like to enter into a dialogue with state governments on behalf of state universities regarding the posts and schemes which its own committees would recommend on merit. This would create tension between the affected departments and the university administration.[22] Such examples are, again, many.

(v) Finally, the UGC will also have to streamline its own procedures of work with a view to achieving speedy action, the lack of which adds to the administrative problems of universities. For example, there is no reason for a delay in clearing the creation of posts which have been approved by the Finance Committee, which, in the case of at least the central universities, have both a Secretary/Joint Secretary from the Ministry of Education and a Secretary of the UGC attending the meetings as official invitees.[23] Again, the UGC/state governments could evolve a procedure by which instalments of dearness allowance could be disbursed simultaneously to government and university employees and thus avoid unnecessary pressure on the Vice-

---

[21] These illustrations embody my experience as Vice-Chancellor, Banaras Hindu University, Varanasi.

[22] This has been my experience as Vice-Chancellor, Rajasthan University, Jaipur.

[23] In fact, this observation was made by one of the Joint Secretaries of Education when I (as Vice-Chancellor of Banaras Hindu University) complained of the delay in the clearance of posts by the UGC.

Chancellor. Further, visiting committees which assess the development requirements of a university should be sent in the early stages of a five-year plan (and not in the last two years as it sometimes happens) so that the none-too-efficient university administration can fill the sanctioned posts and spend money on equipment, building, and so on, judiciously and in time.[24] One could easily continue listing such examples.

The Internal Dynamics

We shall now discuss the more important trends in the internal administration of a university outlined against the systemic framework because in this context, the lines between the external and the internal are really blurred.

(*i*) **The Office of the Vice-Chancellor.** The Vice-Chancellor is the key-stone of university administration and the success or failure of the latter depends, to a large extent, on the former. There are, however, many imponderables attached to his role. *First*, the question is: how is his office being viewed and treated by the powers-that-be? Is it being taken as a political office, or a bureaucratic office[25] or the office of a scholar/teacher-administrator, on the one hand, and an office of dependence or accountability, on the other? *Second*, how does he perceive his own office? Besides the categories already noted, he has also to decide whether he would like to be a factional leader or an independent non-partisan Vice-Chancellor; whether he would like to follow a policy of appeasement, irrespective of whether the demands are reasonable or not, so that he survives in office or say 'No' to unreasonable demands even though this may cost him his job or may lead to the closure of the

---

[24] This refers to my experience as Vice-Chancellor of Rajasthan University and Banaras Hindu University.

[25] The office does not become bureaucratic only when a civil servant is occupying it. A teacher-Vice-Chancellor can also behave in a bureaucratic fashion and may decide to run a university in a mechanical way according to the rules. It cannot be denied, however, that the bureaucratization of administration is, in fact, partly inherent in the university scene because the moment a Vice-Chancellor makes even a genuine exception, he is in the dock for partisan action, unless he is prepared to make the exception a general rule.

university;[26] whether he would just somehow run the university or also be obliged to work for its academic development;[27] whether he would like to centralize all power in himself or evolve a decentralized system of administration;[28] whether he would always manipulate for his own survival in office or be prepared to quit when he cannot serve honourably; and so on. *Third*, it is also a matter of debate whether the office suffers from a lack of power, or external fetters on their exercise, or want of will and courage on the part of the office-holder or weak governmental support or all of these, together. At any rate, there is too much dependence on the office of the Vice-Chancellor by the university system—who ultimately has to decide on his own whether to fight the battle or take the university system down the drain. This is a crucial choice and the Indian experience illustrates that the choice is not easy, though both the options can be (and have been) exercised in actual life.

(*ii*) **Politicized Campuses and University Administration.** The politicization of university campuses is another feature. All political parties try and develop cadres in universities. The emergence of teacher-politicians who use students as pawns in their game is another well-known phenomenon. Student unions and trade unions among teachers and *karamcharis* [clerks] provide regular forums for the formulation and expression of demands and,

---

[26] The Indian experience tells us that a totally inflexible attitude towards demands is not possible; some compromise is inevitable. The point at issue here is whether the compromise is on basic parameters of the governance of a university or its peripheral aspects and whether the Vice-Chancellor is himself clear about the limits of indulgence and whether he has made them known both in words, and more important, in practice.

[27] It should be mentioned in this context that a Vice-Chancellor has a hand-to-mouth existence and is usually bogged down by just running a university, even when he may consider its academic development an important part of his role. However, the perception of this facet as part of the self-image of his role is the point at issue here, as this would have a bearing, however limited, on the empirical profile of his performance.

[28] My experience has been that even when power is decentralized, the heads, principals, directors and the deans, more often than not, would like to pass the responsibility back to the Vice-Chancellor instead of taking decisions themselves for which they are legally competent. Worse still, they even tell the faculty members, students and employees, as the case may be, that they had forwarded the case under reference to the Vice-Chancellor for a decision—little realizing that, in the ultimate analysis, the university administration would either sink or swim together.

ultimately, through agitations, hold the university to ransom. The time and energy of the university administration is wasted in dealing with demand charters and containing agitations. The silent majority of teachers and students suffer and withdraw, though they continue to work. This is responsible for whatever remains of the university system in India today. On the whole, the consequence is:

> Even significant educational reform creates more problems than it solves because the pressures are difficult to withstand—providing a large variety of diploma and certificate courses has often been misused by groups of students who just want to prolong their stay in hostels or the university to either live cheaply or earn leadership and make mischief; internal assessment which is the most appropriate form of evaluation for many kinds of academic performance has often been misused to inflate the marks either uniformly for all or selectively for those who can threaten teachers with dire consequences. The pursuit of rights is so strong that duties often go by the board; even teachers cannot be made to work.[29]

Even an official document on educational policy concedes that

> political issues might be debated within the precincts of the university at the intellectual level but the administrative system of the university should not be used or subverted for the ends of any political party. This view would necessarily predicate the exercise of self-restraint by all concerned, *i.e.*, the central government, the state governments and also by other parties not in power. There is an urgent need of establishing a consensus on the issue. Whether any legislative measures are called for also needs consideration.[30]

Leadership in post-independent India has so far failed on this score; leaders appear to have, in fact, given up.[31] Can they rise to the

---

[29] *Conference of Vice-Chancellors, op. cit.*, p. 41.
[30] *Challenge of Education, op. cit.*, pp. 115–16.
[31] As a member of the Commission on Status of Teachers in Higher Education, I asked Mrs. Indira Gandhi, then Prime Minister of India, in the discussion that followed her forthright address to a joint meeting of the two national commissions on the Status of Teachers in India, 'Can we depoliticize university campuses?' Her reply

challenge now and save the educational system from a total collapse? This is an open question. Can the silent majority of students be mobilized in favour of depoliticization, which they really want? This is the only hope, though again an open question. One can recall here an interesting experiment which Charan Singh tried successfully in Uttar Pradesh: to make membership of the students' union optional. Unfortunately, the experiment was given up later.

(*iii*) **Rotation of Headship and Democratization of University Governance**. The rotation of headship and the process of democratization of university governance have, at best, yielded mixed results and, at worst, these have failed. The unity of perspective in the academic planning and development of a department have been lost in the wake of the rotation of headship, though in some cases it has put an end to the continued tyranny of a bad head. While, in a few cases, democratization has resulted in the much-desired participative management, it has, more often, provided institutional forums for factional warfare and unwanted criticism of the head by non-serious academics, on the one hand, and distribution of work on the basis of non-academic criteria, like raising of hands, on the other. Perhaps these innovations better suit the democratic milieu of the West than the feudal societies of the Third World. Thus, there is a need to re-think this question also. The basic issue here is whether the experiment has not been given a fair trial or whether it has failed. The question is: Can democracy and educational administration exist together; and, if so, in what form and to what extent?

(*iv*) **Poor Finances and Growing Dependence on Government**. The financial position, particularly of the state universities, is very weak. To aggravate the problem, a real boss has emerged here in the guise of the finance officer who has little appreciation of the demands of educational administration as, more often than not, he brings to bear just an accountant's perspective on financial administration. The lack of planning at the university level

---

was, 'You know it better than I do. We cannot do so now. We failed to do it when one could have done so.' I wondered what the available alternative was, in that case. Should we give in and give up? This remains one of the basic challenges facing educational policy in India today.

for the scientific distribution of scarce financial resources further aggravates the crisis. The want of managerial skills to put these resources to optimum use further worsens the situation. On the whole, as mentioned elsewhere also, the Vice-Chancellor is usually reduced to the position of an errand boy for the collection of funds. As M.S. Gore has put it:

> While the danger of nationalistic, religious, class and political interest factors impeding the right of the academic to free enquiry cannot be altogether denied, they do not, to my mind, constitute the major problem area in the relationship between the government and the universities today. The most common problems that arise between the two seem to be in the somewhat more mundane areas of the structuring and finance of university education and the formulation of education-related policies.[32]

(v) **Myth of University Autonomy**. There can be no denying the fact that university autonomy is a prized feature in any university system, provided it is buttressed by a sense of self-discipline and accountability. However, the absence of this is more pronounced today than ever before. The concept of university autonomy can hardly survive in the wake of tensions between the Chancellor and the Chief Minister about the choice of a Vice-Chancellor,[33] though

> it is hardly likely that a governor will choose a Vice-Chancellor for a university without consulting the government—particularly the Chief Minister and Education Minister—and it is extremely

---

[32] *University News*, Vol. 24, No. 3, 16 January 1986, p. 1.

[33] Even a lay observer of the university scene knows that while a Vice-Chancellor would sometimes cultivate a Chief Minister or a Governor (Chancellor) for his survival, at other times, the Chief Minister and the Chancellor would differ about the appointment of a Vice-Chancellor in a state university. In both cases, the office becomes a political office which is antithetical to the concept of university autonomy; nor does it leave the Vice-Chancellor free to govern a university independently without political interference though with a sense of accountability. However, a Vice-Chancellor 'may at times find that the Chancellors' office and the government between them provide him with an excuse for not doing what he does not wish to do. But a Vice-Chancellor who makes a habit of so playing one centre of influence against the other will in the long run find himself in difficulty because he will have lost the confidence of both.' M.S. Gore, 'Universities and the Government,' *op. cit.*, p. 2.

unlikely that he will choose a person who is unacceptable to the government. That would not be wise either, since in the last analysis, the Vice-Chancellor cannot function without cooperation from the government.[34]

This is even more true when universities have to turn to the government almost every day for the maintenance of law and order on the campus, on the one hand, and for finances for survival, leave alone development, on the other. As stated earlier, whatever still remains of university autonomy is doomed when teachers, instead of setting their own house in order, run to the government frequently, to inform them that the university administration is being mismanaged and they should come to its rescue. It should be remembered, however, as the Gajendragadkar Committee put it, that:

> ... university autonomy does not suggest that universities are a state within a state, and a law unto themselves. The concept of university autonomy, however, means that it would be appropriate on the part of democratic legislatures not to interfere with the administration of university life, both academic and non-academic. The claim for autonomy is made by the universities not as a matter of privilege, but on the ground that such an autonomy is a condition precedent if the universities are to discharge their duties and obligations effectively and efficiently as regarding imparting and advancement of knowledge, and also making their unique contribution to the life and development of the nation. There are two aspects of university autonomy—(*i*) autonomy within a university, and (*ii*) autonomy in relation to agencies and authorities external to it, the most important of which is the state.[35]

Towards the Future

The discussion here should neither be taken to mean that the university sub-system in India has completely

[34] *Ibid.*, pp. 1–2.
[35] Quoted by Amrik Singh in 'University Structure: Autonomy and Other Issues,' published in *Higher Education in the Eighties: Opportunities and Objectives*, New Delhi: Lancer International, 1984, pp. 190–97.

failed, nor that it has reached the point of no return in a situation of relative decay today. In fact, the purpose of the essay has been to highlight the nature of the challenges and dilemmas that the university administration in the country is facing at present. It will also not be out of place here to mention that, though the political will of the ruling elite and a gentleman's agreement on the part of political parties 'to leave the universities alone' will be helpful (if these could be achieved), the real and lasting reforms in university administration will emanate only from within, from the joint efforts of the faculty members, students and the administration. External props cannot help for long; nor can externally induced reforms endure. Till this happens, the educational sub-system, particularly the university sub-system, can at best serve as a barometer for the spill-over effects of social change, and quite often only superficially. They cannot become spontaneous agents of induced social change of a positive kind (which is characterized by a balanced and happy blending of what is best in tradition, as symbolized in the country's composite culture) and modernity (as reflected in the onward thrust towards science and technology).

4

Education: Politics and Social Structure

Poromesh Acharya

This paper studies the problems of popular education in an agrarian society. It examines the implications of the vast expansion of educational facilities in West Bengal in relation to particular social and political developments since Independence. It highlights the structural and attitudinal roots of unequal participation of different strata of rural society in the existing program of primary education. In conclusion, a search has been made for an alternative course to universal elementary education.

West Bengal, one of the constituent states of India, is predominantly agrarian. It has an area of 88,752 sq. kilometres and a population of 54 million. Here, 73.51 per cent of the total population lives in the rural areas and there are 38,074 inhabited villages. The agrarian sector provides employment to 62 per cent of the total working population. Thirty-seven years after Independence, universal primary education is still the unfinished business in West Bengal that it is in the rest of India. This is despite the gigantic expansion in educational facilities during this period. The relation between political development, a differentiated rural society and the growth of a segregative system of education in West Bengal after Independence is the focus of this paper and this may afford a better insight into the problems of development.

Growth of Education Since Independence

In 1950–51, there was only one university, 90 colleges of general education, 19 professional colleges, 1,107 high schools, 1,261 middle schools and 14,783 primary schools in West Bengal. The total number of students was nearly 2.1 million while the total number of teachers was about 71,000. Expenditure on education during 1951–52, was only 9.3 per cent of the total expenditure in West Bengal for the same period (NCERT, 1961, p. 680; Government of West Bengal, 1959, p. 11).

In 1980–81, after thirty years, there were 8 universities, 281 general colleges, 45 professional colleges, 5,067 high schools, 3,157 middle schools and about 50,000 primary schools in West Bengal (Government of West Bengal, 1981, Table 3). Nearly 41,000 primary schools are located in the rural areas, while more than 8,000 are in urban areas. It is commonly believed that most of the villages in West Bengal have a primary school. There are almost 0.28 million teachers in West Bengal. The expenditure on education has also increased considerably and is now about 30 per cent of the annual budget of the state. According to the Director of Public Instruction (Government of West Bengal, 1981, Table 3.3), the total number of students was about 8.6 million in 1980–81. This data, however, should not be taken at face value. These figures have been collected by head teachers from school records. It is well known that school records are not properly maintained by head teachers, particularly in rural areas. The common practice is to inflate the number by fictitious enrolment. Hence, an error of 15 to 20 per cent may reasonably be assumed. In any case, there is no doubt that the number has increased considerably. More important is, however, unequal enrolment and its structural and attitudinal roots. This may give us some insight into the implications of the growth of educational facilities.

A program of universal education has three components—universal facilities, universal enrolment and universal retention. Universal facilities may not ensure universal enrolment and universal enrolment, in turn, may not guarantee universal retention. On the other hand, differential participation may render the growth of education instrumental to social differentiation. In that case, education becomes an instrument of change but in a different direction.

Differential Participation and Its Implications

According to the Fourth All India Educational Survey (NCERT, 1982, Table 170) conducted in 1978, 70.86 per cent of the children in the age group 6 to 11 years in the rural areas were enrolled in schools. In a survey conducted the same year in four villages of Bankura and Malda districts in West Bengal, it was found that contrary to official claims, only 49.51 per cent of the children in the age group 6 to 11 years were enrolled. The findings of this survey are very revealing in regard to the differential participation of different strata of rural society in the existing program of school education.[1]

It has been found that there is a very close correlation between educational achievement (in terms of literacy and enrolment) and agrarian class structure. There is also a correlation between educational achievement and caste status and income level. In fact, the frequency distribution of families to agrarian class, caste and income level as has been found in the survey, indicates a close relation (if not a perfect correlation) between them. Literacy and enrolment rates decline very steeply in accordance with the hierarchical order of agrarian society.

At the primary level, 84.11 per cent of the total number of enrolled students belonged to the three upper strata of agrarian society, namely, the *jotedars*, rich peasants, and middle peasants (who constitute only 52.24 per cent of the total population). At the secondary level, 98.70 per cent of the total number of enrolled students belonged to the three upper strata. It is even more interesting to note that 100 per cent of the children in the age group 6 to 11 years belonging to *jotedar* families were found to be enrolled in contrast to only 5.66 per cent of the children of the same age group belonging to agricultural labourers. As for other groups, 84.34 per cent of the children of the same age group from rich peasant families, 50.84 per cent from middle peasant families and 21.34 per cent from poor

---

[1] I conducted this survey in connection with the research project—'Problems of Education of the Weaker Section of Rural Community'—jointly sponsored by the Indian Council of Social Science Research, New Delhi, and the Indian Institute of Management, Calcutta. In this paper, I have extensively used the findings of the survey from the two reports of the project, namely, *Education and Agrarian Relations* and *Structural and Attitudinal Hindrances to Popular Education* (cyclostyled).

peasant families were found to be enrolled. Not a single student in Class V came from a family of poor peasants or agricultural labourers. Only 5.26 per cent of the students in Class IV belonged to poor peasant families and none to agricultural labourers. There is an abrupt break in enrolment in Class II for agricultural labourers while enrolment for poor peasants falls abruptly in Class III.

The two upper classes—namely, the *jotedars* and rich peasants—no doubt, fare much better in regard to enrolment and achievement than the two classes at the bottom—namely, the poor peasants and agricultural labourers—through all the successive stages of education. It has also been found that 25.17 per cent of the total number of non-enrolled children in the age group 6 to 16 years are gainfully employed as child labour while 98.67 per cent of the child labour belongs to the three agrarian classes—agricultural labourers, poor peasants and lower-middle peasants. Above all, teachers and members of local school committees and local *panchayats* [a village-level council for local self-government] also generally belong to the top two agrarian classes (Acharya, 1981a).

It is worth noting that agrarian class status has been determined in the survey by the nature of participation in the production process. *Jotedars*, at the top of rural hierarchy, do not take part physically in cultivation, but unlike 'landlords as a pure rentier class,' supervise field labour regularly and bear the entire cost of cultivation, including the cost of hired labour. Rich peasants are those who not only supervise but also participate manually in at least one major operation of crop production. In the rural hierarchy, they are second to the *jotedars*. The middle peasants rely mainly on family labour to cultivate their holdings, but may also employ a few outsiders. Poor peasants cannot subsist on the earnings from their small holdings and are obliged to work on other people's land. Agricultural labourers are even worse off, being entirely dependent on earnings from agricultural work on other people's land.

The results of other surveys also largely corroborate the findings of the fore-mentioned survey. In another survey conducted in three villages of Burdwan district during the summer of 1974, it was found that 'school-age children from poor peasant and agricultural labour families constituted 18 and 23 per cent respectively of the total; yet only 10 per cent, equally divided between these classes, of the total school-going population came from their midst.' It concluded that 'the existing school system barely caters to the needs of the children from the economically weaker sections' (Chandra, 1983, p. 257).

Another survey, conducted by the Scheduled Castes and Tribes Welfare Department (1971, 1972) of the state government in 44 villages of 7 districts in West Bengal, holds that 79 per cent of the children in the age group 6 to 10 years and 88.7 per cent in the age group 11 to 17 years belonging to Scheduled Caste and Tribe families were non-enrolled. This indicates the extent to which existing educational facilities have been appropriated by the classes which stand higher in the social hierarchy. This unequal participation has contributed to the process of structural and cultural differentiation in India after Independence.

Structural Differentiation: Political Development and Culture Gap

It is apparent that the upper strata of rural society in West Bengal has reaped almost all the benefits of the gigantic expansion of educational facilities. In fact, they have been benefited in various ways. Not only are their children the sole beneficiaries, but as teachers they have appropriated a major part of the huge expenditure incurred by the state for the expansion of educational facilities. In West Bengal, there are now nearly 0.28 million teachers. They comprise nearly 1.65 per cent of the total working population. The number of primary teachers has increased from 43,000 in 1950–51 to 149,000 in 1980–81. In the rural areas, this has strengthened the position of the *jotedars* and rich peasants in the hierarchy. Educated members of these classes have adopted the teaching profession as a subsidiary occupation. They generally invest their cash earnings from their subsidiary occupation in land for double-cropping high-yielding varieties and thus enhance their social and economic position. However, they do not need to pay much attention to their subsidiary occupation once in service, as their employment is secure.[2]

---

[2] In rural West Bengal, for example, a number of primary teachers do not even come to school regularly. In fact, there is a practice in many areas, called *pari lagano*, i.e., attending duty by rotation. In other states, like Punjab, substitutes are employed

After Independence, a large number of colleges and universities were established by the government in mofussil areas to meet the growing demands of the rural neo-elites. These are, however, second-rate institutions which mainly train teachers and other white-collar workers. Looking at how the program of primary education works, one doubts whether the expansion of educational facilities was meant for educating children or for providing teaching jobs to educated unemployed young people from the upper and middle strata of society. It is unfortunate that in the present system of education from above, these teachers and members of school committees (who come from the upper and middle strata) are expected to fill the gap between the government and the masses below. This may be one reason for the non-participation of the labouring classes in the existing program of universal primary education. It is obvious that they play a rather negative role in regard to the education of children from the lower strata. The lower strata in rural society generally maintain that these teachers, leaders of village institutions and government officials are either against or reticent about the education of the lower strata (Acharya, 1982a, p. 32).

The vast expansion of educational facilities has, in fact, helped to sharpen the differentiation in rural society rather than reduce it. The resultant uncongenial social condition has made the process of universal education even more complicated. Before Independence, peasant politics centred around the issue of *zamindari* abolition. In fact, peasants, in spite of differentiation, were more or less united against the landlords or *zamindars*, who were their common foe. Leadership was surely in the hands of the big *ryots* and *talukdars*, without 'permanent rights on fixed rent' in land. After the abolition of the *zamindari* system in the 1950s, a section of the big *ryots* and *talukdars* rose to form the rural neo-elites.[3] The so-called green

---

at a nominal pay by primary teachers who keep the profit without doing any work. This is similar to subinfeudation in land (as developed after the introduction of Permanent Settlement by Cornwallis). Uma Shankar Dikshit, Governor of West Bengal, in a convocation address at Jadavpur University stated, 'Apart from lack of adequate infrastructural facilities in primary schools, there often was widespread indiscipline, absenteeism, double employment and deputation of substitutes who shared a part of the regular teacher's salary' (*The Statesman*, 1 January 1985).

[3] *Talukdars* were landholders in Bengal, during the colonial period, who generally enjoyed permanent rights on land taken from a *zamindar* usually as a lessee, but not always on fixed rent.

revolution accelerated the process. It may be noted that the fruits of the green revolution are largely confined to the higher strata of the agrarian society (Swamy, 1983, p. 265). The growth of the tertiary sector (particularly the growth of education), helped the process further. Universal franchise also contributed to changing the structure of political power in rural society. It is interesting to note that the number of farmers grew over successive parliaments. They composed the largest single group in the last four Parliaments.

Culture Gap

The spread of English liberal education among the upper strata of agrarian society has also widened the culture gap between classes. Before Independence, liberal education (however appropriate for the leisure class) was mainly limited to the urban gentry and a small coterie of rural elites, the *zamindars* and other privileged people of a higher caste. It is interesting to note that only 35.09 per cent of university and college students came from the rural areas in 1950–51. The antipathy to labour implicit in liberal English education or pre-British Brahmanical Sanskrit education was still to extend below the landlords and the privileged people of higher caste, who were numerically a very small group. *Ryots*, big or small, who composed of the bulk of the rural society were cultivators and used to productive labour on land. The anti-labour culture of English liberal education did not spread as it has today.

It is interesting to note that even during the 1920s and 1930s, peasants (including the big *ryots*) generally treated school education and indigenous education differently. A story narrated by Abul Monsur Ahmed, a contemporary literary and political figure, is revealing in this regard. Abul Monsur and his fellow-students once requested a peasant who was ploughing a field, to allow them to plough the field for a while. The peasant refused to oblige because, according to him, educated people should not touch the plough.

Ryots were generally cultivators who enjoyed only occupancy rights on land as subjects of the *zamindars*. The rent payable to the landlords or *zamindars* could be enhanced by them on various grounds. Besides, there were various types of *abwabs* (illegal extortions) from the *ryots*.

Abul Monsur belonged to a family of big *ryots*. He argued, citing the example of his elderly relatives who were quite learned in Arabic and Persian but ploughed their own land. The peasant, however, was not convinced. According to him, there was a difference between school-goers and *maktab*-goers [an elementary school run by, or in association with, a local mosque]. To him only school-goers were educated (Ahmed, p. 55). In fact, education and *babu* [commonly refers to a lower class male, usually a lower level civil servant] culture became synonymous after the introduction of the English system of education in the nineteenth century.

It is significant that colonial rule created conditions congenial to the growth of a new class known as *bhadralok* [the middle class in Bengal]. It is to cater to the needs of these *bhadralok* that the modern system of education developed during the nineteenth century in Bengal. Modern Bengali language developed during the nineteenth century as the language of the *bhadralok*. Modern language text-books developed as a corollary to the new system of education and reflected the cultural world of the *bhadralok*. In the process, indigent people who had participated in the indigenous vernacular system were left out of the elementary system of education that took its place. Education became the exclusive preserve of a *bhadralok*. In fact, the new education system of the *bhadralok* developed in relation to the destruction of the indigenous system of the indigent people (Acharya, 1984, p. 23).

During the colonial period, there emerged a class of English educated people in Bengal. There was a sharp cleavage between the English educated few and the illiterate rest. After Independence, there developed a three tier system—a few at the top with an elite English schooling, a large group of neo-elites in the middle with education in ordinary Bengali schools and the vast majority of illiterate labourers at the bottom. It is evident that a segregative system of education grew in accordance with the social differentiation and political development since Independence.

The Problem in Perspective

It is apparent that mere expansion of educational facilities and external incentives—like free books or mid-day meals—may not be sufficient for resolving the problems of popular education in an agrarian society. On the contrary, expanding educational facilities may make the situation more complex. As Philip Foster (1971, p. 29) has rightly observed: 'Quite obviously, formal education insofar as it is unevenly distributed contributes to the process of structural and cultural differentiation. But substantial problems arise if privileged groups "capture" the educational system in such a manner as to use it as an instrument for maintaining existing status differentials.'

It appears that, in an agrarian society, structural and attitudinal obstacles to popular education are much more important than others (such as, the so-called 'cost factor' or 'standard of education'). Unequal participation of the different strata in the existing program of education in West Bengal and the close correlation between the agrarian class structure and educational achievement (as has been found in the survey of four villages in the state) surely corroborates the point. It may be noted that in the survey, the classification of rural society was made on the basis of the work process and degree of exploitation involved. It was reasonably assumed, therefore, that the conflict of interests of the various agrarian strata was largely responsible for the differential responses to the existing education program.

The Attitudes of Different Strata

The attitudes of different strata of agrarian society may illustrate the problem better. It is interesting to note that only 19.70 per cent of the respondents in the four villages surveyed, covering all strata, opted for universal compulsory elementary education while 54.64 per cent were against it. The classwise break-up of the respondents shows that the overwhelming majority of the upper strata (namely, the *jotedars* and rich peasants) were against universal compulsory elementary education. It is also evident that the lower strata as well were not favourably inclined towards the introduction of universal and compulsory elementary education. However, 14.86 per cent of the respondents were ambivalent in this regard. The two upper strata mentioned earlier did not show any such ambivalance, by and large, while the lower strata suffered most.

ATTITUDE OF THE UPPER STRATA

The attitude of the upper strata is significant, particularly since 100 per cent of the children in the age group 6 to 11 years belonging to *jotedar* families and 84.31 per cent belonging to the rich peasants were already enrolled. Compulsion or not, it would make little difference to the education of their children. Why then did they respond so overwhelmingly against compulsion?

The reasons are very simple. They were against compulsion because they feared that universal and compulsory enrolment would deprive them of the easy supply of child labour. In that case, they would be forced to hire adults instead at a higher wage. This would increase their cost of agricultural production. Besides, they feared that labour relations would deteriorate if the labour classes were educated. The general feeling was that the labour classes would refuse to submit to the authority of the higher strata and would try and assert their rights and privileges once they were slightly educated. The upper strata in rural West Bengal were in favour of the traditional authority pattern and would resist any measure which was in any way likely to upset this.

It is even more interesting to note that 90 per cent of the rich peasants, 80 per cent of the *jotedars* and 62.06 per cent of the upper-middle peasants responded in the affirmative when asked whether universal and compulsory education would cause any inconvenience to them. In fact, 53.93 per cent of the total respondents belonging to the higher strata opted for employing illiterate field labourers in preference to literate field labourers; only 22.47 per cent preferred employing literate labourers; 46.06 per cent opined that field labourers would not like to work as labourers if they were educated while 37.07 per cent considered that this would not happen. A majority (61.97 per cent) of the respondents feared that field labourers would demand higher wages if they were even partially educated. The most important question is, however, the question of labour relations. This is a very sensitive issue in the villages and the upper strata usually refrains from discussing such issues with outsiders. It is significant that one-fourth of the respondents evaded the question in regard to labour relations; 38.20 per cent feared that labour relations would deteriorate if the labour classes received elementary education and 35.95 per cent did not subscribe to this view.

So it can be safely concluded from the responses of the upper strata to different related questions that the overwhelming majority are against educating the lower strata. The reasons, as just observed, are deep-rooted in the existing relations of agrarian production. E.E. Biss (1921, p. 7) may not be wrong when he observes: 'One more unspoken objection to universal education is perhaps well answered in the words of Diderot: "There is no doubt but that it is more difficult to suppress a peasant who can read than any other man".'

The structural hindrances in promoting the educational interests of the lower strata as noted in the foregoing may be termed hindrances from above. There are hindrances even from below, i.e., in-built hindrances from the lower classes themselves. It is interesting to note that Hodgson Prat, Inspector of Schools, South Bengal, in 1857, observed:

> The poorest classes, those who form the mass, do not want schools at all because they do not understand the use of education, because they are too poor to pay schooling fees and subscriptions, and because the labour of their children is required to enable them to live. The middle and upper classes will make no sort of sacrifice for the establishment of any but English schools. (Stark, 1916, p. 78).

It appears that his observations are still valid.

ATTITUDE OF THE LOWER STRATA

We have already mentioned that the lower strata too were not very favourably inclined towards the introduction of universal and compulsory elementary education. Only 18.29 per cent and 16.88 per cent of the respondents belonging respectively to the class of agricultural labour and poor peasants favoured the introduction of universal compulsory education while 43.90 per cent and 48.05 per cent respectively expressed themselves against it. It should be noted that a large number of respondents from the lower strata were ambivalent in this regard. This is unlike the *jotedars* and rich peasants who had a more positive stance. A majority (65.55 per cent) of the respondents belonging to the lower strata—comprising agricultural labourers, poor peasants and lower-middle peasants—considered that the introduction of compulsion would cause inconvenience to them.

Regarding the non-enrolment of their children, most of the respondents had more than one reason. These were, mainly: (a) poverty, (b) lack of interest in education, and (c) the necessity for their children to work for the family. It is interesting that 41.11 per cent of the total respondents belonging to the lower strata (the largest number) expressed lack of interest in education as one of the major reasons for not sending their children to school. In fact, 15 per cent of the respondents did not enrol their children in school simply because they were unwilling to educate them. Another 26.11 per cent indicated lack of interest in education as one of the reasons for the non-enrolment of their children.

The other major reason for non-enrolment is that children are required to work for the family. Of the total number of respondents belonging to the lower strata, 32.79 per cent felt this was one of the reasons for the non-enrolment of their children while 10.55 per cent felt this was the only reason. It is interesting that 19.44 per cent of the respondents stated poverty to be the reason for the non-enrolment of their children but only 5 per cent stated poverty as the only reason.

An examination of the responses regarding what non-enrolled children do during school hours, reveals that the largest number of respondents stated that these children either help in housework or hire out their labour for some extra income for the family. It is significant that 29.44 per cent of the total number of respondents from the lower strata stated that their non-enrolled children were gainfully employed. Further, except for 7.77 per cent of the total number of respondents belonging to the lower strata who stated that their non-enrolled children simply while away their time during school hours, the rest, in fact, maintained that their non-enrolled children were required to work for the family.

It is evident that child labour and labour relations are the two main issues which create most of the problems in popular education. In an agrarian society, employers are against universal education as they fear a deterioration of labour relations and the withering of an easy supply of child labour. On the other hand, the labour classes suffer from internal contradiction between individual interest and class interest because of child labour. Some families are likely to be deprived of their children's earnings under universal education.

But, on the whole, the total income of the labour classes is likely to go up as adult labour will be hired in lieu of child labour at a higher wage if child labour is withdrawn from the market. There are, however, other reasons for the reticent attitude towards universal education. One is that these classes are unsure of the benefits of education and apprehensive of their employer's wrath.

Alternatives to Elementary Education

The crucial question for a program of universal elementary education is how to motivate the labour classes towards education. It follows from the foregoing discussion that though the majority of the lower strata could not be motivated towards education till now, this is not an impossible task. Basic education or the *nai talim* of Gandhi may be said to be the answer. In fact, *nai talim* or 'education through profit-yielding productive labour' is likely to resolve many of the problems peculiar to agrarian society. It will strengthen the bargaining power of the labouring class by resolving their internal contradictions. The loss to individual family incomes through sending earning children to school may be largely compensated as children will earn while they learn. Besides, the labour component of the education system is likely to make it relevant to their life situation. The existing program, on the contrary, with its anti-labour-culture component is more suited to the leisured classes.

The education program, as formulated after Independence, only aggravated the crisis instead of resolving it. If Gandhi's creed of *nai talim* (or basic education) had been adopted as the sole educational process for our country by the framers of our Constitution, the entire course of education would have taken a different turn. It would have been easier to adopt basic education as the only system at the elementary level and a common school system at the secondary level since differentiation among peasants was not as sharp then as it is now. The political unity of the different strata of agrarian society vis-a-vis the *zamindars* and their affinity to manual labour could have been conducive for adopting such a course of education. It is unfortunate that our policy-makers failed to uphold the cause of the labour classes.

It should be noted that basic education was not acceptable to many political leaders. M.A. Jinnah rejected the scheme as communal. A.K. Fazlul Huq, the first Premier of undivided Bengal, considered it objectionable as, according to him 'the scheme would turn schools into factories or ashrams'. Congress leaders were also not eager to give it anything more than lip-service. Nirmal Bose (1962, p. 204) lamented:

> It is also interesting and significant that after Congress came into power, several expensive schools were established in different parts of the country. And these were modelled after the public schools of England . . . . In other words, a grave blow to the new educational system of Gandhi was delivered from within than from without.

The Central Advisory Board (CAB) of Education, just before Independence, accepted the Gandhian concept of basic education 'but without its acid test of self-sufficiency'. Our Constitution mentions only 'free and compulsory education and makes no reference of the type of education—basic or non-basic' (Naik, 1966, pp. 3, 5). In fact, the CAB killed the soul and our Constitution buried the body of basic education. Now there are few even to hold a lamp at the crumbling tombstone.

Education through profit-yielding productive labour, or basic education, is still the only conceivable alternative course for the labour classes, particularly, in an agrarian country like India. But, without solving the problem of instrumentality it is not possible to successfully implement such a program. The course of development after Independence has made the task much more difficult.

It appears that our system of primary education has reached a point where no piece-meal measures are likely to work. We should start afresh if we want any tangible results. It is unfortunate that instead of opting for basic education, we have depended more on piece-meal measures to solve the crisis of universal education. The recent attempts made by the West Bengal government to abolish English at the primary level and withdraw the language text-book, *Sahaj Path* (by Rabindranath Tagore) as the only text-book, from primary schools may be cited as examples of such piece-meal measures. The failure of the West Bengal government to even implement such measures are only natural. The strong resentment expressed by the privileged classes (particularly, the urban middle class) and the agitation organized by them to protest against these measures ultimately compelled the government to compromise and abandon its radical stance (Acharya, 1981b; 1982b).

Political developments in India since Independence have contributed largely towards determining the course of educational growth. There developed a differential system of education to satisfy the needs and aspirations of different strata of society. Nobody cared about the people at the bottom of the social hierarchy who are considered to be the rejects of society. In fact, a resistance syndrome has already developed. The upper and middle strata (who have reaped all the benefits and almost captured the system of education) are likely to oppose, either overtly or covertly, any attempt to change this differential system. As a result, it can be fought only politically. It is only at the political level that the problem of instrumentality can be resolved.

After thirty-seven years of lop-sided educational development, the only course open for a universal system of education is to rouse the labouring classes to demand and organize an education for themselves. In fact, initiative from below is a pre-condition for the successful implementation of any program of popular education. The labour classes must become aware of their invulnerable political strength as against their economic weakness. A program of non-formal education guided by such an aim could be a viable strategy for encouraging initiative from below. This could be a program for training educational workers from the weaker sections of the rural community who, in turn, could organize programs of political awareness for adults and literacy for children in the age group 6 to below 9 years. It should be noted that children below 9 years are not generally employed as child labour.

A two-phase program has been envisaged here. In the first phase, the program will aim at training educational workers from the weaker sections of rural society and a take-off level of literacy for children from the weaker sections. In the second phase, universal elementary education through profit-yielding productive labour will be aimed at. A *panchayat*, composed of people exclusively from the weaker sections, will be entrusted with the task of supervising the progress made. Unfortunately, the existing peasant organizations and *panchayats* are not only unwilling but incapable of taking up this task in West Bengal. And this is in spite of the declared policy of the West Bengal government to process all rural developmental work through *panchayats*. An alternate peasant leadership imbued with the partisan attitude of a crusader is the need of the day.

References

AHMAD, A. 1978. *Atmakatha*. Dacca: Khosroj Kitabmahal.
ACHARYA, POROMESH. 1981a. *Education and Agrarian Relations, Part I: Report, A Study of 4 Villages in West Bengal*.
——. 1981b. 'Politics of Primary Education in West Bengal.' *Economic and Political Weekly*, Vol. 24, pp. 1069–75.
——. 1982a. *Structural and Attitudinal Hindrances to Popular Education, Part II: Report*.
——. 1982b. 'Abolition of English at the Primary Level in West Bengal.' *Economic and Political Weekly*, Vol. 4, pp. 124–28.
——. 1986. 'Development of Modern Language Text-Books And The Social Context in Nineteenth Century Bengal.' *Economic and Political Weekly*, Vol. 21, No. 17, 26 April.
BISS, E.E. 1921. *Report on the Expansion and Improvement of Primary Education in Bengal*, Calcutta.
BOSE, NIRMAL. 1962. *Studies in Gandhism*. Calcutta: Bose.
CHANDRA, NIRMAL. 1983. 'Agricultural Workers in Burdwan,' in Ranjit Guha, ed., *Subaltern Studies*, Vol. 2, pp. 228–58.
FOSTER, PHILIP. 1971. 'Access to Schooling,' in Don Adams, ed., *Education in National Development*. London: Routledge and Kegan Paul, pp. 13–33.
GOVERNMENT OF WEST BENGAL. 1959. *Quinquennial Review on the Progress of Education in West Bengal*, Calcutta.
——. 1981. *Statistical Handbook*. Calcutta: Bureau of Applied Economics and Statistics.
NAIK, J.P. 1966. *Elementary Education in India, the Unfinished Business*. Asia Publishing House.
NCERT. 1961. *A Review of Education in India. First Yearbook of Education (1947–61)*. Delhi.
——. 1982. *Fourth All-India Educational Survey*. Delhi.
STARK, H.A. 1916. *Vernacular Education in Bengal from 1813 to 1912*. Calcutta.
SWAMY, S. DALIP. 1983. 'Differentiation of Peasantry in India' in S.A. Shah, ed., *India: Degradation and Development, Part II*. Hyderabad: M. Venkatarangaiya Foundation, pp. 259–78.
THE SCHEDULED CASTES AND TRIBES WELFARE DEPARTMENT, GOVERNMENT OF WEST BENGAL. 1971. *On Educational and Economic Achievement*. S.K. Basu, R.N. Saha, Special Series No. 13, Calcutta.
—— 1972. *Twenty Villages of West Bengal*. B. Chakraborty, P. Roy, Special Series No. 14, Calcutta.

5

Education and Social Stratification—An Illustration from a Metropolitan City

Suma Chitnis

A Difficult Transition

Education in pre-independence India was categorically exclusive. Several forces converged to create this exclusiveness: First, the notion that knowledge is sacred and, therefore, not to be imparted to the ritually impure lower castes. Second, the fact that the country had very limited use of formal schooling. A small, educated manpower was required for administration, and there was some room for the functioning of scribes, scholars, doctors, lawyers, mathematicians, and so on. But, on the whole, the economy had not advanced beyond a rudimentary division of labour and family-based skills and crafts adequately served most of the needs of a society that lived by simple subsistence or feudal agriculture. Third, the fact that neither the native princes who had preceded them, nor the British colonial rulers, were committed to schooling the masses and the British, in particular, consciously subscribed to what was known as the 'downward filtration theory' or the conviction that benefits provided to the masses would eventually trickle down to the rest of the population. Finally, and perhaps most significantly, the fact that until very recently the Indian consciousness and conscience had not really been invaded by sentiments of equality, by a sense of the social and political obligation to provide for education, both as a basic human right and as an instrument of social mobility, and by the awareness that universalization of schooling is the cornerstone of economic advance and social development.

Inspired by dreams of economic development, through the application of technology and industrialization, and fired by the ideals of democracy, equality, abolition of caste and by the vision of their country as a strong, integrated and advancing nation, the planners for independent India set high store on education. They saw it as a basic human right and as an instrument for economic, political and social change and development—the Indian Constitution initially promises free and compulsory education to all children, up to the age of 14 years.[1] The constitution also promises equality of opportunity for education at all levels, and special provisions for the educational advancement of some of the weaker sections of society, such as, the Scheduled Castes (former Untouchable Castes) and Scheduled Tribes, traditionally excluded from schooling.[2]

The transition has been extremely difficult. The backlog of illiteracy and inherited educational disparities of various kinds—for instance, between the rural and urban population, between men and women, between children from families involved in agriculture or in urban labour and children from families in white-collar occupations, between the upper castes and the lower castes and, of course, between the rich and the poor—have proved to be much too forbidding to overcome.[3] Efforts to universalize schooling and to establish equality of opportunity for education have been thwarted by many factors—for example, the sheer inability of the rural as well as the urban poor to spare children for school, or the inability of the government to ensure efficient administration of the facilities provided; and, above all, the inability to halt the new forces towards

[1] Article 45 of the Constitution of India.
Subsequently, the immediate target has been scaled down to the less ambitious goal of universalizing education up to the completion of primary school.

[2] Article 46 of the Constitution of India.

[3] Only 16.7 per cent of the population of the country was literate when the First Five Year Plan was launched in 1951 in Independent India. Between 1950-51 and 1980-81, the number of children enrolled in primary school increased from 1,91,54,457 to 7,26,87,840, but the percentage of literacy increased to only 36.2 per cent.

inequality that seem to have been let loose as the massive expansion, or virtual explosion, of education in the country has led to a dilution of standards, devaluation of qualifications and cut-throat competition for admission to the few courses that carry social prestige and value in the employment market.

In the circumstances, the task of sorting out the current relationship between education and social stratification in India is complex. It calls for an unravelling of the subtle interplay of both the old and the new forces that make for inequalities in and through education, and for a sensitive interpretation of the dynamics of their interaction. This paper does not attempt anything so ambitious. It merely presents some facets of the situation with respect to the urban poor and Scheduled Castes with illustrations from the metropolitan city of Bombay.

Provisions for Schooling

Bombay was one of the first cities in the country to adopt a policy of free and compulsory primary education (1927), and the municipal corporation has provided free primary education since 1907.[4] Currently, 1,298 (out of a total of 2,036) primary schools in the city are owned and managed by the municipality. Except for two owned by the central government, the rest are owned and managed by private bodies.

Provisions for secondary school education for the poor in Bombay are much less liberal. Only 51 out of a total of 795 secondary schools are owned by the municipality. The rest are privately owned and managed. Together, the 1,298 municipal primary schools serve about 1,00,000 children who constitute roughly 72 per cent of the total number of children availing of primary education in the city. They provide instruction in ten vernacular languages and charge no fees. In contrast, except for a few schools run as charities, private schools charge fees that range from four or five rupees to more than Rs. 300 a month. Under the circumstances, Bombay should be rated as one of the cities that is well provided with facilities for primary schooling, and favourably poised to provide equality of

[4] See *Milestones in the History of Compulsory Education* and *Census of Children in Bombay*, in Suma Chitnis, *Drop-outs and Low Pupil Achievement among the Urban Poor in Bombay*, Bombay: Tata Institute of Social Sciences, 1982 (mimeo).

educational opportunity for the urban poor. However, a closer look suggests that the situation is far from satisfactory.

Disparities in the Quality of Schooling

To an extent, high fees merely ensure 'exclusiveness'. But they also cover the cost of superior physical amenities and surroundings, better teaching aids, laboratory, library and other academic facilities, a smaller teacher-student ratio, more varied choices in the courses offered, more diversified and better-organized extra-curricular activities, exposure and experience—all of which add up to the better 'all-round development' of the student and to a better performance at the School Leaving Certificate examination (SSC) that is crucial in deciding a student's chances of admission to, and placement in, more favoured courses at the university.*

As may be expected, parents who can offord to do so send their children to private schools which offer these 'extras'. Since such parents happen, inevitably, to be educated and occupationally well-placed, the schools gain in strength since they acquire a body of students who come from backgrounds that are highly favourable to schooling. In contrast, free municipal schools, and of course private charity schools that charge little or no fees, are used by the mass of children from working class backgrounds, who are generally first generation learners, from educationally disadvantaged homes. Even as these schools struggle to stretch their physical facilities and amenities to accommodate the large numbers that seek free education, they are confronted with the problem of dealing with pupils who are altogether unprepared for the discipline of schooling and who have very little or no help at home to develop the qualities required. Irregular attendance, poor performance and heavy drop-out rates combine to create a climate that is hardly conducive to survival within the school system, much less to achievement and performance of the quality required for admission to institutions of higher education, particularly to the more prestigious ones.

* Figures collected for this paper indicate that whereas municipal schools in the locality visited spent a total of Rs. 357 per year per child, the per capita expenditure of the elite missionary school in the same locality was as high as Rs. 954 per annum.

Tables 1, 2, 3 and 4 illustrate the social class dependence of the distribution of children in the three different kinds of schools in the city, viz., municipal, private aided, and private unaided. They have been drawn from a carefully designed study of primary education in the city conducted by Lindsey.[5] This covers a randomly selected sample of the three kinds of primary schools in the city. The indicators for social class used in this study and presented in the tables were systematically tested for validity in the population sample covered by the study.

While Lindsey's data generally indicate the social class differences in the composition of the three types of schools, they do not indicate

Table 1: School Sponsorship and Occupation of Parents

Occupation Group	Municipal Schools	Private	
		Aided	Unaided
Lumpen Proletariat	0.622	−0.220	−0.402
Wage Labourers	0.446	−0.140	−0.306
Artisans	−0.088	0.446	−0.357
Shopkeepers	−0.166	0.208	−0.042
White-collar Workers	−0.536	0.149	0.387
Ideological Occupations	−0.278	−0.443	0.720

(X^2 [10] = 536.01, N = 4433)

Table 2: School Sponsorship and Income of Parents

Income Per Month	Municipal Schools	Private	
		Aided	Unaided
0–99	0.883	−0.366	−0.518
100–199	1.362	−0.347	−1.015
200–299	9.726	0.002	−0.730
300–399	0.469	−0.025	−0.449
400–599	−0.324	0.062	0.262
600–999	−1.058	0.344	0.714
1,000 +	−2.059	0.329	1.730

(X^2 [12] = 1541.96, N = 4172)

[5] J.K. Lindsey, 'Primary Education in Bombay—Introduction to a Social Study,' *Evaluation in Education—International Progress*, Vol. 2, No. 1, Oxford: Pergamon Press, 1978.

Table 3: School Sponsorship and Education of Father

No. of Years of Schooling	Municipal Schools	Private	
		Aided	Unaided
0	1.197	−0.714	−0.482
1–4	0.778	−0.078	−0.700
5–7	0.357	−0.046	−0.311
8–10	−0.128	0.325	−0.997
11	−0.609	0.220	0.369
12–20	−1.595	0.293	1.303

Table 4: School Sponsorship and Education of Mother

No. of Years of Schooling	Municipal Schools	Private	
		Aided	Unaided
0	1.658	−0.675	−0.963
1–4	0.975	−0.143	−0.832
5–7	0.479	−0.088	−0.390
6–10	−0.217	0.070	0.147
11	−1.131	0.412	0.718
12–20	−1.764	0.624	1.348

the contrast between municipal schools, on the one hand, and elite schools, on the other. This is brought out in Tables 5 and 6 which offer a comparison between the social class background of children in an elite school and a municipal school which I made for a study conducted for the ILO in 1982.[6]

Municipal Schools as a Clue to the Education of the Poor

Since the fact that children from socially and economically disadvantaged sectors of the population in the city are largely found in municipal schools is thus well established, we may focus on municipal school children to understand the situation

---

[6] Suma Chitnis, *Drop-outs and Low Pupil Achievement among the Urban Poor in Bombay*, Bombay: Tata Institute of Social Sciences, 1982 (mimeo).

Table 5: School Sponsorship and Monthly Joint Income of Both Parents

Monthly Joint Income of Both Parents (Rupees)	Type of School	
	Municipal School	Elite School
Up to Rs. 50	3 (0.46)	0 (0.00)
51–100	9 (1.38)	0 (0.00)
101–150	16 (2.45)	0 (0.00)
151–200	28 (4.28)	0 (0.00)
201–300	106 (16.21)	0 (0.00)
301–400	140 (21.41)	0 (0.00)
401–500	134 (20.49)	0 (0.00)
501–600	56 (8.56)	0 (0.00)
601–800	66 (10.09)	2 (0.68)
801–1,000	41 (6.27)	12 (4.05)
1,001–1,500	14 (2.14)	16 (5.41)
1,501–2,000	6 (0.92)	42 (14.19)
2,001–3,000	0 (0.00)	62 (20.95)
3,001–4,000	1 (0.15)	52 (17.57)
4,001–5,000	0 (0.00)	53 (17.91)
5,001–7,500	0 (0.00)	27 (9.12)
7,501–10,000	0 (0.00)	7 (2.36)
10,001–15,000	0 (0.00)	8 (2.70)
15,001–20,000	0 (0.00)	1 (0.34)
20,001 & above	0 (0.00)	4 (1.35)
Not Specified	28 (4.28)	9 (3.04)
Not Applicable	6 (0.92)	1 (0.34)
Total	654 (100.00)	296 (100.00)

regarding the schooling of the poor in Bombay city. Data from a major study on drop-out, failure, stagnation and absenteeism from schools conducted by the education department of the Bombay Municipal Corporation 1981 offer some valuable illustrations.[7]

This study covers a highly representative sample—95 (7 per cent) of the 1,298 municipal primary schools—and offers a detailed follow-up of the students admitted to Std. I during the academic years 1972–73, 1973–74 and 1976–77. Forty-five of these 97 schools provide schooling up to Std. VII. Others provide education only up to Std. IV. The sample of the former was stratified to distinguish those with a relatively 'better' performance record from those with an 'average' performance record. Data are given in Table 7.

[7] Data were obtained from the unpublished report on census and survey conducted by the education department of the Bombay Municipal Corporation.

Table 6: School Sponsorship and Father's Education

Father's Education	Type of School	
	Municipal School	Elite School
Illiterate	94 (14.37)	1 (0.34)
Unschooled but Literate	2 (0.30)	0 (0.00)
Primary School	138 (21.10)	0 (0.00)
Below SSC*	278 (42.50)	2 (0.68)
SSC or Equivalent	91 (13.91)	29 (9.80)
SSC + Technical Diploma	0 (0.00)	11 (3.72)
Some College Education	13 (1.99)	23 (7.77)
Non-professional Graduation	10 (1.53)	72 (24.32)
Professional Graduation	1 (0.15)	84 (28.39)
Non-professional Post-graduation	1 (0.18)	19 (6.42)
Professional Post-graduation	0 (0.00)	38 (12.84)
Doctorate/Post-doctorate	0 (0.00)	13 (4.39)
Not Specified	13 (1.99)	2 (0.68)
Not Applicable	13 (1.99)	2 (0.68)
Total	654 (100.00)	296 (100.00)

* SSC = Secondary School Leaving Certificate

DROP-OUT AND FAILURE

Since the municipal corporation data provided no details on the status of those who failed, some primary data was collected from one of the three municipal schools observed. These data may not be representative of all municipal schools; nevertheless, they illustrate the likely form of stagnation. In this school, 395 children were enrolled in Std. I in 1975–76. After seven years (i.e., in 1982), only 22 (5 per cent) had reached Std. VII. As many as 244 (62 per cent) had dropped out or left school with transfer certificates, at various points. The remaining 129 (33 per cent) had failed repeatedly and were lingering on in the lower classes as follows:

	No.	Per Cent
Std. I	Nil	(—)
Std. II	3	(2)
Std. III	12	(9)
Std. IV	18	(14)
Std. V	55	(43)
Std. VI	41	(32)
Total	129	(100)

Table 7: Annual Enrolment, Drop-out and Performance of Municipal School Students in Bombay

(Percentage)

Batch	Academic Year	Standard	Left with Certificates	Left without Certificates	Passed and Promoted	Failed and Held Back
A* Enrolled 1972–73 (17 Schools)	1972–73	I	1	22	55	22
	1975–76	IV	9	32	20	39
	1978–79	VII	14	33	9	44
	1973–74	I	3	26	63	8
B* Enrolled 1973–74 (25 Schools)	1976–77	IV	11	35	24	30
	1979–80	VII	18	36	11	35
C† Enrolled 1976–77 (55 Schools)	1976–77	I	3	18	55	24
	1979–80	IV	11	25	18	46

* Students from the two upper primary schools.
† Students from lower primary schools.

Thus, 33 (8.4 per cent of the original number) of those who joined Std. I in 1975–76 were still in school and had yet to complete primary school in 1982. No one knows how long it will take them to do so nor how long the 96 students (25.3 per cent), stuck in Stds. V and VI, will take to be promoted to Std. VII and to complete that class. Will these students finally finish school? Or will repeated failure undermine their future? If so, at what cost to themselves and their families?

IRREGULAR ATTENDANCE

While drop-out constitutes total withdrawal from school, irregular attendance may be viewed as partial withdrawal, particularly when it occurs continuously. A cursory observation of poor children's schooling reveals their poor attendance. Unfortunately, there is very little systematic information available on the issue. But the data in Table 8 which I collected for a study conducted for the ILO illustrates the problem.

Table 8 shows that between 10 and 20 per cent of the students are usually absent for more than 10 days a month in Std. I, Std. II and Std. III throughout the year. Another 5 to 10 per cent are absent for around five to nine days. Those absent for more than ten days a month are from the higher standards. Nevertheless, absenteeism is quite high throughout the school, particularly at the beginning of the school year in July.

The table shows absenteeism as a percentage of 'average' enrolment. In municipal schools, enrolment for each class is not constant throughout the year. Students are admitted and drop out at any time. Enrolment is generally lowest at the beginning of the year in July and August, increases between September and December, and declines thereafter. In Std. I, in the school shown in the table, enrolment was 339 in July, 394 in August, 406 in September, October, November and December, dropped to 386 in January, and was 367 in February and March. Enrolment obviously picks up as the academic year advances. It declines from January onwards, possibly because seasonal employment attracts children or because their interest flags after a few months of school.

Table 8: Children Absent According to Standard and Month

(Percentages)

		July	Aug.	Sept.	Oct.	Nov.	Dec.	Jan.	Feb.	Mar.
Standard I	3–5 days	8.5	5.6	4.0	1.2	6.2	6.6	4.1	3.8	8.7
	6–9 days	5.0	3.8	1.2	1.7	3.0	0.5	2.3	4.1	4.9
	10+	30.6	15.7	17.3	13.8	20.2	19.0	21.2	13.9	10.6
Standard II	3–5 days	4.0	7.1	8.9	4.8	6.8	7.5	4.9	1.9	2.2
	6–9 days	1.7	1.8	3.0	0.6	2.4	2.7	2.5	2.2	2.2
	10+	28.2	19.2	11.9	10.7	16.2	16.4	14.8	14.7	15.0
Standard III	3–5 days	3.5	8.3	3.5	4.3	6.2	6.7	1.5	2.0	4.3
	6–9 days	0.8	1.2	1.6	3.5	3.5	1.9	1.2	0.4	2.4
	10+	16.5	11.1	10.9	10.95	12.4	11.1	11.2	9.4	8.7
Standard IV	3–5 days	5.7	4.8	10.3	1.2	13.5	11.1	6.9	9.6	5.7
	6–9 days	2.8	3.6	2.4	1.6	1.6	1.2	1.2	2.9	1.2
	10+	17.0	12.3	5.1	4.3	6.3	9.1	7.7	5.3	2.5
Standard V	3–5 days	0.4	5.4	5.3	0.4	12.6	6.6	9.1	7.2	4.0
	6–9 days	4.6	3.1	1.4	—	5.0	4.6	3.9	1.6	0.4
	10+	15.5	4.2	3.4	3.8	5.7	5.4	5.5	3.6	1.6
Standard VI	3–5 days	8.8	4.2	7.7	1.6	12.8	2.8	8.6	9.7	4.0
	6–9 days	3.1	5.8	1.7	—	5.6	3.9	3.4	3.4	—
	10+	17.5	11.1	7.7	3.8	10.0	7.8	6.9	2.9	4.6
Standard VII	3–5 days	10.1	6.4	13.5	—	18.2	6.4	5.5	3.8	1.9
	6–9 days	1.8	4.6	4.5	1.8	5.4	2.7	0.9	0.9	2.9
	10+	17.4	8.3	—	7.2	8.2	5.4	8.3	8.6	4.8

LATE START

In addition to the problems of drop-out, failure, stagnation and absenteeism, another major shortcoming in the education of poor children is their late start. In India, a child is normally expected to enrol in Std. I as soon as he is 5 years old. Of the 393 admissions to Std. I in 1975 in one municipal school, 153 children (39 per cent) were 5 years old, 145 (37 per cent) were 6 years old, 50 (13 per cent) were 7 years old, 24 (6 per cent) were 8 years old and 21 (5 per cent) were between 9 and 12 years old. A late start and repeated failure combine to cause inordinate delay in the education of poor children. Table 9 gives the age composition of children in Stds. I, II, III and IV in the school mentioned. Only 51 to 61 per cent of the children in Stds. I–III and 71 per cent of the children in Std. IV are in the correct age group. Stds. I, II and III seem, in particular, to have a large percentage of children who are overage. Few, however, are overage in Std. IV. This suggests that Stds. I, II and III constitute difficult hurdles to cross. Given the high percentage of failure in Std. I as also in Stds. II and III, it may well be that children from poor families are eliminated before they reach Std. IV.

The massive incidence of failure and drop-out in municipal primary schools is devastating evidence of the quality of schooling of poor children. Data collected for the ILO study referred to earlier suggest that drop-out is a problem with schools that serve the poor, the working class and the lower-middle class and does not exist in schools that serve the middle and upper classes. Even the problem of failure affects the latter only marginally. These students are better prepared for schooling when they enter school. They attend school more regularly and are better supervised both in school and at home. Schools inform parents if they notice a child's performance is poor or declining. Parents, in turn, readily provide extra coaching so that their children do not lose a year.

Explanatory Factors

Research studies analyzing the situation indicate a combination of social, economic, psychological, educational and administrative factors. Poverty emerges as by far

Table 9: Age-wise Distribution of Students in Stds. I-IV in a Municipal School

	5–6 Years	7–8 Years	9 Years	10 Years	11 Years	12 Years	13–14 Years	15–16 Years	17–18 Years	19+	Total
Std. I (appropriate age 5 to 6 years)	234* (55)	142 (34)	22 (5)	11 (3)	5 (1)	— (—)	4 (1)	4 (1)	—	—	422 (100)
Std. II (appropriate age 6–7 or 8 years)	23* (7)	180* (54)	66 (20)	35 (11)	16 (5)	6 (2)	1 (0)	—	3 (1)	1 (0)	331 (100)
Std. III (appropriate age 7–8 or 9 years)	2 (1)	74* (28)	61* (23)	54 (21)	44 (17)	19 (7)	9 (3)	1 (0)	—	—	264 (100)
Std. IV (appropriate age 9/10/11 years)		25 (9)	61* (21)	82* (29)	61* (21)	22 (8)	27 (9)	5 (2)	2 (1)	—	285 (100)

Figures in brackets indicate percentages.
* = students in appropriate age groups.

the most important factor. It operates as a handicap to education in many ways. In the first place, children need to earn. According to the Census of India (1971), as many as 37 per cent of the children in Bombay between 0 to 14 years are earning. In fact, in many cases it is they who keep the wolf from the door. In one municipal school in Bombay which I observed, students were absent *en masse* each time the neighbouring factory had a peak period of production.[8]

More directly, poverty implies continual hunger, malnutrition, ill-health and illness which interfere with regular attendance at school and with the ability to learn. In Bombay city, it also means houselessness, or at best meagre shelter, exposure to the extreme heat in summer and to continuous wind and rain during the monsoon. Even those who have shelter live in places where toilet facilities are negligible or non-existent, drains clogged, flooded and overflowing and certainly without a place to study or a light to read by at night. Poverty also means that children are shunted back and forth between the city and the village as the parents keep moving in search of work. Or it means frequent shifts of residence within the city as parents move from one construction site to another, or from one slum to another as their 'illegal' shanties are demolished and the slums in which they reside 'cleared'. In addition, there are the usual well-known correlates of poverty, such as, language or mathematical disability, the inability to deal with abstract concepts and to classify, comprehend and recognize patterns.

The crux of the problem is that in spite of the national commitment to their education, the school system has not really adapted to the shortcomings of the poor. There is a tendency to attribute their poor performance to 'poor capacity' or to the 'indifference of parents'. There is a visible inability to fully recognize the implications of children's social disabilities for their performance; a failure to build upon their strengths, to harness the unique maturity that exposure to poverty and to life in the raw cultivates in these children and, conversely, the practice of forcing them through moulds and paces set for middle and upper class children from white collar and upper class homes. There is a total failure to provide these children with learning materials and syllabi appropriate with their situation and needs, to work with them in the spoken dialects of their illiterate

---

[8] See Suma Chitnis and C. Suvannathar in P.J. Richards and A.M. Thomson, *Basic Needs and the Urban Poor—An ILO-WEP Study*, London: Croom Helm, 1984, pp. 189–207.

sub-cultures, to help them graduate to abstract concepts, to adapt school timings and requirements to fit in with their other obligations and to enable them to overcome the fear and diffidence they suffer as their home lives are continuously affected by death, usury, unemployment and uncertainty of every kind. A couple of small experiments aimed at helping municipal school children in the city to overcome their problems have met with spectacular success. But, by and large, the administration of education in the city is too rigid and bureaucratic to allow for the kind of creativity, initiative, drive and confidence that teachers must bring to the task if the transition is to be accomplished.

Education and Employment

The irony of the situation is that while the education of the poor continues to be beset with problems, the educational requirements for employment are continually rising, particularly in the cities.[9] Several studies relating to employment in Bombay city clearly reveal that both employment stability and size of earnings are positively correlated with education. For instance, a 1981 study on the stability of employment reveals that whereas barely 48.5 per cent of the illiterate wage earners surveyed work for more than 25 days a month, the corresponding percentage for those who have more than four years of education goes up to 62 per cent. An ILO study of patterns of employment in the slums of Bombay done in the same year, shows that education is an important factor in securing employment in the relatively more stable, better-organized and definitely better-paid 'formal sector' where earnings are, on an average, 60 per cent more than in the informal sector. It also shows that education is a positive asset in self-employment.[10]

The same study shows that the educated earn better than the uneducated, both in the formal and informal sector. Cumulative figures for the two sectors show that whereas the mean income of those who have no education is Rs. 290 per month, those who have one to four years of schooling earn up to Rs. 327 per month. Those

[9] V.N. Kothari, 'Employment Dualism and Education Policy in India,' *Manpower Journal*, Vol. 14, No. 2, New Delhi: Institute of Manpower Research, 1978.

[10] Brahm Prakash, *Patterns of Employment among Slum Dwellers*, Report on ILO Project, Bombay: Tata Institute of Social Sciences (mimeo).

in the next category of education (viz., five to ten years of schooling) earn about the same as those with only five years school education. But education up to or above the SSC level (school leaving stage) brings substantial economic gain. The mean income of those with an SSC degree is Rs. 428 per month. For those educated beyond the SSC level, it is Rs. 492 per month. Thus, the earnings of those with an SSC degree are nearly one-and-a-half times the earnings of those who have no education; the earnings of those educated beyond SSC are about 15 per cent more than the earnings of those who have done their SSC.[11]

Higher Education

The foregoing discussion underlines the value of university education. Perhaps one of the most unhappy consequences of the limitations to quality in the school education of the poor is that the chances of their upward mobility through university education are seriously affected. The massive expansion of higher education after Independence has been accompanied by the emergence of sharp hierarchies in terms of courses and institutions—medicine, engineering and technology are considered prestigious courses, leading to high income, high status occupations. Arts and humanities are regarded as inferior. Similarly, in each city and in each field of study it is possible to identify 'elite' institutions. They produce superior results, provide distinctive grooming and contribute subtly as an 'advantage' in the process of social selection. Admission, both to the prestigious courses and to elite institutions, is ruthlessly competitive. Only a small fraction (i.e., the best performers at the SSC level) gain admission to these institutions.

The extent to which children from poor families are likely to lose out in the competition to gain admission to institutions of higher education may be gauged from a comparison of the performance of students from a randomly-chosen sample of municipal, private aided and private unaided schools, respectively, in the School Leaving Certificate examination. The examination is conducted by the State Board of Secondary Education and constitutes the qualifying

---

[11] See *ibid.* Also see Lalit Deshpande, *Bombay's Labour Market*, Department of Economics, University of Bombay (mimeo).

Table 10: Performance at the SSC Examination of Children from the Three Categories of Schools

	Municipal School	Aided School	Unaided 'Elite' School
No. Securing First Class with Distinction	1 (0.28)	1 (0.93)	Nil
No. Securing First Class	34 (9.63)	33 (32.35)	30 (43.48)
No. Securing Second Class	92 (26.06)	46 (45.10)	38 (55.07)
No. Securing Third Class	73 (20.68)	9 (8.82)	1 (1.45)
No. Failed	153 (43.34)	13 (12.75)	Nil
Total Appearing	353 (100)	102 (100)	69 (100)

Figures in brackets are percentages.

requirement for admission to higher education. It may be recollected that while municipal schools serve the poor, private aided and unaided schools serve successively more affluent sections of the population.

Reservations for the Scheduled Castes

In a sense, the policy of 'reservation' for the Scheduled Castes and Scheduled Tribes in higher education anticipates this situation. Briefly, the policy ensures that a fixed percentage of admissions are reserved, in all institutions of higher education, for persons belonging to the Scheduled Castes and Tribes. Admission is granted to them in this quota, as long as they fulfil the basic qualifying requirements, regardless of their position vis-a-vis the total body of applicants competing for admissions. Over the years, the Indian government has become more demanding and vigilant with respect to the implementation of the policy of reservation. Nevertheless, it has been difficult to overcome disadvantage.

This point may be illustrated with reference to 'reserved' admissions for Scheduled Caste and Scheduled Tribe students in the IIT, Bombay. As per government requirements, the IIT reserves 54 (25 per cent) seats for students from these communities each year.

Massive concessions, in terms of lower admission requirements, are offered to Scheduled Caste and Tribe students in order to utilize these reserved seats. However, data for the years 1973–80 indicate that there were only 15 admissions in 1973, 37 in 1974, 27 in 1975, 27 in 1976 and 21 in 1980. Data for 1978 and 1979 are not available. Despite a carefully designed program of special coaching, students who were admitted were not able to complete the course requirements. Table 11 shows the number of students who dropped-out and those who remained.

Table 11: No. of SC/ST Students Admitted Each Year and Retained through the Period 1973–77 in IIT, Bombay

1973–74	1974–75	1975–76	1976–77	1977–78	No. of Students at the various stages of the 5-year B.Tech. Program	
15 (100)	10 (66.7)	9 (60)	5 (33.3)	5 (33.3)	Fourth yr.	3
					Third yr.	2
	37 (100)	32 (86.5)	26 (70.3)	26 (70.3)	Fourth yr.	1
					Third yr.	6
					Second Yr.	19
		27 (100)	23 (85.2)	23 (85.2)	Third yr.	3
					Second yr.	8
					First yr.	12
			27 (100)	20 (74.1)	Second yr.	10
					First yr.	10
				42 (100)		

Note: Figures in brackets show the percentage of students who remained at the end of each year.
Source: 'Report of the Committee Appointed to Consider the Problems of Scheduled Caste/Scheduled Tribe Students,' Bombay: IIT, 1977.

Many of the students who have remained are in a precarious position. For, at the IIT, academic performance is evaluated on a 10-point grading system. A student is expected to maintain a minimum Cumulative Performance Index (CPI) of 5.5 throughout. If a student fails to maintain this index, he is given a warning and a chance to improve his academic performance within a prescribed period—in other words, the student is kept on probation. If the student fails to improve his performance within the prescribed period, he is advised to leave the Institute. Table 12 illustrates the different stages at which SC/ST students were on probation or advised to leave the Institute.

Table 12: Number of SC/ST Students Either on 'Probation' or 'Advised to Leave' or 'Withdrawn' at the End of Each Semester

Year of admission	Total No.*	1st Semester	2nd Semester	4th Semester	6th Semester	8th Semester	Information Month
1	2	3	4	5	6	7	8
1973	15	3	2	4	5	2	July 1977
1974	37	—	2	10	8	—	
1975	27	—	3	11			
1976	27	—	1				

* In the first row, the figures in columns 3, 4, 5, 6 and 7 add up to more than the total because the performance of some of the students on probation was not satisfactory and so they were eventually advised to leave or withdraw. They have been recorded for each of these stages and therefore, counted twice, or even three times.

Source: Same as Table 11.

Another relevant illustration is the study which I conducted in 1972.[12] Although the data is more than twelve years old, there is reason to believe that the situation of Scheduled Caste students has not changed substantially since then. The data collected for the study indicates that there were 2,176 Scheduled Caste students studying for degree courses in Bombay in 1972. Of these, 1,616 (74 per cent) were enrolled for degree courses in arts and science. A detailed analysis of 1,480 (91 per cent) of these 1,616 students revealed that they were distributed over 15 arts and science colleges in the city. Graded on the basis of the performance of their students in the university examinations, these colleges could be easily categorized into four grades—A, B, C and D. Colleges with the highest level of performance fell in Grade A. Those with the lowest level fell in Grade D. As many as 1,122 (96 per cent) of the 1,480 students observed were enrolled in the colleges in Grade D. Almost 55 per cent were enrolled in one college which stood third from the bottom in the list ranking the fifteen colleges. In contrast, only five students

[12] Suma Chitnis, 'Education for Equality,' in *Economic and Political Weekly*, Vol. 7 (31-33), Special Number, August 1972.

were enrolled in the college ranked first and barely 5 per cent were enrolled in the colleges in Grade A.

There are many such illustrations. What emerges is that the struggle uphill is tough, both for the economically disadvantaged as well as the socially disadvantaged sectors of the population in India. Education has certainly brought an unprecedented measure of social mobility to these sectors. But, as the forces of competition gather strength and as polarization in Indian society grows, the limits to its efficacy as an instrument for the 'just' allocation and redistribution of occupational placement, political power or social prestige are increasingly evident.

Solutions need to be worked out at several levels. The issue is in a sense simplest, conceived of in terms of 'learning disabilities' at the pedagogic level. In fact, at this level, some startling successes have been achieved by individuals and groups who are experimenting with remedial programs and interventions that combine specially designed instruction with counselling and, perhaps, most significantly with simply care, warmth and concern. The problem here is one of the extent to which these programs can be replicated and extended. Although 'packages' aimed at replication are being developed, one cannot but be sceptical, considering not merely the physical resources but the sensitivity, flexibility and dedication required of the personnel involved.

At another level, the problem is one of sprucing up the administration of school education and revamping and revitalizing it to serve more effectively the needs of children whose learning requirements go far beyond instruction in the three 'R's. Here the problem is not merely one of revising and redesigning school hours, age requirements, entry points, attendance requirements, learning materials, evaluation methods and so on, with a greater sensitivity towards the needs of children from disadvantaged backgrounds but of developing strategies to obtain the more dynamic involvement of school administrators and teachers. Although there is a good deal that can be done at this level, both with respect to the administration of school and university education, the limitations that inevitably surface lead to the third, and perhaps the most critical, level.

At this level one is compelled to reflect upon the objectives of education in the country. It is necessary to examine whether it is realistic to try and combine, within the system, the conflicting goals of excellence and social justice, as we have been trying to do over the past two decades. It is necessary, further, to examine carefully the increasing bureaucratization of education within the country and to question whether transformations of the kind that are desired can be achieved without the zeal required to fire a social movement. Do we have the zeal, the political will; or the economic resources or the social commitment required to use education effectively as an instrument of social change and development? The quest for an answer leads us into the complex labyrinths of the politics, economics, sociology and philosophy of education in India.

Economic, Scientific and Technological Issues

6

Education and Economic Growth: Lessons from India

A M Nalla Gounden

The concept of human capital was rediscovered in the late 1950s; it was a rediscovery in the sense that eminent classical economists like Adam Smith, Irvine Fisher, Alfred Marshall and others saw the relevance of education in what they had written. Smith included all the acquired and useful abilities in fixed capital; he considered the improved dexterity of a workman as similar to a machine or an instrument of trade. Marshall observed that 'knowledge is the most powerful engine of production' and 'the most valuable of all capital is that invested in human beings'. Yet human capital did not play an important role either in economic theory or practice till the late 1950s, perhaps because of Marshall, who said that it would not be in keeping with the market place to treat human beings as capital.

In the 1950s, growth economists encountered certain questions to which the rediscovery of human capital may be attributed: (i) The income of the US had been increasing at a much higher rate than the combined amount of land, labour and capital used in production, the growth of these three inputs (as conventionally measured) explained hardly 35 per cent of the growth of national income. One important clue to resolve the question of the residual 65 per cent was found in the improvement of human quality as represented by more education, training and better health; (*ii*) The US, a capital-rich country, was found exporting labour-intensive goods. This is, again, a puzzle for economists because it is contrary to the received theory of international trade. The US was found rich in human capital also; (*iii*) Japan, Germany and other European countries suffered severe loss of plant, equipment and structure during World War II, yet these countries speedily recovered from war destruction, contrary to the estimates of economists. On the other hand, India and other underdeveloped countries, in spite of heavy investment in physical capital, did not grow fast. These contrasting experiences of growth were again explained in terms of differences in the quality of human agents of production. Thus, all three questions are related to development and human capital was rediscovered to resolve them. Human capital gained such popularity among economists in the 1960s and 1970s that it became one of the fastest growing subjects.

A major part of human capital is formed by education and training and the rest by medical care. The attitude of planners has changed; instead of considering education as consumption they regard it as investment. For example, only in the Third Five-Year Plan was this investment aspect of education emphasized: 'Education is the most important single factor in achieving rapid development and technical progress' (Third Five-Year Plan, 1961). Economists do not deny the consumption value of education. Most human capital economists consider that education has both consumption and investment value. However, most of the studies have treated education as investment. The Central Statistical Organization (CSO) has classified educational expenditure by households under 'private final consumption expenditure' along with recreation, entertainment and cultural services.

When education is accepted as investment, certain questions are raised: How much is invested in education? How is the total investment in education distributed among different levels and types of education? How do the rates of return compare with those from other investments? Does education promote economic development? Does it help reduce inequality of income and wealth? In this paper, I have tackled some of these questions using the Indian experience to illustrate. In the next section, I will discuss investment in education and its efficiency. The following section deals with the growth of the Indian economy and the contribution of education to growth.

Investment in Education

Before discussing human capital formation and returns on it, some preliminary remarks are in order. Human beings are producers as well as consumers of goods and services. Our focus is on human beings as producers. Individuals spend time, energy and money to acquire knowledge, skills and talents. Health is also acquired but has not been dealt with in this paper. People invest in education with a view to increase their productive capacity and thereby increase their consumption bundle. It is a recognized fact that education also increases consumption efficiency.

Education capital (knowledge, skills and work capacity) can be formed in many ways. The most obvious is through formal education—starting from primary school, continuing through secondary school and going on to higher education like college, university or a technical institute. Another equally important method is on-the-job training, sometimes systematically provided within the work environment. In addition to these, individuals develop themselves through reading, independent study, observing and learning from others and personal experience. Thus, human/education capital formation is a life-long process for most people. It covers work-oriented activities in schools, factories, farms, government, armies, political organizations and trade unions. At an early age, the family is the most important source of education for children.

Formal education connotes age-specific, full-time classroom attendance in a graded system geared to awarding certificates, diplomas or degrees. It is associated with the young, it is easily identified, its costs are measurable and its outputs are easily recognized.

It is worth remembering that formal education in India and other countries is expected to perform many functions—to manifest the perfection already in man and woman and the enrichment of human life. Generating values and creating an awareness and sensitivity to the community and humanity is another function of education. Education is expected to identify and select the brilliant young ones and develop their capacities fully. Formal education has many functions and human capital is formed from many resources. Thus, organized formal education and human capital formation are not the same thing.

Economists borrowed the concept of capital from physical capital and applied it to education/human resources. However, human capital and physical capital, though similar, differ in certain respects (Parness, 1984, pp. 34–37). One of these is worth noting, in particular. The productive capacity of human capital depends upon the volition of the individual in whom it is embodied: a machine can be relied upon to work as it is designed to work, once it is started, but there is no similar assurance on the part of human capital. Consequently, there tends to be great variance in the productive capacity of a given amount and kind of education capital whereas in the case of physical capital the variance will be much less. The innate ability and prior experience of human beings may be one of the reasons for greater variance. Another important source of variance is differences in initiative, motivation and other personality traits. Systems of reward and punishment play a crucial role in influencing productivity.

Individuals as well as society invest in education. The cost of and benefits from education, when looked at from the point of view of individuals, are called private costs and benefits. Similarly, there are social costs and benefits of education. Society, through the government, subsidizes education because it is believed that education has an external economy. So, if left entirely to individuals, there would be an under-investment in education. For individuals, the cost of education covers fees and other payments made to schools and colleges to acquire the privilege of attending classes, expenditure on books, stationery and the income foregone. The last item is called opportunity cost while the other items are direct costs. Economists view post-tax earnings as the private benefit of education. They recognize the non-monetary and non-market benefits of education, but little work has been done on these returns. Social costs refer to the cost of all resources—human and non-human—that are used in schools and colleges. The annual expenditure on these resources form the social cost. Economists view pre-tax earnings as the social returns of education. Little attempt has been made to include external economics and/or diseconomies. Later, I shall cite the results of non-market benefits.

Measuring physical capital stock is a complicated problem and there is no consensus of opinion on this aspect. In the light of the features of education, human capital stock is no less difficult to measure and returns on it are also difficult to identify and measure. In spite of the limitations of the measures, attempts have been made to estimate the cost and benefits of education. The studies cited later all have some limitations.

There is no official estimate of the investment in education in India. Official publications like *Education in India* give information about the number of educational institutions, enrolment, teachers, expenditure, examination results and so on. The expenditure given in the official documents is not the total investment in education but much less because the rental value of fixed assets, household expenditure on education (except fees), and the income foregone by students are not included in it. In the absence of official data on investment in education, I shall use studies made by individual scholars.

Table 1: Investment in Education in India (Rs. Million)

Year	Household Expenditure	Institutional Expenditure	Column 3 as % of National Income	Social Expenditure	Column 5 as % of National Income
1	2	3	4	5	6
1950–51	—	1,153	1.2	—	3.6*
1956–57	—	2,062	1.8	—	5.2*
1959–60	—	2,997	2.3	—	6.5*
1960–61	—	3,443	2.6	—	—
1965–66	—	5,863	2.4	—	—
1970–71	8,960	11,180	3.1	20,140	5.5
1975–76	12,530	21,050	3.2	33,580	5.1
1979–80	20,920	35,000	3.9	55,920	6.2

* estimates by Kothari.
Source: J.B.G. Tilak and G.K. Butt, *Costs and Supply of Education*, New Delhi: NIEPA, 1984.

Table 1 gives the estimates of investment in education from 1950–51 to 1979–80. It provides household expenditure on education, institutional expenditure and social expenditure which is the sum of the first two items. It also gives the percentage of institutional and social expenditure in national income. Institutional expenditure, in current prices, increased from Rs. 1,153 million in 1950–51 to Rs. 35,000 million in 1979–80. Over this period, the average growth of institutional expenditure was 15.7 per cent, which is much larger than the growth of national income or population. As a result of this growth, expenditure as percentage of national income increased from 1.2 per cent in 1950–51 to 3.9 per cent in 1979–80. As mentioned earlier, this is an underinvestment. For the years prior to 1970–71, little attempt was made to estimate the household expenditure on education. Kothari's estimate (see Tilak and Butt, 1984) is given in column 6. From 1970–71, more systematic attempts were made by the CSO and the derived figures are given in column 2. When household and institutional expenditure are added to get social expenditure, the proportion of national income invested in education increases to 5.5 per cent in 1970–71 and 6.2 per cent in 1979–80. Even this sum of Rs. 55,920 million is an underestimate, in the sense that it does not include income foregone by the students.

Income foregone by the students at different levels of education for the year 1979–80 was calculated as follows: primary level Rs. 10,493 million, middle level Rs. 6,564 million, secondary level Rs. 10,876 million and at a higher level Rs. 10,049 million. The total income foregone totalled Rs. 37,982 million (which is 4.2 per cent of the national income). If this amount is added to social expenditure, gross investment in education comes to 10.4 per cent of the national income in 1979–80 (Tilak and Butt, 1984). Rati Ram and Schultz's estimate of investment in education is 11 per cent of the national income in 1970–71.

It is argued that in India, where unemployment is fairly high and increasing, the opportunity cost of students is almost zero because the alternative to schooling is unemployment. There are arguments for and against opportunity cost being included in cost calculations. Makhija (1980) and Duraisamy (1984) have calculated the contribution of children of school-going age to family income. They have found that where the opportunities to work and earn are higher, other things being the same, it is less likely that children will go to school. Measures of opportunity cost also indicate one dimension of private effort to acquire education.

Another way of relating expenditure on education to national income is to estimate the income elasticity of expenditure on education. Income elasticity is defined as the proportionate change in expenditure on education divided by the proportionate change in national income. The income elasticity of institutional expenditure in relation to national income, for the period 1970–71 to 1979–80, was 0.78; for social expenditure 0.88 and for private household expenditure 1.02. In the case of private elasticity, the total household expenditure on all items was used in place of national income.

Income elasticity is interpreted as the marginal propensity to invest in education. If this definition is accepted, private propensity to invest in education is higher than social or institutional propensity.

The cost per student year varies with the level and type of education. Table 2 gives the unit cost of education by levels; here, the unit cost refers to institutional expenditure. Two observations are worth

Table 2: Unit Cost of Education (Institutional Expenditure)

Year	Primary	Middle	Secondary	University	College General	College Professional
1	2	3	4	5	6	7
A: At Current Prices						
1950–51	19.9	37.1	72.9	1,905.6	231.2	739.2
1960–61	27.6	40.5	91.7	2,524.2	302.4	813.4
1970–71	57.0	84.9	168.4	4,141.2	421.6	1,179.0
1975–76	95.9	114.2	237.7	5,993.6	572.5	1,539.9
Growth Rate	6.5	4.6	5.2	4.7	2.5	2.8
B: At 1970–71 Prices						
1950–51	41.9	78.1	153.5	4,011.7	486.7	1,640.4
1960–61	50.1	73.5	166.4	4,851.1	548.8	1,476.2
1970–71	59.0	84.9	168.4	4,141.2	421.6	1,179.0
1975–76	55.2	83.3	148.9	3,664.5	330.9	890.1

Source: J.B.G. Tilak and G.K. Butt, *Costs and Supply of Education*. New Delhi: NIEPA, 1984.

mentioning. When one moves from primary to university level education, the unit cost increases both in current and constant prices. The unit cost at the university level is the highest, followed by professional colleges, while primary education is the cheapest. Secondly, with the passage of time, the unit cost at all levels increases at current prices. The rate of increase was 6.5 per cent at the primary level, 4.6 per cent at the middle, 5.2 per cent at the secondary and 4.7 per cent at the university level, 2.5 per cent at colleges for general education and 2.8 per cent at professional colleges. However, in real terms (at 1970–71 prices), there was a mild increase of 1.1 per cent at the primary school and 0.3 per cent at the middle school level. At other levels, there was a fall in the unit cost between 1970–71 to 1979–80. A falling unit cost is normally interpreted in economics as increasing efficiency. In this case, I am inclined to think that the education system has not become more efficient over these years. If this is accepted, the falling unit cost implies that the expansion of resources used for education did not match with the institutions and students.

The relative unit cost at various levels may be expressed in a different way, i.e., how many children could be educated at the primary level for one student at each of the other levels. This is illustrated as follows:

	Middle	Secondary	University	Art-Science Colleges	Professional Colleges
1950–51	1.9	3.7	96.0	11.7	38.9
1979–80	1.2	2.5	62.4	6.0	16.0

With the cost of educating one student at university in 1950–51, 96 students could have been schooled at the primary level.

Not many studies are available on estimates of profitability of education in India. Rates of return on education at different levels collected from eight studies are given in Table 3. The table indicates two tendencies—the marginal rate of return declines and the private rates of return exceed the social rates of return. Although the absolute values of the rates of return vary, the relative ranking is maintained in all the studies. Primary education is the most profitable investment while education in the arts stream at the university level is the least profitable. An engineering course has a favourable rate of return. Second, private rates of return are higher than social rates of return at all levels where both figures are available. Perhaps this is a reason for higher private propensity than social/institutional propensity to invest in education. Social costs exceed private costs by a wide margin because of heavy subsidy, while pre-tax earnings exceed post-tax earnings marginally. The proportion of the tax-paying labour force is very small; for those who do not pay income-tax, social and private returns are the same. This explains the difference between social and private rates of return.

The question that is relevant from the point of view of efficiency of investment is how these rates compare with those from other investments. Since I do not have any data on the rates of return in other sectors of the economy, we shall have to use interest rates available on long-term savings. If a 12–15 per cent interest rate is accepted, then most of our education seems to have a favourable rate of return (except, perhaps, arts education at the college level).

Table 3: Differential Rates of Return on Investment in Education in India

Source	Social					Private				
	Primary	Middle School	Matriculation	B.A. College	Engineering College	Primary	Middle School	Matriculation	B.A. College	Engineering College
Blaug (1972)	13.7	12.4	9.1	7.4*		16.5	14.0	10.4	8.7*	
Psacharapoulos (1973)	20.2	16.8**		12.7*		24.7	19.2**		14.3*	
Harberger (1965)	—	10*‡		16.3*						
Nalla Gounden (1967)	16.8	11.8	10.2	7.0	9.8					
Kothari (1967 and 1970)	—	—	20	14	25.0				10.0	25.0
Husain (1967)	—	—	37.0**	4		—	—	48‡	12.0	
Pandit (1976)	13.4	15.5	—	10.7		17.3	18.8	—	—	
Shortlidge (1974)	—	—	—	10††		—	—	—	16.2‡‡	
Average	16.0	13.3	13.1	10.3	17.4	19.5	17.3	10.4	12.2	25.0

* Type of degree unspecified.
** Level of secondary education unspecified.
‡ Rate of total return—i.e., matriculation over zero years of schooling.
†† B.Sc. aggregate over matriculation.

Source: S.P. Heyneman, *Investment in Indian Education*, World Bank: Staff Working Paper No. 327, 1979.

According to Malenbaum (1957, p. 146) and V.K.R.V. Rao (1966, p. 68), 'it is an economic waste to use scarce resources to educate young people' because 'expenditure on education is not giving a positive return'. They have based their observations on the high incidence of unemployment. Table 3 does not support their view. The rates of return are positive and, at some levels, they are favourable.

Criticisms have been levelled against the rates of return on education. First, the returns are confined to money earnings. Since education is embodied in human beings, it should influence their behaviour in other areas as well. So the calculated rates of return are underestimates. Duraisamy (1984) identified two areas which are non-monetary and non-market—fertility behaviour and agricultural productivity. He used the framework of new household economics to investigate fertility behaviour. Children ever born was regressed against a set of variables, including father's and mother's education. The coefficient of the variable—education of parents—turned out to be negative as expected, but only the father's education was statistically significant, not the mother's education. This hypothesis was invariant when Duraisamy replaced a single equation with structural equations for fertility, demand for children's education and labour force participation by the mother. He tested the role of education in agricultural production, which is a self-employed sector. The marginal productivity of education was positive in production function and education had a negative coefficient in allocative error function. Education was regressed against the difference between the value of the marginal product of an input and the price of that input. The interpretation is that educated farmers are less likely to commit an error of allocative resource use. The positive contribution of education remained unchanged when Duraisamy replaced production function with profit function. He also estimated the rate of return on education in agriculture as 4 per cent, which is very low. This may be the reason why people migrate from rural to urban areas to seek salaried jobs.

Another criticism against human capital is the calculation of social cost benefit analysis, as distinct from private cost benefit calculations. Arrow (1973) argued that schooling, particularly at the college level, contributed nothing to increase capabilities for productive activity; what schooling did was to sort out people according to traits that ensured their high productivity even without schooling; differentials in earnings associated with schooling indicated nothing about any contribution of schooling to the social product, even though schooling might be a good private investment. This type of argument has come to be known as the screening hypothesis. It is essentially a problem of information about the capability of potential employees. When the employer and job-seekers are different persons, some screening is necessary. But when persons are self-employed, there is no need for a screening. Using such an argument, I (1982) fitted the earnings function separately for the public sector, private sector and self-employed sector. The chow test was used to check whether the structure of earnings in the private sector was different from that in the self-employed sector. There was no statistically significant difference between the two earnings structures. The same result was found between the public and self-employed sectors. This exercise encourages us not to reject the human capital theory; Duraisamy's (1984) findings about agricultural productivity as well as that of Jamison and Law (1982) also support this theory. However, this does not mean that qualifications have no screening role in India.

All the studies cited in Table 3 are dated; they refer to the early 1960s. Till the middle of 1960s, the magnitude of educated unemployment in relation to the work force did not increase: the ratio of educated unemployed to total educated workers remained more or less constant. However, during the last twenty years the problem of unemployment has been getting worse and is becoming more serious. In these circumstances, how much faith can we place in these figures of rates of return? What might be the rates of return on education in 1987? Will they be as much as those in the 1960s? Research is required to answer these questions. The UGC, NCERT, and NIEPA conduct educational surveys in India, but in none of the four all-India surveys conducted were efforts made to collect data necessary for estimating the rate of return nor for analysing equality of education opportunities.

Education and Economic Growth

There is no simple definition of economic growth which adequately reflects the experience of countries in the process of development. Growth being a complex process, it involves not only economic but also social, political, technological, cultural and managerial changes. The primary goal of economic growth is to increase the welfare of the people. Welfare may be increased by producing more goods and services and distributing them more equally among the people. Production of goods and services can be increased by the fuller and better utilization of all the productive resources, and by augmenting the productive capacity of the resources by research and development. The latest attempt to measure growth is MEW, i.e., measure of economic welfare. This includes goods and services produced during the year minus 'bads' because the production process also has external diseconomies (such as, pollution of water, air, etc.) which reduce welfare. As growth takes place, working hours get reduced and so leisure time increases; leisure being a normal good the value of leisure time is added to the value of goods and services. However, I have used the growth of national income or its variant as a measure of economic growth; this is, of course, a conservative measure but a widely used one and correlated with other indicators of development. I have also considered distribution of income and full employment as a part of economic growth.

Net domestic product (NDP) is used as a measure in most of the studies on growth in India (Rao, 1983). NDP represents the unduplicated value of all goods and services produced in the economy at any given period of time, the net of depreciation of capital. This NDP is measured either at current or constant prices. When the value of the yardstick of money itself changes, it is desirable to use NDP at constant prices as an index of growth. Rao used 1960–61 prices while Ahluwalia used 1970–71 prices (Ahluwalia, 1984).

NDP for the Indian economy as a whole grew at a rate of 3.5 per cent per annum during 1956–81, at 1970–71 constant prices. This 3.5 per cent compound growth rate cannot be considered high: however, compared with secular growth in the developed countries, India's growth is not unsatisfactory. Population has also grown at the rather high rate of about 2.3 per cent between 1951–81. When we express the growth of real NDP in per capita, per capita real income growth is only marginal. The growth rate has varied from period to period—it was 3.5 per cent from 1956–57 to 1981–82, 2.9 per cent from 1956–57 to 1965–66 and 4 per cent from 1966–67 to 1981–82. Similarly, the agricultural and industrial sectors also showed fluctuations in growth; agriculture growth was 2.0 per cent from 1956–57 to 1981–82, 0.5 per cent from 1956–57 to 1965–66 and 3.17 per cent from 1966–67 to 1981–82; industrial performance for the same periods were 4.9 per cent, 6.4 per cent and 4.5 per cent respectively. While agriculture showed no deceleration after 1966, industry showed deceleration. Construction and railways also decelerated after 1966. However, the service sector did not show any change in growth rate.

Agriculture is an important sector in India because it supplies food to the growing millions, raw material to agro-based industries, absorbs a vast majority of the labour force and creates a demand for the output from the industrial sector. The growth of foodgrains, commercial crops and all crops were compared for different sub-periods from 1950–80, and a statistical test was applied. From this exercise, no evidence of a slowdown in the growth of production of foodgrains or agriculture as a whole after the mid-sixties was found (Ahluwalia, 1984); no doubt the growth was slow throughout the period. Value added in agriculture grew at 2.3 per cent per annum throughout this period. Imports of foodgrains were substantially reduced and the net availability of food increased; the per capita net

Table 4: Country-wise Economic Growth Rate and Contribution of Education (Percentages)

Country	Economic Growth Rate	Contribution of Education
Japan		
1955–68	10.1	2.3
1961–71	9.3	5.7
1953–61	8.1	6.2
Venezuela	7.7	4.3
Germany	7.3	2.5
Mexico (1950–64)	6.0	6.6
Italy	6.0	10.9
Chile (1950–64)	4.2	12.8
Denmark	3.5	6.6
Norway	3.5	11.3
U.S.A.	3.3	23.5
Belgium	3.2	21.9
Argentina	3.2	27.6
U.K.	2.3	20.5

availability of foodgrains per day increased from 448 grams in 1959–60 to 478 grams in 1983–84.

There was a significant slowdown in the growth of the industrial sector after the mid-sixties. The manufacturing sector (which forms 80 per cent of the industrial sector) and mining (which forms about 9 per cent of industry) suffered a setback in the growth rate. This was true of electricity generation as well.

The structure of the economy changes with economic growth—the share of the primary sector declines while that of the secondary sector increases with economic growth. In India the primary sector contributed 56.3 per cent to NDP in the year 1950–51 and the share declined to 35.5 per cent in 1980–81. During the same period, the secondary sector increased its share from 16.9 per cent to 25.7 per cent and the tertiary sector from 26.9 per cent to 38.9 per cent. The structure of the economy, in terms of the labour force employed, showed little change during the same period.

What was the role of education in India's economic growth? How much does education capital contribute to economic growth? To answer such questions, economists have developed a framework known as the 'growth accounting equation'. A production function for the economy as a whole is assumed; the relation between the rate of growth of output of the economy, on the one hand, and investment-output ratio, marginal product of capital, the rate of growth of the labour input, the share of labour in total income, on the other, is derived. Investment in education is brought into the accounting framework and its contribution to growth is estimated. However, there are two variables in the computation of the contribution of education to growth—one developed by T.W. Schultz (1961) and the other by E.F. Denison (1962). These are equivalent under certain conditions and they give approximately equal results. The Schultz procedure requires information about the changes in the stock of education capital over the period and about the rates of return on education. The contribution of education capital is calculated by multiplying the two. Denison's method requires data on changes in the employed labour force (classified by education) and data on earnings (classified by education category). By multiplying the changes in the labour force with various education categories and each by the corresponding income and aggregating them, one can obtain the contribution of education to economic growth.

In the past, three attempts have been made to estimate the

contribution of education to economic growth in India. All these studies refer to the 1950s. I have (1967) used the Schultz-type procedure and estimated that about 7 per cent of the growth of income from 1950 to 1960 was accounted for by education. Selowsky (1969) used the Denison-type calculation and concluded that 6 per cent of the growth of income was attributable to the growth of education. Psacharapoulos (1972) estimated that of the total contribution of education, primary education accounted 35 per cent, secondary education 50 per cent and higher education 15 per cent. It should be noted that the rates of return as well as the contribution to national income growth are low for higher general education. Dholakia (1974) used Denison's method and estimated that education contributed between 9 to 25 per cent to income growth for the period from 1948–49 to 1968–69. The relative contribution of education to economic growth for different sub-periods, according to Dholakia are 14 per cent from 1948–49 to 1968–69, 10 per cent from 1948–49 to 1954–55, 9 per cent from 1954–55 to 1960–61, 25 per cent from 1960–61 to 1968–69 and 16 per cent from 1954–55 to 1968–69.

What was the contribution of education to growth in the 1970s and 1980s? Since the industrial sector has slowed down after the mid 1960s and educated unemployment has been increasing during the last twenty years, is it reasonable to expect that the rates of return would have diminished and contribution to growth fallen? An international comparison of the rates of return on education and the level of per capita income failed to find a statistically significant relationship. Again, across countries we find that there is no relationship between the rate of growth of the economy and the contribution of education to growth. For example, England experienced more or less the same rate of growth of the economy (2.3 per cent) but the estimated contribution of education to growth was much higher (20.5 per cent) than India. Japan experienced much faster economic growth (8–10 per cent) than India but the contribution of education to economic growth was approximately equal (2 to 6 per cent) to that of India. More studies on India are required to answer the question.

Equal distribution of income and wealth is one of the important goals of planning; equity, fairness or justice is desired as an end in itself as well as a determinant of growth. What changes have occurred in the pattern of income distribution over the last thirty years in

India? The lack of data on household income is a serious obstacle in providing a firm answer. Many observers using partial and indirect evidence (such as, percentage of landless labourers to total population, degree of concentration of land holdings and trends in real wages of agricultural labourers) asserted that income distribution over time has become worse; inequality has increased. Though income inequality is more in urban than in rural areas, most observers have neglected urban problem. The NCAER survey data from 1960 to 1975 and the NSS data on average per capita monthly consumption expenditure and its distribution do not lend support to the assertion of worsening income distribution. The Gini co-efficients calculated from the NCAER data for various years are listed below (Ahluwalia, 1977).

Year	Urban	Rural	All Areas
1960	0.45	—	—
1962	—	0.42	—
1964–65	—	—	0.35
1967–68	0.46	0.46	0.46
1968–69	—	0.43	—
1969–70	—	0.39	—
1970–71	—	0.38	—
1975–76	0.42	0.39	0.42

The per capita expenditure from 1960–61 to 1973–74 also supports the contention that distribution has not become worse. The Gini co-efficients are listed here (Dutta, 1980).

Year	Rural	Urban
1960–61	0.32	0.35
1965–66	0.30	0.35
1970–71	0.28	0.33
1973–74	0.28	0.30

How much does education contribute to income inequality? Since we have no relevant study on this question, I have referred to the results of micro-studies on variance of earnings of persons based on sample surveys. Sample studies on India show that education and on-the-job training explains about 30–35 per cent of the variance in the earnings of the sample population (Usha. 1981; Malathy, 1984; Nalla Gounden, 1983).

Earnings functions were fitted with sample data. Using human capital theory, earnings in natural log form were regressed against education, division obtained, experience, sector of employment, occupation and other variables. In the next exercise, earnings from the first job were added to the explanatory variables. It was found that the R^2 increased, the co-efficient of the first earnings was statistically significant and its value was higher than that of many other variables. In another exercise, the sample was classified into 10 year groups. The first earnings from the first employment of each group was regressed against education, division obtained, foreign or local degree, sector of employment, occupation and period of job search. The co-efficient of the job search period turned out to be statistically significant (Prasad, 1982; Nalla Gounden, 1982). In another study on the cost and demand for education (Arumugam, 1984), it was found that the economic status of the family—as measured by family income, size of land holdings, etc.—was the most important variable associated with schooling of children. Duraisamy's (1984) study also supports Arumugam's findings. Further, other things being the same, opportunities to work and earn are negatively related to schooling of children. Putting all these conclusions together, I venture to guess that education in India has not helped to reduce inequality. This view is based on the following reasoning: children from poor families are less likely to go to school, more likely to drop out, when they complete a given level of education and enter the labour market, they are less likely to invest in a good job. As a result, their first earnings (as well as life-time earnings) are likely to be low. On the other hand, children from rich families are more likely to go to school and continue their education further. When they enter the labour market, they are more likely to invest in a good job—one with a high starting salary, scope for promotion and stability. Consequently, their life-time earnings are more than those of poor children.

Another method of linking education to economic growth is manpower planning. This method seems to be popular among decision-makers and planners, judging from the number of studies conducted, whereas cost-benefit analysis is popular among research scholars. After the Planning Commission was established, a number of working groups on manpower were set up. In 1956, a special manpower division was created which was later merged with the Perspective Planning Division. The Institute of Applied Manpower

Research (IAMR) was established in 1962 to conduct studies on supply of and demand for different categories of manpower. The Education Commission (1964-66) also commissioned a manpower study. As a result, there are a number of forecasts on manpower in India. The rationale for manpower forecasting comes from the observation of shortages and surpluses of different types of manpower persisting simultaneously; such imbalances are undesirable for individuals (since they suffer losses in earnings) and also for the economy (as the growth of the economy is restricted by shortages of particular kinds of manpower).

Manpower requirements are estimated assuming a certain rate of growth of the economy as a whole or a sector of the economy; the growth rate is usually given to the manpower planner by the Perspective Planning Division. Secondly, it is assumed in most of the studies that there exists a fixed technological relationship between inputs and output, that is, they allow little scope for substitution between physical capital and human labour or between one type of labour and another.

The question that naturally arises is how far the forecasts of manpower needs have been realized? In other words, does the forecast correspond to the actual achievement in a target year? To answer such questions, we require post-mortem analyses of the forecasts made. Post-mortem analyses are very complicated and I am not familiar with the data or procedure. However, one observation about manpower needs is worth noting. Suppose the forecasted manpower figure differs from the actual figure achieved in the target data, should we attribute this divergence to the method of forecast, to the assumption of fixed co-efficient, or to the assumption of a certain rate of growth of the economy/sector? This is not easy to answer. A more useful way of looking at the utility of manpower forecasts is whether the policy on education is sensitive to manpower forecasts. It seems that in India, whenever a manpower planner forecasted a shortage of a particular manpower, the government, perhaps in response to it, expanded the educational facilities to train that category of manpower. However, in cases where manpower planners forecasted surplus manpower, the government was not sensitive to the surplus because very little effort was made to curtail the educational facilities. This is only natural in the Indian context where it is almost impossible to close an organization even in industrial sector which is profit-oriented; if a firm is sick, it is rarely closed; the government take it over and runs it, meeting the loss from the tax-payer's money. If this is the case in industry, it is not possible to close down an educational institution.

Census and NSS data on unemployment are not alarming; they show that the incidence of unemployment is low. However, data given in the live registers at employment exchange offices indicate that the unemployment situation is serious. Experts on poverty say that about 40 per cent of the population in India live below the poverty line; indeed, the poverty line moves up or down depending upon the author and criteria. It may be that another 20 to 30 per cent are just above the poverty line. Therefore, only about 30 per cent of the population is comfortably above the poverty line (i.e., the middle class and above). In such a situation, educated unemployed persons should have come from well-to-do families. About 5 per cent from this age group attain third level education while 95 per cent do not go to college. They are on the look-out for good jobs because such an investment is a profitable one. Till 1970, the job search period had not increased compared to 1950 or 1960. The problem of unemployment is a result of the fast expansion of education and the slow growth of the economy. Reducing the rate of population growth and accelerating economic growth are the only means of reducing unemployment. I am inclined to think that changing the educational structure and introducing vocational education at the higher secondary level will have only a marginal effect on unemployment.

Concluding Remarks

The Indian Constitution directs that all children up to the age of 14 should have free and compulsory education. Thirty-five years after Independence we have achieved only about 37 per cent literacy, leaving about 115 million people in the age group 15 to 35 illiterate. The cost-benefit analysis indicates that primary education should be the first priority. Since the rate of return on it is the highest among all levels of education, it is relatively inexpensive as well.

Leading educationists and others have been complaining that the quality of Indian education is low; there are no national or state level primary school achievement tests. The International Educational

Achievement (IEA) throws some light on what our children learn in schools. According to reports of the IEA, Indian pupils at the age of 10 learn only 50 per cent as much science and 48 per cent as much reading as those in Japan, Europe and America. The gap in the knowledge of science between Indian students and those in industrial countries is larger at the secondary level than at the primary level. At the upper secondary level, Indian students learn only 28 per cent as much in science and 14 per cent as much in reading as children from industrial countries. The gap between Indian students and others increases despite the fact that the transition ratio from primary to secondary is higher in industrial countries than in India (Heyneman, 1980).

There are no studies on the rate of return to investment in improving the quality of education in India. Therefore, we cannot say whether it is desirable, from the economic point of view, to invest to raise the quality of education. However, common sense tells us that the quality should be improved. Studies from the US demonstrate that quality improvement is as profitable as quantity expansion. This finding seems to be relevant to India as well. Thus, there is a strong case for greater investment in quality improvement at all levels of education.

The latest fad is vocationalizing secondary education. Tamil Nadu is the leading state in the introduction of vocational courses at the higher secondary level. Occupational experience is essential but how this experience should be given is the most important question—whether it should be in ITIs and secondary schools or by organized in-firm training. There is a controversy about the relative advantages of the two methods. Economic analysis of the costs and benefits support training in firms. Foster's study (1965) of Ghana and Fuller's (1970) study of India are enlightening. Fuller compared turners, millers and grinders in a metal cutting factory trained in an ITI with those trained in the firm. Even after controlling variables (such as, schooling, trade experience, socio-economic status, etc.) productivity is higher among those trained in a firm. The social rate of return to training turners in an ITI is 5.9 per cent against that of training in a firm (14.5 per cent). The rates of return for fitters are 7.9 per cent and 11.3 per cent, respectively. These findings suggest that vocational training should be given in the work environment itself and not in an organized institution separate from the firm.

Schools and colleges are expected not only to disburse knowledge to the young but also to identify talented and gifted children and help them grow. In spite of talent search schemes and merit scholarships, my opinion is that our schools and colleges have failed in this respect. Identifying and educating talented children is a prerequisite for later scientific development and technical progress which is the primary source of economic growth. At present, governments at the centre and in the states give incentives and provide special facilities for educating children from disadvantaged groups. This is desirable from the point of view of equality. It is equally desirable, if not more, to provide special incentives and facilities for talented children, irrespective of their family background, from the point of view of efficiency.

More and more students continue in further education because the cost of education is low and the expected earnings even after adjusting for unemployment are high. If we accept that parents and children are not irrational then I should expect that the rates of return will be still favourable for individuals. If private rates of return are relatively high, then there is a case for the discriminatory pricing of education services and reducing earning differentials between educational levels.

References

AHLUWALIA, I.J. 1984. *Industrial Growth in India*, New Delhi: Oxford University Press.
AHLUWALIA, M.S. 1977. 'Rural Poverty and Agricultural Performance in India.' *Journal of Development Studies*.
ARROW, K.E. 1973. 'Higher Education as a Filter.' *Journal of Public Economics*.
ARUMUGHAM, P. 1984. Cost and Demand for Secondary Education in Tamilnadu (unpublished Ph.D. thesis), Department of Econometrics, University of Madras.
BOWMAN, M.J. 1980. 'Education and Economic Growth: An Overview,' in T. King, ed., *Education and Income*. World Bank.
DENISON, E.F. 1962. *The Sources of Economic Growth in the U.S. and the Alternative Before U.S.* N.Y.: Committee on Economic Development.
DHOLAKIA, B.H. 1974. *The Sources of Economic Growth in India*. Baroda: Good Company.
DURAISAMY, P. 1984. Economics of Education: The effect of Education on Fertility, Schooling, Employment of Women, Agricultural Production and Innovation (unpublished Ph.D. thesis), Dept. of Econometrics, University of Madras.
DUTTA, E. 1980. *Inter-Sectoral Terms of Trade and Income Distribution in India 1960–61—1973-74*. New Delhi: I.S.I. Working Paper.

Foster, Philip J. 1965. 'The Vocational School Fallacy in Development Planning,' in A.C. Anderson and M.J. Bowman, eds., *Education and Economic Development*. Aldine.

Fuller, William M. 1970. Education, Training and Productivity. A study of skilled workers in two factories in South India (unpublished monograph), School of Education, Stanford University.

Government of India. 1961. *Third Five Year Plan*. New Delhi.

Heyneman, S.P. 1980. 'Investment in Indian Education: Uneconomic?' *World Development*, No. 8, February, pp. 145–63.

Jamison, D.T. and Lawrence J. Lau. 1982. *Farmer Education and Farm Efficiency*. Johns Hopkins University Press.

Makhija, I. 1980. *High-Yielding Varieties: Schooling and Fertility in Rural India*. Chicago University.

Malathy, R. 1984. Allocation of Time by Married Women to Market and Non-Market Work in Madras City (unpublished Ph.D. thesis), Department of Econometrics, University of Madras.

Malenbaum, W. 1957. 'Urban Unemployment in India.' *Pacific Affairs*.

Nalla Gounden, A.M. 1967. 'Investment in Education in India.' *Journal of Human Resources*.

———. 1982. *Qualifications and Earnings: Human Capital vs. Screening Hypothesis*. Working Paper, Department of Econometrics, University of Madras.

———. 1983. *Discrimination Against Women*. Working Paper, Department of Econometrics, University of Madras.

Parnes, H. 1984. *People Power*. New Delhi: Sage Publications.

Prasad, Eswar. 1982. A Study of the Labour Market for Engineers (unpublished Ph.D. thesis), Jawaharlal Nehru University, New Delhi.

Psacharapoulos, G. 1972. *Return to Education*. N.Y.: American Elsevier.

Rao, V.K.R.V. 1966. *Education and Human Resources Development*. Bombay: Allied Publishers.

———. 1983. *India's National Income, 1950–1980*. New Delhi: Sage Publications.

Rati Ram and T.W. Schultz. 1979. 'Life Span, Health, Savings and Productivity'. *Economic Development and Cultural Change*, pp. 399–421.

Schultz, T.W. 1961. 'Education and Economic Growth,' in N.B. Henry, ed., *Social Forces Influencing American Education*. Chicago: National Society for the Study of Education.

Selowsky, M. 1969. 'On the Measurement of Education's Contribution to Growth.' *Quarterly Journal of Economics* (August).

Tilak, J.B.G. and G.K. Butt. 1984. *Costs and Supply of Education at Micro-Level*. New Delhi: NIEPA Working Paper.

Usha, S. 1981. Male-Female Earnings Differential in the Urban Labour Market (unpublished Ph.D. thesis), Department of Econometrics, University of Madras.

7

Science and Technology Policy in India: Implications for Quality of Education

Dinesh Mohan

Introduction

Almost a quarter of a century ago, I remember standing at attention for the unfurling of the national flag. I could not sing the national anthem because of a lump in my throat. I felt emotionally charged to be participating in yet another Republic Day of India. A free India led by Jawaharlal Nehru. His message was stirring. I was involved in the building of new India. My education was going to liberate me from the evils of casteism, untouchability, dowry and regionalism. We were the leaders of nonalignment and I was going to grow up in a world free of war. We, the school children of India, were going to be adults in a country where no one would be hungry.

Those were heady days for a schoolboy. At least for one who was free from hunger and disease. The Bhakra dam was being built, steel plants and cement factories were coming up, and we were manufacturing our own cars. We were told that factories were the new temples of our country. We even saw the factory smokestack as a symbol of progress. A progress that would make us independent of foreign domination. Our scientists and engineers would make sure that we would make our own things in our own ways for our own needs. What further proof or assurance did a young boy need that things were really moving?

I do not know how the adults felt in those days. I do not really know how young boys and girls view the scene today. I suspect they don't even listen to Republic Day speeches. I certainly don't find much to be excited about. I would like to think it's just middle age blues. But I don't think so. Educational institutions, factories, legal institutions, medical facilities and research laboratories are all facing a crisis, and this crisis has erupted in sores all over our national body politic: closed universities, the slow murder of labourers in unsafe mines and factories, fraud and plagiarism in science, iatrogenic diseases spread by an ignorant and callous medical profession, and the promotion of image-building science and technology on the Indian scene.

There are two lies that are repeated *ad nauseum* by everyone in authority and believed quite readily by almost everyone else: India has the third largest scientific manpower and India is the tenth largest industrial nation in the world. Both these statements reflect the jingoist and hegemonistic tendencies of citizens of large countries who generally like to exert their superiority over others by championing their own achievements in terms of quantity rather than quality. However, it appears that in terms of people who can really be called scientists or engineers, India may be well behind a large number of other countries and in industrial production it ranks, anywhere from twenty-second to twenty-fourth (*World Development Report*, 1982–84). This is just not a matter of quibbling over numbers. I think it reflects a serious malaise in the Indian science and education establishment. It shows that the very people who talk of establishing a scientific culture are not willing to deal with numbers and statistics in a factual manner. It also shows that the educated public at large is not willing to challenge rulers on a purely scientific basis. This problem, in itself, is a microcosm of the successes and failures of science and education in India.

It is a truism to state that for scientific and technological development, a nation needs a well-educated citizenry and for good science teaching a good industrial infrastructure creates the necessary demand. This symbiotic relationship is very important in the development of both science and education. The problem is that even today, the literacy rate in India is one of the lowest in the world and we still do not understand what elements are most critical in promoting self-sustaining industrial development.

The number of educational establishments, research laboratories and scientific institutions have increased manyfold since independence and so have the number of students enrolled in schools and colleges (Table 1). At the same time, all those problems which were expected to disappear with a better educated populace seem to have increased also or at least remained the same: communal violence (Gopal Krishna, 1985), centralization of power (Kothari, 1984), foreign collaborations (Goyal, 1982), and lack of innovation (Bhagawan, 1981). This means that either our earlier expectations were misplaced, or that we really do not understand the mechanics of interaction between science education and social change in India. To understand this we must at least briefly understand our successes and failures and then attempt an analysis of what we can do in the future to improve the quality of science and education in India.

Strengths of the System

The strengths of the system are extolled continuously by the establishment scientists. They generally hold the view that if only scientists had better working conditions with more equipment and clear-cut directions from the government, we could solve almost all the problems of the country. One of the major proponents of this view is P.M. Bhargava (1981). According to him, our investment in many areas of scientific and technical endeavour is subcritical. He is also convinced that because of the scientific and industrial infrastructure available in India, we can find the technological component of the solution to problems concerning health, housing, clothing, education and employment within five years. In his view, the main responsibility for failure in these areas lies with 'the highest echelons of power'—in other words, in the realm of politics. This view justifies the fast expansion of the scientific and industrial infrastructure in India in the early sixties.

India has set up an institutional structure which makes possible the training of a large number of skilled people in science and technology (Table 2). Though the quality or these scientists and engineers is very varied, the fact remains that out of this large

Table 1: Enrolment and Percentage of Enrolment in Classes in Corresponding Age Group and Absolute Increase with Percentage (1961, 1971 and 1981)

Educational Level and Age Group	Enrolment			Percentage of Population in Relevant Age Group Enrolled			Increase (figures in thousands)			
							Number		Percentage	
	1961	1971	1981	1961	1971	1981	1961–71	1971–81	1961–71	1971–81
Class I–V (6–11 years)	34,994	57,045	72,200	62.4	78.6	80.5	22,051	15,155	63.0	26.6
Class VI–VIII (11–14 years)	6,705	13,315	18,700	22.5	33.4	36.9	6,610	5,385	98.6	28.8
Class IX and above (14–17 years)	2,837	6,580	10,876	16.7	18.5	18.3	3,693	4,296	128.0	65.3
Higher Education (17–23 years)	2,590	3,502	5,921	5.1	5.7	6.8	918	2,419	35.2	69.1

Note: Figures for 1981 are provisional.
Sources: *Education in India*, 1961 and 1971, Ministry of Education.
Estimated by IAMR in *National Manpower Accounts*.
CSO, *Basic Statistics Relating to Indian Economy—1950–51 to 1979–80*.

Table 2: Estimated Stock, Number of Economically Active Persons, Unemployment and Employment of Scientific & Technical Persons in 1980 and 1985

(figures in thousands)

Category	1980 (Beginning)					1985 (Beginning)			
	Stock	Number of Economically Active	Unemployment	Unemployment Percentage to Economically Active	Inter-se Percentage of Unemployment rates	Stock	Number of Economically Active	Unemployment	Employment
Engineering Degree Holders	254.5	221.4	15.7	7.09	7.8	306.1	266.3	18.9	247.4
Engineering Degree Holders	378.6	329.4	65.5	19.88	21.9	494.1	429.9	85.5	344.4
Medical Graduates	178.5	155.3	10.1	6.50	7.2	211.9	184.3	12.0	172.3
Dental Surgeons	11.6	10.1	0.2	1.98	2.2	13.4	11.6	0.2	11.4
Nurses (B.Sc)	2.2	2.2	—	—	—	2.8	2.8	—	2.8
Agricultural Graduates	98.8	77.1	8.8	11.41	12.6	115.9	90.4	10.3	80.1
Veterinary Graduates	22.3	19.4	0.7	3.60	3.9	27.3	23.7	0.9	22.8
Science Graduates	961.9	750.3	154.3	20.57	22.6	1,226.3	956.5	196.8	759.7
Science Post-Graduates	278.9	217.5	10.6	4.87	5.4	350.0	273.0	13.3	259.7
B.Sc./B.Ed.	213.2	166.3	24.8	14.90	16.4	284.2	227.7	35.7	191.9
Total	2,400.5	1,949.0	290.7	14.90	—	3,032.0	2,466.1	373.0	2,092.5

Source: Sixth Five Year Plan, 1980–85; Planning Commission, Annexure 13.9, p. 220.

number a few individuals end up being very well trained and are very competent. This would be true for almost all areas of scientific and technical endeavour. This makes it possible for society to be reasonably confident that it can undertake any complex technical task and find people to carry it through. This is a very important prerequisite for good plans to be feasible in practise.

INDUSTRIAL AND SCIENTIFIC INFRASTRUCTURE

India is one of the very few countries in the world today where almost every consumer product is manufactured or at least assembled within the country. Though there are signs that this situation is likely to change in the near future and India will allow more and more foreign technology to enter in order to 'catch-up,' a vast majority of items needed by most people will continue to be manufactured in India. This large structure keeps up a constant demand for technically skilled persons and thus influences the value system in the educational process. A technical or semi-technical training is seen as a sinecure for a comfortable middle class life. This keeps up the pressure on the politicians to provide science and technical education.

At the time of Independence there were only 19 universities in the country. By 1984 India had over 140 institutions of university stature. While most of the laboratories have come up after Independence, some research organizations were started before Independence: the Council of Scientific and Industrial Research in 1942, Indian Council of Agricultural Research (as Imperial Council of Agricultural Research) in 1929, Indian Council of Medical Research (as India Research Fund Association) in 1911. Even in these organizations, the main expansion has taken place after Independence. The CSIR now supports 38 national laboratories, three complexes and two research associations. The ICAR runs 33 research institutes and four project directorates; the ICMR has 18 institutes and six regional medical research centres. After Independence, the major departments set up were the Department of Atomic Energy, Department of Electronics, Department of Environment, Department of Ocean Development, Department of Space, Department of Defence Research and Development and the Department of Non-conventional Energy Sources. A concise summary of all these institutions and their functions has been compiled by A. Rahman (1984). In addition, a large number of research organizations have been established in the social sciences also.

The Department of Science and Technology had also recognized research and development units in 714 private industries by December 1983. At least in numbers this is a very impressive infrastructure. While many of the institutions included in this list may not have very useful equipment or professionals of much competence, many do possess very useful and sophisticated instrumentation. Therefore, as a national resource, the infrastructure is quite impressive and affords possibilities of a great deal of useful work and training.

Scientists in almost all Third World countries look upon this infrastructure with envy. Industrial production in India has increased from about 10 billion dollars in 1960 to about 70 billion dollars in 1984. Just in terms of quantity and variety this means a tremendous expansion of skills. This would necessarily exert a demand on the system which makes growth in scientific and technical learning automatic.

FREEDOM FOR EXPERIMENTS AND POLITICAL ACTIVITY

A large number of innovative academic, industrial and institution management experiments have been attempted by some very gifted people. These include tremendously successful health programs and science teaching experiments implemented successfully in rural areas. This list would contain rural development programs by voluntary organizations and Gandhian institutions, labour organizations (like SEWA), rehabilitation experiments (like the one which made possible the Jaipur Foot) and popular science movements (like the Kerala Shastra Sahitya Parishad). The experiences of these individuals and groups are there for us to draw upon specifically with the idea of planning for the future. This is possible because there is still a reasonable degree of political freedom which allows such experiments to take place and innovative ideas to emerge. In addition, professionals and bureaucrats are still under the strong influence of politicians. This gives us hope that it should be possible in the future to improve the scheme of things through the political process.

It is because of this that it may be possible for the varied experiences of activist groups to be made useful by linking education-science-culture-politics with survival.

PLURALITY OF CULTURE AND SURVIVAL OF TRADITIONAL CRAFTS AND SCIENCES

India's large size and the existence of a vast hinterland with a great deal of geographical and cultural variety ensure that traditional culture and science survive here. It may be possible to channel this storehouse of experience and expertise into some novel ways of solving our problems. They may even be able to tackle some of the basic production challenges of the late twentieth century.

The existence of a large number of distinct languages and cultural practices helps one to view the same problem in different ways. This has partly helped the vast majority of the Indian people not to fall into the monoculture trap of the elite.

BOTTOM HEAVY POPULATION DISTRIBUTION

In the decades to come India will retain a population distribution in which young people will constitute a majority of the population. This could ensure the emergence of youthful ideas and exuberance if the young today are given special attention and encouraged to think differently.

Weaknesses of the System

LOW QUALITY OF SCIENTIFIC AND TECHNICAL PERSONNEL

I have dealt with the quality of scientific and technical personnel in some detail elsewhere (Mohan, 1981) but will mention the essential points here.

In the total number of papers published in all areas of science and technology (in journals indexed in *Current Contents*), India ranks eighth after the USA, UK, USSR, W. Germany, France, Canada and Japan. But, in quality, India appears worse than Swedan, Belgium, Switzerland, Denmark, Australia, Japan, Israel and Italy as well (not including the communist nations).

One way of assessing the quality of publications is to see how often they are cited. In a study of 100 most-cited articles of the 1960s in pre-clinical basic research and another 100 in clinical research, not one paper came from an Indian institute (Table 3).

Most of the journals included in *Current Contents* are published in English so such studies probably have a bias towards scientists publishing in English. Since all scientific work in India is published in English. Indians should not have any problem on this score. Data for all the other fields gives similar results: no Indian institution produced any significant paper which was widely cited in the 1960s.

An argument can be levelled that the real advances were made in India in the 1970s and 1980s, so our institutions should be producing better work now. However, Table 3 shows that even if we consider only papers published in 1977, we do not have any Indian institute producing a significant paper in the physical or life sciences. Similar studies for other years and other disciplines show that there is no Indian institution which produces high quality work consistently. Very sporadically, the Tata Institute of Fundamental Research in Bombay and the Indian Institute of Science in Bangalore manage to get included.

No article in any discipline which has been highly cited has been published in an Indian journal. There are many ways of assessing the quality of a journal: how often its articles are cited in other journals (impact factor), how often it cites articles in other journals and how quickly other journals cite its articles (immediacy factor). Eugene Garfield, who publishes *Current Contents* and *Science Citation Index*, does such analyses regularly. His analyses show that there is no Indian journal in any field which ranks in the top twenty according to any of these criteria. A more detailed analysis of Indian physics journals (Arunachalam, 1979) indicates that they publish articles of a routine nature with very little conceptual originality.

No matter how we try to assess the quality of Indian scientists working in Indian institutions, we reach the same conclusion: Indian science is not making important contributions to international science in any field, experimental or theoretical. This runs counter

Table 3: Institutional Origin of the Hundred Most-Cited Papers in Various Disciplines

Study	More than Four Papers	Four	Three	Two	One
Pre-Clinical Basic Research (Most-Cited in the 1960s)	USA (35) UK (8) Sweden (5)	—	Belgium Canada Switzerland	Japan	Austria Denmark West Germany France Norway
Clinical Research (Most-Cited in the 1960s)	USA (52) UK (9)	Sweden	Canada	West Germany France New Zealand	Denmark Austria
1977 Articles (Most-Cited in 1977–79) Life Sciences	USA (52) UK (9) Denmark (5)	Sweden	Canada	France West Germany	Israel, Italy Japan, Kenya Norway Switzerland Netherlands
1977 Articles (Most-Cited in 1977–79) Physical Sciences	USA (41) West Germany (11) France (5) UK (5)	—	—	Italy USSR Switzerland	Belgium, Chile Denmark Japan Spain, Sweden

Source: All data from studies reported in *Current Contents*.

to the often made argument that Indian scientists are good at theory and work on the problems of Western countries. If they are, scientists in Western countries are not noticing them.

It is very difficult to assess the quality of Indians abroad as no articles mention the place of birth of the authors. Neither do institutions mention the place of birth of their employees. So any analysis can at best be approximate. I have tried to do this by counting articles authored or co-authored by scientists who have Indian-sounding names. This of course has its pitfalls—I could miss those Indians who have foriegn-sounding names, and at the same time include foreign-born Indians, African Indians, West Indians, Pakistanis, etc. However, the numbers are so small that I don't think these errors cause any significant problem.

I have tried to compare the contribution of scientists with Indian-sounding names with that of scientists with Chinese-sounding names, Arab- and Iranian-sounding names and Japanese-sounding names (see Table 4).

I have again used two studies of the 100 most cited articles of 1977 as examples. Both in the physical and life sciences there was only

Table 4: Authorship of Highly Cited Articles by Ethnic Background of Author

Study	Number of Papers							
	Arab/Iranian-Sounding Names		Chinese-Sounding Names		Japanese-Sounding Names		Indian-Sounding Names	
	Principal Author	Co-Author	Principal Author	Co-Author	Principal Author	Co-Author	Principal Author	Co-Author
1977 Articles Most-Cited in 1977–79 Physical Sciences	4	1	2	10	2	2	1	2
Life Sciences	2	0	3	10	3	8	1	2
Citation Classics 1980	3	1	3	4	11	2	3	2

See text for sources of error.
Source: All data from *Current Contents* (1980).

one paper each authored by a scientist with an Indian-sounding name. There were two more which had Indian names as co-authors. A very small number, indeed, considering that there are such a large number of Indian scientists with a good grasp of English working in the US and the UK.

The pattern is similar in other studies of highly cited articles. What is interesting is that there seem to be as many scientists with Arab- and Iranian-sounding names who are cited often as if they were Indians. In general, scientists with Chinese and Japanese names seem to do better than Indians according to this criterion. Every week each edition of *Current Contents* has a 'Citation Classic' which is a highly cited publication from previous years. *Current Contents* has six editions—agricultural, biological and environmental sciences; clinical practice; engineering, technology and applied sciences; life sciences; physical chemistry and earth sciences; social and behavioural sciences. So, in a year, there are approximately 312 citation classics. Out of these citation classics, in 1980 there were only three authored and two co-authored by scientists with Indian-sounding names (Table 4). Of these, two were books. So even if we take a long-term perspective, we do not see Indians outshining any other comparable group even when they work abroad.

These are just a few ways of looking at the problem. If one uses other indices the conclusions are similar: that the average quality of Indian scientists is very low. This tends to affect the productivity of even the better ones both directly and indirectly.

An analysis of this kind is always criticized for using Western criteria to judge the competence of Indian scientists. The reason I use Western criteria is because all our scientific institutions are based on Western (largely American and British) models. One of the main criticisms against scientists levelled by nationalists is that Indian scientists only work on Western problems and are inspired by the need for publication in Western journals. If *this* is so, then Indian scientists must also be evaluated by Western yardsticks. I do not believe that Indian scientists *should* work on problems considered important by the West or that we *should* use Western yardsticks. However, we cannot have it both ways; we cannot accuse Indian scientists of working on Western problems and then want to judge their quality by some mythical Indian yardstick.

WIDESPREAD DISHONESTY

The culture of science considers the following values very important: equality, curiosity, individuality, courage of conviction and absolute honesty. All these values are discouraged in a hierarchical tradition-bound and status quo-oriented society. Honesty is thought to be a personal issue. When a faculty member of a prestigious technical institution went to the director of his institute to inform him of the rampant dishonesty in research in his department he was rebuffed for trying to act 'like Christ'. He was told that he should not worry about what happened around him but just do his own work honestly. He was lucky. In some other institute he would have faced serious problems after that. But honesty is a crucial issue. Each scientist's work constitutes a building block to be used by other scientists. If there is a lack of real or perceived honesty, there can be no building blocks. Genuine scientific work cannot thrive in isolated pockets.

A large number of senior scientists in important laboratories in India have, at one time or another, been accused of outright fraud, plagiarism or exaggeration. Even if these accusations are not correct at times, this is a serious matter since there is then an absence of role models and it encourages widespread cynicism among the younger ones. So, there is little attempt to do any serious work. In some institutions it is suspected that at least 70 per cent of the research projects are of dubious quality involving plagiarism, invention of data, and plain unscientific methodology and analysis. These badly trained young scientists then end up being senior scientists.

UNWIELDY HIGHER EDUCATION SYSTEM

Figure 1 shows the phenomenal rise in higher education in India. In all probability, elementary education statistics are less reliable than the university enrolment statistics and, therefore, the disparities may be worse. Looking at the plan allocation figures, it appears that higher education has been given a disproportionate amount of importance in India. It is only in the Sixth Plan that elementary education has been given a relatively higher allocation. But we must remember that basic education and higher education share a symbiotic relationship—if basic education is bad then students going into higher education would be of poor quality; if higher education is of poor quality, secondary school teachers would be of poor quality. In an extreme situation this would result in a downward spiral in both sectors. In higher education there are many other issues involved. Are the finances adequate? Is there a demand for the products of universities? Is the education relevant? Which section of the population is being served? Do universities impart needed skills, idealism and motivation?

All these are inter-related questions and none of them independent of the political and economic structure of the nation. I believe that it would be very difficult to resolve any other issues unless the need and demand for higher education is sorted out first. Solutions to other problems would be easier after that.

Figure 1 shows that as enrolment in higher education increased in India so did the number of Indian students in the USA. I do not think that this relationship is entirely fortuitous, though factors such as immigration laws in the USA do influence it. However, it does indicate that highly trained persons in India may be in excess and they do not find adequate outlets in India.

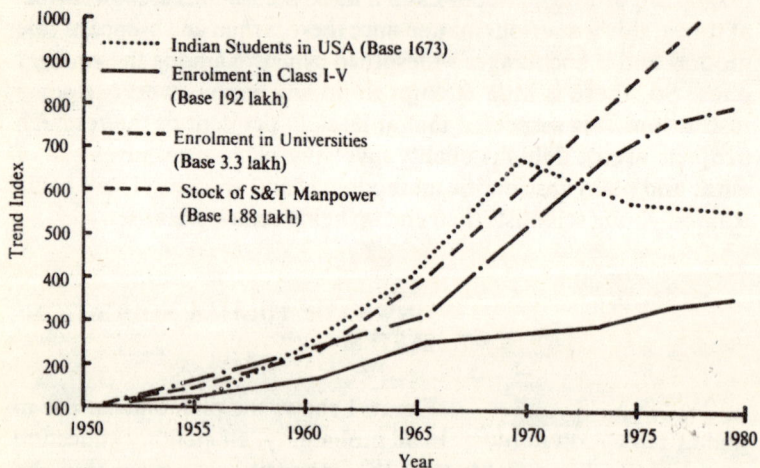

Expenditure on Education in Crores

	4th Plan	5th Plan	6th Plan
Elementary	240	410	905
University	214	450	762

Figure 1

Figure 2 shows that though expenditure on education as a percentage of GNP is low in India, enrolment at universities as a percentage of the labour force in industrial and labour sectors is very high. Enrolment at the third level (beyond secondary school) as a percentage of population has not been used because I think it is mainly an index of poverty and lack of industrialization. Since university or professional graduates seek jobs mainly in the industrial or service sector, the ratio used in Figure 2a may give us a better indication of the relative demand for higher education. In the industrialized countries the expertise level required in the service sector and the skilled to unskilled ratio in the industrial sector is much higher than that in India. The data in Figure 2a indicates that third level enrolment may be far too high in India for current socio-economic conditions.

Industrial and service sector employment would have to increase manyfold before university graduates in India could find meaningful employment if our development is based on current models. Since we do not have capital and resources to waste, we may need much lower ratios than even the UK.

Another way to look at the same issues is to compare the number of scientific personnel as a ratio of the industrial product instead of the total population. The former ratio may give some idea of current need whereas the latter just indicates the level of poverty. Figure 3 shows these statistics in India, the USA and the UK. India produces about ten times as many engineering graduates per billion dollars of manufacturing product as the UK. Even if the price differentials are taken into account, it is clear that either India produces too many engineers, or that most of the engineers may not be of good quality, or that many of these graduates do not work as engineers, or all of the above.

The disparities are not as large, but a similar situation seems to be true for the number of scientists and engineers involved in R & D (Figure 3). These statistics could indicate that the country is supporting far too many scientists for the level of manufacturing in the country, or that those listed as R & D personnel are really not involved in R & D. Conversely, one could even say that since these ratios are so lopsided in India, it is not surprising that these scientists cannot be supported adequately.

What I have demonstrated in the foregoing has been discussed qualitatively by many. The demand for delinking jobs from degrees

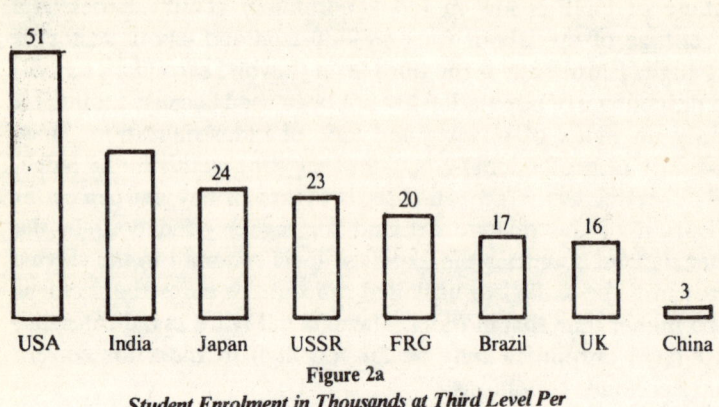

Figure 2a
Student Enrolment in Thousands at Third Level Per Million Labour Force in Industrial and Service Sectors

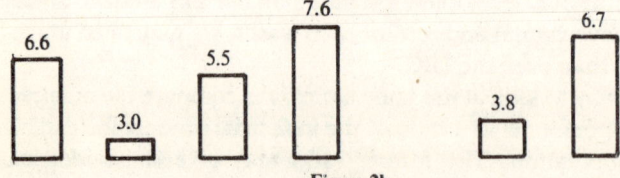

Figure 2b
Total Public Expenditure on Education as a Percentage of GNP

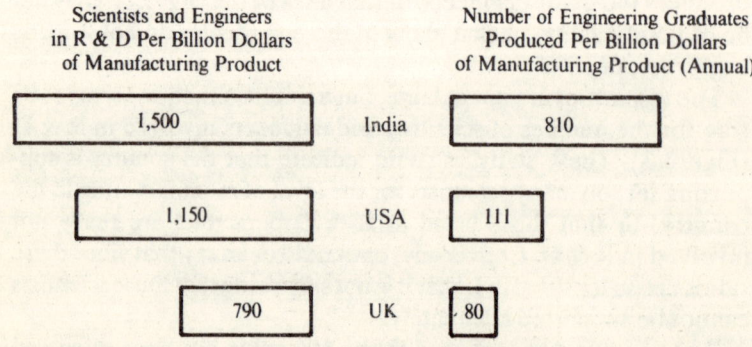

Figure 3
Scientists and Engineers in India, USA and UK as a Ratio of Manufacturing Product

actually is an assertion that there are not so many jobs as there are degree holders. But delinking is not the issue. It cannot be done as long as there are colleges which have openings for admission.

The employment exchange data give ample evidence of the overproduction demonstrated earlier. But no serious thought has been given to the magnitude of this problem, quantitatively or qualitatively. The indices I have used in Figures 2 and 3 clearly show that the higher education sector in India has expanded far too rapidly in relation to economic and industrial development. This expansion has had some very deleterious qualitative effects on the educational establishment as a whole. Some of these are discussed below.

EFFECTS OF UNREASONABLE EXPANSION OF HIGHER EDUCATION

Sometime back I interviewed a first class graduate in electronics from G.B. Pant University. I quickly realized that asking him technical questions would not get me anywhere. So I asked him where his hometown got its power. From 'the power house, sir,' he replied, with complete confidence.

Such experiences are not uncommon whether the person being interviewed is seeking admission to a post-graduate program, a faculty position in a university, or a sales job in a company. They indicate the tremendous lowering of standards that has accompanied this expansion in higher education.

It is not necessary that lowering of standards will always accompany expansion. Not at all. Not if higher education expands in proportion to industrial, agricultural and societal needs and not at the expense of basic education.

In India, the expansion of higher education has been of a unilateral nature in spite of the 1964–66 Education Commission's observations in this connection: 'There is a general feeling in India that the situation in higher education is unsatisfactory and even alarming in some ways, that the average standards have been falling, and that rapid expansion has resulted in lowering quality.' But the report itself did not deal with this problem of expansion in university enrolments from 1 million in 1965–66 to 4 million in 1985–86. And we have expanded almost as fast as the Commission suggested. It is important to note here that even when the problem of expansion was noticed, no measures—except streamlining and better facilities for students, faculty and staff—were suggested.

The problem is that when there is no real demand for a large number of university graduates, there is no external check on their quality by the users. This makes the students less discriminating and so there is no check on the teacher. The teacher, in any case, is not of the highest standard and this lack of demand, consequently, makes him worse. Under such circumstances, the university administrators, in turn, do not have to worry about quality. Thus it really does not matter if faculty selections are not entirely fair. Quality is no longer the issue; personal gains are. One can't expect fair selections when there is no need to select the best.

Once bad faculty is selected then it is very difficult for good ones to get in. Only the good ones leave as the bad have nowhere to go. The good ones leave for another new institution or for greener pastures abroad. Since the average age of teachers in India is low, universities are then doomed for decades.

In a large country, there are bound to be a large number of bright young people. If they are lucky enough to belong to the higher income groups, they can gain entry to some of the elite institutions and do well with the help of a few good teachers and good textbooks.

However, there are very few openings where these excellent graduates can be used productively. Some, especially those interested in pursuing careers in science and technology, choose to go abroad. The remaining are lucky if they don't end up doing work of a routine nature. Their potential is not challenged in areas they have been trained to think as their realm of expertise. *This internal brain-drain is far more harmful and a greater waste than the external brain-drain we always focus on.*

When bright, trained and educated persons do not use their expertise, society gets an indirect message that specialization and intellectual activity may not be important or necessary. The importance of scholarship is thus devalued in general. This effect is dramatically demonstrated by the fact that very few outstanding students opt for research careers. For example, hardly any of the Indian Institutes of Technology's own graduates return for postgraduate work. A Ministry of Education Committee on higher technical education recently noted that 'it has not been possible to attract a sufficiently large number of bright young people for postgraduate education.' But the authors of the report do not attack the import of technology in strong enough terms nor do they discuss the rapid expansion of higher education as a possible cause of these problems. Figure 3 clearly indicates that we cannot use such large numbers of highly trained persons as long as we use models operating in the West. They seem to survive with relatively fewer experts for their level of development.

Another serious side effect of this rapid expansion, lowering of standards, and insufficient demand, is the widespread prevalence of fraud and plagiarism in institutions of higher learning. Most heads of institutions do not even take reported cases seriously. Hardly any faculty members lose their jobs due to academic dishonesty. Most retort that fraud is common even in America so who are we to get excited? But the proportions here seem to be frightening. In a private conversation, a member of the Medical Council of India estimated that as much as 80 per cent of the M.S. theses may be based on fraudulent data. In another such conversation, an eminent scientist and director of a national laboratory claimed that he does not accept examining Ph.D. theses because the results of 70 per cent are not replicable. These are not matters to be brushed aside. They are devastating for a community and nation that desperately needs to be independent of foreign domination in knowledge and information.

One common argument in favour of rapid expansion of higher education is that this gives a better opportunity to the less affluent for upward mobility. Even this contention is being challenged. In the absence of accompanying political changes and improved basic education this may have the opposite effect. Richards and Leonor (1981) claim that 'the promotion of education, which simply means its expansion, may equally well lead to the opposite of the effect intended, i.e., greater inequality in incomes and overall well being'. One of the reasons this can happen is because, as the system expands unnaturally, only a few institutions maintain standards. These institutions institute admission procedures and aptitude tests which generally favour those coming from better family backgrounds. In the other institutions, since the teachers and facilities are not good it is the students with deprived backgrounds who suffer more. In a very tight job market and an over-inflated supply situation, those with poor backgrounds end up where they started after having wasted time and effort in an endeavour that was supposed to help them in upward mobility. A sure recipe for cynicism and corruption.

There are many other effects of this lowering of standards, but I would like to discuss just one more. As the expansion of institutions has taken place, the quality of academic work has reduced but the number of higher degrees has increased. As these Masters and Ph.D. degree holders get jobs in research institutions and universities they all become equal. They forget that most of them did not do much to earn their advanced degrees. Living conditions being difficult, all of them demand the same benefits that their best colleagues deserve. Initially, some of them manage this by fixing selection committees, and they follow the demands of the unions. Eventually, those groups who have blackmailing power manage to get time-bound promotions and academic evaluation takes a back seat.

In the foregoing analysis I have tried to link many of the ills of our educational system to the rapid expansion it has undergone. I am not suggesting that this is the only reason but only focusing on an aspect that has been neglected too long and little understood. It will not be easy to resolve either but some counter measures have to be contemplated.

DISPROPORTIONATE SUPPORT FOR SPECTACULAR SCIENCE

There is an undesirable and unnatural importance given to "basic" science and spectacular science (Nandy, 1985) in India. This results in all people-oriented projects being neglected to a very large extent. Hence, even applied scientists gravitate towards proving their machismo in mathematical acrobatics of little consequence. This obviously results in science barons (who often are very competent by international standards) using their international prestige and connections successfully to push projects like bio-technology, expeditions to Antartica, fancy physics laboratories and nuclear research. This results in neglect of people-oriented science and technology. This has also resulted in isolating scientists and engineers even more from society.

After three decades of 'catching up,' we are back where we started. We are contracting with foreign companies and governments—for import of designs and processes in most of our industries—power, steel, fertilizer, automobiles, aviation, consumer goods, etc. This is supposed to indicate that we are making concessions to free trade and it will help us produce the latest and the best. There is tremendous pressure for letting in the multinationals, both from inside and outside the country. The fact that we have taken the largest IMF loan which this institution has ever given indicates that the policy-makers have faith in the ideologies of such institutions. This is not an abstract statement. Even before we took the loan, we had increased the number of foreign collaborations allowed from 277 in 1976 to 526 in 1980. These are curious facts considering that we take great pride in our scientific and technological capability.

We claim that we are the tenth largest industrial nation in the world, neglecting our abysmally low per capita production. But as I have stated earlier, even this claim is just a myth. We are also very proud that Indian engineers and technicians work wonders in innovation and adaptation. A belief not borne out by facts or by comparison with other countries (Bhagawan, 1981). Japan is used to justify foreign collaborations, the import of turnkey projects, and the import of obsolete know-how. In personal conversations with me, very senior officials of the Birlas, Modis and Tatas have used the argument that this is the path Japan followed for its advancement. 'Japan never did any research but just copies' they claim. However, according to Shigeru Nakayama (1978), Japanese scientists changed from the old-fashioned generation of academic bureaucrats to the new technically-oriented who advocated planning of scientific research for national goals in the early part of this century.

Let us take the Chinese case. Indians point out with glee that even the Chinese are now turning to foreign know-how. 'See, they have learnt the lesson of their past mistakes. So let us in India now have even more foreign collaborations.' A curious double-think. We conveniently forget that the Chinese do not at present have over 100 multinational subsidiaries operating on their soil and have not already signed over 6,000 collaboration agreements with foreign companies in the last thirty-five years as we have . Even the few agreements that they did sign in the last two or three years are being pruned.

We also like to believe that they have suffered technologically because of their policies. But let us examine the facts. We are proud of our achievements in space, nuclear energy and agriculture. China does not seem to be any worse off in any of these sectors. Even in computer technology they seem to be as good as the Soviet Union

Table 5: Comparison of Industrial Production in India and China

Item	Units	India† Per Million Population	China† Per Million Population
Chemical Fertilizer	thousand tons/year	4	12
Steel	thousand tons/year	9	27
Electric Power	million KVH/year	166	316
Tractors	units/year	96	54
Foodgrain	thousand tons/year	193	322
Cotton cloth	million metres/year	14	15
Trucks	units/year	118	180
Fans	units/year	6,000	10,000
Cement	thousand tons/year	28	86
Radios	total number	29,000*	41,000
TV Sets	total number	1,400*	5,500

† All data normalized by assuming India's and China's population as 673 and 976 million, respectively.
* These figures are probably underestimates.
Source: *India's Economy in Figures*, CSO, 1982; India 1980; *China Reconstructs*, August 1982.

(Sigurdson, 1981), which is better than us. We seem to be much better off in assembling or making under license many of the more elitist consumer products, but China does not seem to have done too badly in the basic infrastructure for mass consumption consumer goods either (Table 5). Even if these figures give only approximate ideas, it appears to me that in technological capability we are probably only at par with China.

The foregoing facts show that we are not particularly better off technically so far as comparable countries are concerned. It appears that we are not utilizing our domestic potential fully and have neglected basic products in favour of toys for the elite. Many have argued that this is bound to happen if the multinational and foreign nexus is too strong. In fact, this seems to have a disastrous effect on the morale of local scientists and engineers and even discourages innovation in products most important for us. M.R. Bhagawan (1981) has done a quantitative investigation into the innovative capabilities of Indian industry and concludes that India has now acquired substantial innovative capacity in the less science-related and the less research-intensive industries like machine tools, but is still very weak in those fields where science relatedness and research intensiveness play a big role. Also, about two-thirds of the innovations cited by the Indian capital goods firms are really quite minor technical changes, adaptations and 'improvements'.

In another study, Iyengar (1982) concludes that the fact remains that the contribution of R & D in industry pales into insignificance against major achievements in other developed countries. As far as the industry is concerned, the basic R & D is still imported either through direct sales or through collaborations. This has resulted in a proliferation of fast-selling formulations which have no relevance to the actual needs of a majority of the population.

Some of my students and I conducted a survey at the Indian Engineering Trade Fair held in New Delhi in February 1981. We questioned almost all the exhibitors about their range of products—whether they had foreign collaboration, in-house R & D and which products they had developed due to their own R & D. Out of the 72 exhibitors sampled, 62 (90 per cent) claimed they did have R & D but 55 (80 per cent) admitted having foreign collaboration.

We could not identify a single product using modern technology which had been made in India without foreign collaboration. Products that were completely indigenous and which could find an export market tended to be those with know-how more than thirty years old obtained even at that time with foreign collaboration. It is not surprising then that Ph.Ds comprise only 8 per cent of the R & D personnel in private industry.

Foreign technology and foreign collaboration still commands a great deal of respect. So much so that almost 70 per cent of more than 170 advertisers in *The Hindu's* Survey of Indian Industry (1981) indicate in one way or another that they are associated with foreign know-how or foreign companies. The main news about modernization in magazines like *Business India* and the *Economic Scene* are about new foreign agreements being signed.

While these magazines have carried major articles on the evils of MRTP and FERA and foreign dumping in India, none of them have really initiated intelligent debate on the quality of indigenous technology, the role of the Indian entrepreneur in innovation and the strengthening of India's R & D base. The tenor of most articles which support greater foreign collaboration and import of foreign technology is that this will help us catch up. It is not clear that even this purpose is served.

The Indian railways imported know-how for electrical and diesel locomotives about two decades back and are planning to do so again. The railways are again so far behind that they are contemplating import of know-how even for power transmission, signalling and various other systems. This is, of course, made very much easier with the availability of the World Bank and IMF loans. Few people know that some Indian railway technology was abreast of the world as far back as 1925. The Bombay, Baroda and Central India Railway had the capability of designing and manufacturing locomotives as good as anywhere else in the world. But we have not kept up hence the need for this periodic shot in the arm from abroad.

We are doing now what we were doing in 1965—importing a modern infrastructure. If politicians, professionals and the industrial elite are allowed to continue their present policies, then in the year 2000 we will be back again to 1965.

LANGUAGE AND COMMUNICATION

The existence of English as a medium of scientific, academic and serious communication among the elite has probably retarded our science education process. In their early years, children, instead of exercising their curiosity to the maximum and imbibing exciting and unusual ideas, have to concentrate on learning a foreign language. Form becomes the most important factor and substance recedes into the background. This process also keeps average children of middle class and lesser income families out of the good education system because almost by definition, good schools teach in English and it is almost impossible except for the elite to have a comfortable knowledge of English. Therefore, a majority of the people are excluded from knowledge exchange and upward mobility. The language also focuses our attention only on the UK and USA as sources of knowledge or information.

It should be quite clear that it is not possible or feasible to teach English to a vast majority of the people. So, the demand of the elite that all should be taught English is actually a clever ploy to maintain the status quo.

It is also true that information dissemination in science, technology, vocational know-how and other societal issues is very weak in India. A study done by Erik Baark (1983) indicates that India lags behind China in the information dissemination system. In particular, in India, the information systems seem to remain locked in their bias towards scientists' needs and they show little concern with focusing services in areas of national priority in technology and economic policies.

LOW LITERACY RATES

India has one of the lowest literacy rates in the world and the primary school drop-out rate is still very high. Therefore, the educated base is very small for the size of the population while higher education facilities have gone through a great deal of expansion. Thus, there is little selection of people continuing into the secondary and tertiary stage, except financial circumstances. Low priority to primary education is bound to result in bad schools, bad students and bad science.

Implications for Education

In spite of the Science Policy Resolution and the Technology Policy Resolution, the scientific and technologic advancement of India has not forced its educational establishment to become first rate.

Places of learning in most societies are held in sacred respect and all attempts are made to protect them from corruption and decay. We are, on the other hand, reduced to just viewing our universities as a law and order problem. We must be the only country in the world where a University Grants Commission can make the most routine academic practices into important guidelines: 'Students will be required to study the entire syllabus, marks are to be awarded for completion of work. Only those abstaining do not get any marks.'

It seems that no one is really happy with what happens on our campuses. The rulers and administrators profess that they are unhappy because the campuses are not quiet enough or productive enough, the parents are peeved because at the end of a few years in college their wards pick up bad habits and get no jobs, the teachers are upset because they don't have enough money to manage their own lives or the power to control the students, the students are adrift and bored by their uninspired professors, courses and miserable surroundings. For all this, everyone suggests facile solutions like delinking degrees from jobs, ending political interference on the campus and restructurig of courses.

This assumes that the changes needed are simple and require only administrative and political will. Very few recognize that universities in India in their present form are almost beyond redemption. Even our present societal values do not give priority to scholarship. It is not surprising that the Director of IIT, Madras, could publically exclaim, 'Obviously in our society the most intelligent student is deemed to be worthless against a Mercedes Benz car and perhaps that is why we export our brightest students and import these cars.'

The recent change in technology policies is forcing our education system to react similarly: take the simple way out as long as it is high profile.

For example, the Government of India has started a program called CLASS (Computer Literacy and Studies in Schools). In this program, 250 schools (only) in India will be gifted a microcomputer to fulfil the following objectives.

1. Provide students with a broad understanding of computers and their use.
2. Familiarize students with the range of computer applications in all walks of human activity and the potentiality of the computer as an information processing tool.
3. Demystify computers and develop a degree of ease and familiarity with computers which would be conducive to developing individual creativity in identifying and developing applications relevant to the immediate environment of the child.

The policy-makers felt that the computer would have a liberalizing influence in schools, by making teachers sensitive to and ultimately capable of utilizing the computer for improving the effectiveness of instruction.

Lofty objectives but far removed from the dirt and tears of the overwhelming majority of India's school children. The project is symptomatic of our science and technology policies. As long as we stay up with the rich of the world in an isolated laboratory we are happy. Reality need not interfere. Even in this case, there was no real debate and the real issues of the benefits/harm of such computer education not really discussed in depth.

In brief, the science and technology policies in India have influenced education in the same way as scientific laboratories. Equity and quality are not important. Success, quality and pride are ensured for a few in the high profile areas; the rest can be happy with large numbers.

SOME IDEAS FOR THE FUTURE

Most solutions would follow automatically from the discussion under the section on weaknesses of the system. In particular, English would have to go as a medium of instruction, primary education will have to be given far greater importance, and B.A./B.Sc. and M.A./M.Sc. programs will have to be cut down drastically. The same buildings and teachers would have to do much more work in teaching short-term courses of all types, especially for continuing education, adult education, consumer education and other training disciplines not normally covered by the university system.

Technology policy would have to be changed to curtail the import of technology in areas of strength (like agricultural technology, railways, etc.). This has to be done to make local scientists and engineers feel wanted. Just like we have missions in space, nuclear energy or to the Antartica, it is high time we had missions in public transportation, medicine, health, housing and clothing. Time-bound, all-inclusive design and production missions will have to be defined to produce a time-bound change in improving the quality and quantity of products in these sectors. It is only such missions which will force people to do meaningful research. These will act as a spur for actual basic research which will be subject to quality control since it will have some local relevance. It is only in such conditions that not only will educational standards be forced to improve in a self-regulatory manner but we may even spawn geniuses now hibernating because of disuse.

It is only when our technology policies change in the above direction that our education will become relevant for our science and technology. Even better still, then we could use technology for the betterment of our education and communication system. In Dr. Yash Pal's words (1984):

> Specifically in regard to communication, we are in the midst of a tremendous adventure. If, after a number of exuberant initiatives

we lapse into an attempt to create a few corners in our country which look exactly like pieces of real estate in America or Europe, we would fail our responsibility. Considering our great needs, and fair capabilities, we can evolve systems which would do more for a large segment of the human race than anyone anywhere else has done for any other segments. We can introduce systems and services which are appropriate to our requirements, and the basic technology for which has arrived too late for all the developed world. We can have a country-wide message system at a cost which is miniscule compared to the cost of installing a few million telephones. We can colocate people-based information and support systems to help the large number of development programmes we are involved in. We can give voice to those who are seldom heard, create human stories not only from big towns but also hundreds of thousands of hamlets in which this country resides.

We can use simple equipment to create images of our land, thoughts, desires, hopes and pleasures of our people. We can involve the same people in generating these images, which can then jump the skies and touch us all. We can move away from the groves where T.V. means just extravaganzas, movies and matches, and where the infrastructure is based in large cities only. The problems and pleasure of continuous learning, adult education, and much else can be woven in. If we proceed this way we will need to worry about structures too. Responsibilities for communication, broadcasting, education, health and family welfare, etc., cannot stay divided. Many new organisational innovations would be required.

The exciting fact is that we can really do it now, ourselves. Technologically and, I hope, even organisationally. Then we will etch out new groves. Then we shall awake to a new freedom. We would have used what is available from the world, combined it with our own innovations and truly exercised a choice. A choice, not only from amongst the available, but also from the world of the possible.

References

AGARWAL, B.L. 1985. 'Nexus between Jobs and Degrees,' in J. Veera Raghavan and K. Singh, eds., *Higher Education in the Eighties*. New Delhi: Lancer International.

ARUNACHALAM, S. 1979. 'Why is Indian Science Mediocre?' *Science Today*, February 1979.
BAARK, ERIK. 1983. *Information Infrastructures in India and China*. Lund: Research Policy Studies.
BHAGAWAN, M.R. 1981. 'Innovations in Industry,' *Seminar*, Vol, 258, pp. 26–35.
BHARGAVA, P.M. 1981. 'Deficiencies and Corrections.' *Seminar*, Vol. 250, pp. 20–25.
GOYAL, S.K. 1982. *New Industrial Licensing Policy—An Empirical Assessment*. New Delhi: Indian Institute of Public Administration.
IYENGAR, M.S. 1982. *The Status of Research and Development in the Private Sector*. New Delhi: M.S. Iyengar Assoc.
KOTHARI, RAJNI. 1984. 'The Aftermath: What Does the Future Hold for Indian Politics in the Wake of Mrs. Gandhi's Assassination?' *Illustrated Weekly of India*, 23 December, pp. 8–11.
KRISHNA, GOPAL. 1985. 'Communal Disturbance in Delhi.' *Economic and Political Weekly*, Vol. 20, pp. 61–74.
MOHAN, DINESH. 1981. 'A Sea of Mediocrity.' *Seminar*, Vol. 258, pp. 36–42.
NAKAYAMA, SHIGERU. 1978. *Characteristics of Scientific Development in Japan*. New Delhi: CSIR.
NANDY, ASHIS. 1985. The Shadow State. *Illustrated Weekly of India*, 24 February–2 March, pp. 20–25.
RAHMAN, A. 1984. *Science and Technology in India*. New Delhi: National Institute of Science, Technology and Development Studies.
RICHARDS, P. and M. LEONOR. 1981. *Education and Income Distribution in Asia*. London: Croom, Helm.
SIGURDSÓN, JON. 1981. 'China's Tortuous Road to Autonomy in Technology and Science.' *Endeavour*, Vol. 5, No. 2.
THE WORLD BANK. 1982–84. *World Development Report*. Washington, D.C.: Oxford University Press.

Strategies to Overcome the Constraints

8

Importance of Female Primary Education for Fertility Reduction in India

Anrudh K Jain and Moni Nag

The purpose of this paper is to review the relationship between female education and fertility in India and to suggest the most effective strategy to reorient the Indian educational structure in order to have a significant impact on fertility. Female education (rather than male education) has been selected for two reasons. First, the education of the wife is usually lower than or, at most, equal to the education of the husband. Thus, with an improvement in female education, male education improves. The reverse, however, is not true. The level of female education in India, for example, still lags far behind that of male education. Moreover, in reviews of Indian (Mandelbaum, 1974) and international (Cochrane, 1979, 1983) literature on the subject, female education has been shown to be more important than male education in regard to its effect on fertility.

Two themes emerge in the international literature on female education and fertility: (*a*) a small amount of education in least literate societies might initially increase fertility (Cochrane, 1979), and (*b*) the magnitude of the individual level fertility effect of education varies from country to country (Hermalin and Mason, 1980). A lack of uniformity in the education and fertility relationship across countries is usually interpreted as reflecting the differences among countries in the average fertility of educated women. However, in a recent study based on World Fertility Survey data collected from 11 less developed countries, the cumulative marital fertility of educated women is shown to be similar in different settings (Jain, 1981a). This study demonstrates that the effect of education on fertility differs from country to country more because of the differences among countries in the average fertility of women with no education rather than because of the differences in the average fertility of women with relatively higher education. It also demonstrates that the curvilinear nature of the relationship between education and marital fertility is attributable to the relatively low fertility of illiterate women with the higher prevalence of fertility inhibiting factors such as breast-feeding. This means that the explanation for a curvilinear relationship between education and fertility should be sought in the factors which suppress fertility of women with no education.

Extent of Ambiguity in Education-Fertility Relationship in India

The results of two national surveys conducted by the Office of the Registrar General of India in 1972 and 1979 are summarized in Table 1. The total marital fertility rate (total number of children born per married woman throughout her reproductive period) estimated from both surveys increases consistently with the increase in educational level in the urban sector of India. In the rural sector, however, although the rate estimated from the 1978 data shows a linear decrease with the increase in educational level, the 1972 data show a curvilinear relationship between education and fertility. In 1972, the total marital fertility rate (7.1) of rural literate women (including those with any education less than matric) was slightly higher than that of illiterate women (6.9) as well as those with at least matric level education (5.0). A similiar curvilinear relationship between education and fertility was also found in a few other country-level (India, CS, 1967; Sharma and Misra, 1978) and state-level (India, RG, 1982; Bhattacharjee,

Table 1: Estimated Total Marital Fertility Rates (1972 and 1978) Per Woman in Rural and Urban India

Level of Education	Total Marital Fertility Rate* 1972		1978	
	Rural	Urban	Rural	Urban
Illiterate	6.9	6.3	5.5	4.9
Literate†	7.1	5.0	5.0	4.5
Primary			4.9	4.2
Matric & above	5.0	4.5	4.7	4.0
All Women	6.8	6.0	5.4	4.6

* Data for 1972 and 1978 are not strictly comparable; these comparisons overestimate the magnitude of fertility decline during the 1970s.

† In the 1972 survey, women with primary school education were classified as literate, a category which also included women with less than primary school education.

Sources: India, RG, 1976, p. 7; India, RG, 1982, pp. 4–7.

1984; Zachariah, 1984, pp. 152–54) studies. In most of the studies, however, fertility of the literate group is not substantially higher than that of the illiterate group.

One reason for the curvilinear relationship between female education and fertility has to do with the quality of data. It is well known that data on the number of live births or births which take place in a specified period of, say, one year prior to interview collected retrospectively are affected by recall errors. The magnitude of these errors among respondents without any education is likely to be higher than among literate respondents. If so, it would differentially underestimate the fertility level for the illiterate group and would give an erroneous impression of higher fertility for the literate group. Another reason has to do with the classification of women with little education. In some cases, women who do not complete primary level education (Grade V), i.e., who drop out from primary school, are included with illiterates, and in other studies they are included with those who have completed primary school education. These women are different from those who have no education, as well as from those who completed primary school education and, therefore, should be classified separately. These reasons can explain small differences in the marital fertility of literate and illiterate women. However, to better understand why this can happen, one has to learn the mechanisms through which education can influence fertility behaviour. These mechanisms are discussed in the next section.

Causal Links between Education and Fertility

The synthesis framework, developed by Easterlin (1978), with modifications to incorporate proximate factors identified by Bongaarts (1978) and intervening variables between modernization and fertility (Nag, 1983), is used in this paper to explain the causal links between female education and actual fertility (number of live births). As shown in Figure 1, actual fertility is seen as determined by the use of contraception, fecundity, and age at marriage. The use of contraception is seen as determined by the demand or desire for children and costs associated with the use of contraception. Education is seen to affect fertility by influencing the family size desire, costs associated with contraception, fecundity (physiological capacity to reproduce), and age at marriage. We shall review here the relationship between education and fertility generated through variables that are most relevant to these four intervening factors in the Indian context.

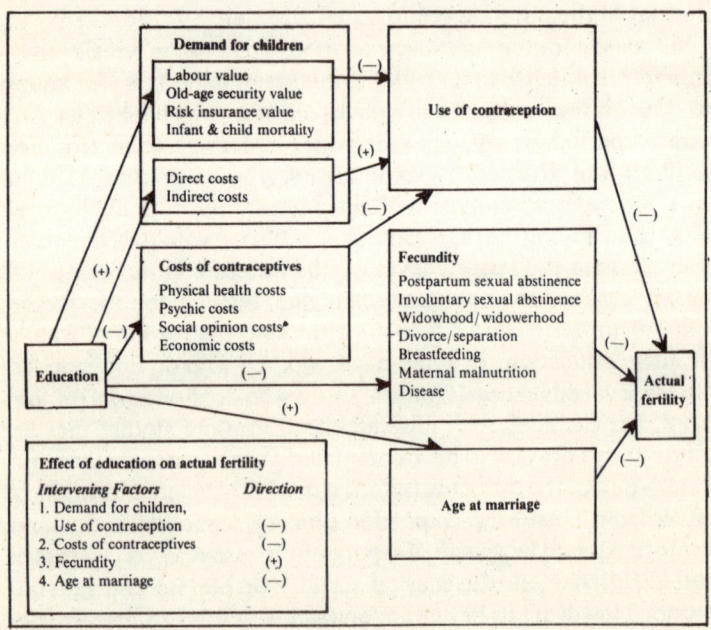

Figure 1
Schematic Representation of Causal Links between Education and Actual Fertility

Family Size Desire. A review of relevant literature suggests that a shift from a large to small number of children occurs along with (a) a decline in the labour value of children, (b) a decline in children's value as old age security, (c) an increase in economic costs of raising children, and (d) a decline in infant and child mortality. Some empirical findings regarding each of these four associations and the effect of education on the fore-mentioned variables are discussed below.

In a Punjab village (where in 1970 the farmers cited the labour value of children, particularly sons, in agriculture as the prime reason for having large families), the green revolution along with a few other institutional changes has drastically reduced the labour value of children, and, as a consequence, their desire for large families. The next important reason for a decrease in family size desire in the same village is the actual as well as perceived decline in the old age security value of children (Nag and Kak, 1984). In this village, as well as in the nine villages in Karnataka state studied by Caldwell et al. (1985; pp. 33-34), higher aspiration of parents for their children's education (as a result of an increase in non-agricultural job opportunities) is an important factor for the decrease in the labour value and old age security value of children.

The financial burden of direct costs (e.g., education, food and clothing) of children is commonly cited by respondents in less developed countries when they are asked about their reasons for not wanting any more children or for limiting their family size (Arnold et al., 1975). Educated parents are expected to be motivated more than the uneducated ones for the actual and perceived costs of their children. For example, in urban India the increasing aspirations of middle class parents for educating their children in private schools and colleges and the rapidly rising costs in these institutions relative to their income are primary reasons for their motivation towards small families.

It can be presumed that unless parents have become reasonably assured of their children's survival, they are not likely to adopt the small family norm and use contraceptives. Using data from the survey conducted by the Operations Research Group in 1970, Jejeebhoy (1984) has shown that in ten Indian states infant and child mortality among users of contraceptive methods was much lower than among non-users. An analysis of the 1978 data collected by the Registrar General's office has shown that the level of infant mortality in a state is inversely associated with the level of fertility (Jain, 1985). Although mechanisms that link education and mortality are not well known, recent evidence from several less developed countries suggests that maternal education plays a major role in determining the level of infant and child mortality (Caldwell, 1979; D'Souza and Bhuiya, 1982; Preston, 1980). In the Karnataka villages studied by Caldwell et al. (1982), the largest differentials in the infant mortality rate were by mother's education, with a level of 130 per thousand where the mother had not been to school, 80 where she had only primary schooling, and 70 where she had some secondary schooling. A similar relationship between female education and infant mortality has also been shown for rural as well as urban areas of almost all major states (India, RG, 1984).

Costs of Using Contraception. Even where couples want to limit family size or to postpone the next birth, they do not always use contraception. The reasons for such non-use are usually designated as costs of using contraception. In the absence of any family planning program, the economic cost of using contraception may be a deterrent. Even if they are made available free, all modern contraceptive methods involve some cost to their users in the form of minor side effects and/or potential health hazards. Progress in education, particularly of women, increases the use of contraception by reducing unrealistic fears of the side effects and by enabling couples to utilize the family planning program facilities more effectively.

One common psychic constraint on the use of contraception is its conflict with the religious belief of one or both partners. Education helps towards reducing such conflict. When one spouse is in favour of using contraception and the other is not, or when a couple is in favour of using contraception but some members of its social influence group are not, the actual use of contraception involves the cost of challenging the spouse or the social influencing group. An educated wife can face the challenge more successfully than an uneducated one.

Extent of Contraceptive Use. We have shown in the foregoing that education decreases the demand for children by reducing the labour value, old age security value of children as well as by reducing infant and child mortality and by enhancing the direct and indirect costs of children. A decrease in the demand for children through these processes increases the use of contraception. Out of four categories of cost of contraception, the only one which is significantly affected by education is the physical/health cost. Education increases the use of contraception by reducing the physical/health cost. Thus, the net effect of education on the use of contraception through both demand for children and costs of contraception variables should be negative. Also, the relationship between education and demand for children, on the one hand, and between education and use of contraception, on the other, should be both linear. The empirical data collected in two national sample surveys conducted by the Operations Research Group in 1970 and 1980 (presented in Table 2) and a few other surveys corroborate these relationships (Sarma and Jain, 1974; Zachariah, 1984; Khan and Prasad, 1983; Jain, 1985).

Table 2: Ideal and Desired Number of Children and Proportion using contraception among Married Women (20–39 years) by Level of Education

	Illiterate	Primary	Secondary	College	Total
Mean ideal number of children: 1970	3.8	3.5	3.2	2.7	3.7
Living plus mean additional desired number of sons: 1970	2.3	2.2	2.0	1.4	2.2
Mean number of children considered small: 1980	3.4	3.1	2.9	2.5	3.2
Per cent currently using contraception (including sterilization):					
1970	7.8	19.4	34.1	53.9	12.2
1980	27.8	46.4	53.0	64.4	34.7

Source: Sarma and Jain, 1974 for 1970; 1980 figures are estimated from data included in Khan and Prasad, 1983.

In Table 2, the 'mean ideal number of children' and the 'living plus mean additional desired number of sons' reflect the demand for children, as expressed by currently married women in the 1970 survey. In both of these measures, the demand decreases, as expected, monotonically as the level of education increases, in contrast with the ambiguity observed in the relationship between education and fertility. The percentage of women using contraception also increases monotonically, as expected, with the increase in the level of education. Only 7.8 per cent of illiterate women in 1970 were using contraception compared to 19.4 per cent among primary-, 34.1 per cent among secondary-, and 53.9 per cent among college-educated women. The 1980 survey data also show a similar relationship between educational level and the use of contraception.

The use of contraception in Kerala, according to a survey conducted in 1980, was found to increase with female education; 31.2 per cent of currently married women with no schooling were using contraception (25.2 sterilization and 6.0 conventional methods) in comparison to 53.1, 55.0 and 59.8 per cent of women with 1–4, 5–9, and 10 + years of schooling (Zachariah, 1984, p. 153). At the state level, the use of contraception has been shown to increase with an increase in the extent of adult female literacy; the correlation coefficient between the two was found to be 0.63 (Jain, 1985).

Fecundity. Of the seven fecundity variables which are shown to affect fertility directly in Figure 1, breast-feeding is noteworthy in terms of its effect on fertility and the effect of education on it. A number of recent investigations have confirmed that prolonged and frequent breast-feeding reduces the chances of pregnancy by delaying the return of menstruation as well as the return of ovulation in women after childbirth. The data for developing countries from the World Fertility Survey have indicated a negative relationship between the duration of breast-feeding and fertility (Jain and Bongaarts, 1981). At least up to 1974, the contraceptive protection provided by breast-feeding in less developed countries is estimated to have been greater than that achieved through family planning programs (Rosa, 1975). Hence a decline in the practice of breast-feeding can increase fertility, if it is not controlled by other means (Nag, 1980). Based on an analysis of Taiwanese data, Jain et al. (1970, p. 269) estimated that in a high fertility society where lactation is virtually universal 'the prevalence of lactation may prevent as many as 20 per cent of the births that would occur if there were no lactation.'

A number of recent surveys in less developed countries, including the World Fertility Survey, have indicated a negative relationship between education and breast-feeding even after controlling income and other variables (Jain and Bongaarts, 1981; Butz and DaVanzo, 1981). In a recent WHO survey of middle income women in an urban area of India, 72 per cent of secondary-educated women were breast-feeding their children at 6–8 months compared to 90 per cent of primary-educated women (WHO, 1979). A more recent survey in India showed that infants of 68 per cent of educated mothers in the Bombay metropolitan area, 32 per cent in the Calcutta area and 44 per cent in the Madras area were being exclusively breast-fed until they were 3 months old as against 80 per cent, 57 per cent and 61 per cent in the corresponding poorly educated groups (Gopujkar et al., 1984). Specific mechanisms by which education affects breast-feeding remain a subject requiring further study.

Age at Marriage. There is a consensus that an increase in the age at marriage and proportions never-married substantially contributed to fertility decline in those less developed countries that have experienced considerable decline during recent decades. The most important reason for the association is that later marriage reduces the total duration of fecund exposure to sexual activity and shifts it to the older ages of lower fecundity. A review of studies done in India generally confirms the negative association between age at marriage and fertility (Sharma and Misra, 1978). At the state level, the female age at marriage has been shown to have a negative influence on the birth rate, independent of the effects of other factors (Jain, 1985). The effect of age at marriage on fertility is evident from the comparisons shown in Table 3, of the total marital fertility rate and total fertility rate by educational level, as estimated from the 1978 data collected by the Office of the Registrar General of India in 1979. The total fertility rate (total number of children born per woman throughout her reproductive period) is considerably lower than the total marital fertility rate for each educational level. The difference is attributable to the effect of age at marriage and of non-marriage on fertility, since for the calculation of the total marital fertility rate non-married women of reproductive age are excluded.

Several surveys in India have confirmed that educated girls tend to be married at a later average age, some of them late enough to have fewer children. For example, the 1961–62 National Sample Survey data show that among couples living in urban areas, the average age at marriage of illiterate wives was 16 years while that of college graduates was 22 years (India, CS, 1970; p. 7). At the state level, the average age at marriage has been shown to increase with an increase in adult female literacy; the correlation coefficient between the two was found to be 0.81 (Jain, 1985).

Table 3: Estimated Total Marital Fertility Rates and Total Fertility Rates Per Woman (1978) in Rural India

Level of Education	Total Marital Fertility Rate	Total Fertility Rate
Illiterate	5.5	4.7
Literate	5.0	3.9
Primary	4.9	3.6
Matric and above*	4.7	2.5
All Women	5.4	4.6

* Includes those who have passed the matriculation examination (after Grade X) and/or those who have been enrolled in higher level institutions.
Source: India, RG, 1982, pp. 4–7.

Schooling may be a direct cause for delayed marriage in that girls are not usually married while they are still attending school or college. But it is quite likely that the difficulty of finding appropriately qualified grooms for educated girls, dependence of parents on educated girls who are employed, higher demands for dowry, and a modern attitude among girls who are educated as well as among parents who want their children to be educated are important reasons for the delayed marriage of éducated girls.

Net Effect of Education on Fertility

To summarize, education increases the demand or desire for children as well as decreases the non-monetary costs of using contraception. Both these changes increase the use of contraception, thereby reducing fertility. Female education also decreases fertility by raising the age at marriage. Education increases fertility only by diminishing the fertility-inhibiting effect of breast-feeding. If all three of these effects are taken into consideration, the net effect of education, in theory, at any particular point of time, can be positive, negative or zero.

In India, empirical evidence shows that the net effect is mostly negative because the positive effect of education that operates through fecundity variables is compensated by the negative effect that operates through the use of contraception and age at marriage. It is not surprising that the net effect of education on marital fertility is sometimes found to be 'ambivalent' or 'inconsistent'. In other words, the marital fertility of women with some schooling is sometimes found to be higher than that of women who have no schooling or who have completed primary school education. This does not necessarily imply that they want more children.

The apparent inconsistency can be explained by the fact that for measuring marital fertility the negative effect of age at marriage is not taken into account. Moreover, up to a certain educational level, the positive effect of education (that operates through the decline of breast-feeding) is not compensated by its negative effect through the increased use of contraception, which may be due to the non-availability of contraceptive methods rather than the pro-natalist effect of education *per se*. Any increase in marital fertility is likely to be a short-term phenomenon because there is no theoretical justification for expecting that a small amount of education will increase the demand or desire for children.

Implications for Educational Policies

Women with a small amount (less than primary) of education represent those who drop out of schools before completing at least primary level education and thus, before acquiring minimum reading and numerical skills. Without these skills, such women are unable to assimilate information disseminated through the mass media, especially through printed materials. Hence, they are slower in shifting from traditional (breast-feeding) to modern (use of contraception) forms of behaviour. Does this imply that education policies should give priority to higher education rather than primary education?

Three important determinants of educational achievement in schools are: the rates of admission, repetition in the same class, and drop-out. The critical policy issues are to decide the priority order in which to make improvements and to decide the priority between primary and beyond primary level of schooling. Out of numerous combinations of improvements in the rates of admission and grade-specific rates of repetition and drop-out, Jain (1982) selected about

22 alternatives including *status quo* (or no change in any of the three parameters) and compared their potential direct effects on educational attainment, implied workload and costs, and their indirect effects on the average family size by using the 1972 education-specific marital fertility rates for rural and urban areas of India shown in Table 1. The following points briefly summarize the results of comparing the 22 alternatives in terms of their potential impact upon marital fertility.

1. In comparison to 'no change,' any improvement in the current system of education would decrease marital fertility of the entire cohort. It is important to note that marital fertility is expected to decline even in rural areas, where the relationship between education and marital fertility was observed to be curvilinear.

2. Improvements in all three parameters are more likely to produce a higher decline in marital fertility than improvements in any two of the three, which in turn is likely to produce a higher decline than the improvement in any one of the three parameters. If, however, a choice has to be made, priority should be assigned in decreasing order to decreasing drop-out rates, decreasing repetition rates, and increasing admission rates.

3. Improvements, in terms of decrease in repetition and drop-out rates, at all grades, would produce a decline in marital fertility. But, if a choice has to be made between improvements up to Grade IV and similar improvements beyond Grade V, the former appears to be a superior approach. For example, a 50 per cent reduction in drop-out rates with or without automatic promotion up to Grade IV is likely to produce a higher decline in marital fertility in comparison to similar improvements beyond Grade V.

These comparisons illustrate that, although women with little education may have higher marital fertility than illiterates, concentrating efforts to improve the situation at the lower level is likely to be a better strategy than neglecting the situation at the lower level and concentrating efforts to improve it beyond the primary level. This makes sense because women who do not complete primary education are different from those who do complete it. The implication of the curvilinear relationship between education and fertility at the individual level for educational policies, therefore, is to reduce the number and proportion of women who drop out of primary school and to increase the proportion of women who complete at least primary level education.

It is clear from the foregoing discussion that primary education, particularly of women, deserves the highest priority among all the educational sectors, if fertility reduction is considered a worthwhile objective for national welfare. The framers of the Constitution of India did not, however, consider fertility reduction when they thought it desirable to provide free and compulsory education for all children up to the age of 14 years by 1960; there were many other worthy reasons. It is only in the Sixth Five Year Plan (India, Planning Commission, 1981, p. 375) that the role of education, especially female education, in reducing fertility was recognized. The recommendation that followed from this recognition did not, however, include an emphasis on primary education, but on increasing the enrolment in high schools. The specific focus was on education in health and reproductive biology rather than the broader objective of education in increasing the awareness and widening the outlook of students.

All the Five Year Plans of the central and state governments, however, stressed the importance of making primary education universal as early as possible. In all of them, targets set up for the end of the Plan period were higher than the percentage of enrolments actually achieved by that time. Although the absolute number of boys and girls enrolled increased substantially every year, the rapid rise in population in the 6–11 age group did not allow a corresponding increase in the percentage figures. Table 4 shows the actual increase in primary school enrolment percentages of boys and girls in India as a whole from 1950–51 to 1979–80.

Enrolment ratios are conventionally used to indicate the progress of education, but they do not indicate the level of educational attainment because of a high wastage rate in the education system. The figures shown in Table 4 also overestimate the progress of education because the numerator includes children who are outside the age group included in the denominator. Thus, children of more than 11 years of age enrolled in primary school are included in the numerator but not in the denominator of the enrolment ratios. These data indicate a gradual increase in the enrolment ratios of both boys and girls in the primary schools from 1950–51 to 1979–80. The rate of increase in the enrolment of girls is slightly higher than

Table 4: Enrolment of Boys and Girls in Primary Schools (Grades I–V) in India, as Percentages of the Population in the Age Group of 6–11 Years ('1950–51 to 1979–80)

	Boys	Girls	Total
1950–51	60	25	43
1960–61	83	41	62
1968–69	93	57	76
1979–80	100	66	84
1979–80			
Kerala	103*	102*	103*
Rajasthan	88	30	60
West Bengal	104*	70	87
Uttar Pradesh	91	45	69

* The percentage figures are above 100 since some students enrolled in Grades I–V are likely to be in ages other than 6 to 11 years. In official documents, 11 year-old children are included in the numerator for calculating enrolment ratios in primary as well as middle classes. Presumably, these children are included only once in the enrolment ratios of middle classes.

Sources: India, Planning Commission, 1973, p. 194 for 1950–51, 1960–61, 1968–69; India, Planning Commission, 1981, pp. 362–66 for 1979–80.

that of boys, but since the girls' enrolment ratio (25 per cent) was considerably lower than the boys' ratio (60 per cent) in 1951, it remained far behind (66 per cent) the boys' in 1979–80 when the latter achieved virtually universal enrolment. Obviously, efforts to increase the enrolment of girls in primary schools have to be strengthened substantially to achieve the target of universal primary education among them. Large variations still exist in the state-level enrolment in primary schools. For example, while Kerala has reached universal enrolment for boys and girls, Rajasthan is still far behind with 88 per cent for boys and 30 per cent for girls in 1979–80. In most of the states, the enrolment percentage of girls is still much lower than that of boys. States in which girls' enrolment in primary schools is still less than 50 per cent need special strategies to expedite progress.

In view of the declared emphasis on girls' education in almost all the Five Year Plans, it is worthwhile to examine the trend, if any, in the enrolment proportion of girls in relation to boys during the last three decades. The relevant data, presented in Table 5, indicate an increasing trend in the female/male enrolment in India during the last three decades for both the primary (I–V) and secondary (VI–

Table 5: Trends in Female/Male Enrolment Ratios in Primary (I–V) and Secondary (VI–XI/XII) Schools (1950–51 to 1977–78)

	Primary	Secondary
1950–51	28	19
1960–61	33	23
1970–71	37	28
1977–78	38	31
1977–78		
Kerala	48	47
Rajasthan	24	19
West Bengal	39	38
Uttar Pradesh	31	19

Source: India, CSO, 1982, p. 514.

XI/XII) educational sectors. However, the female enrolment ratio in relation to the male still remains quite low. At the all-India level, in 1977–78 (the latest year for which figures are available), female enrolment in proportion to the male was only a little higher than one-third for the primary sector and a little lower than one-third for the secondary sector. Another disturbing fact is that the rate of increase in the female-male ratio seems to have slowed down in the 1970s, even though the policy documents of both the central and state governments have been stressing the priority of female education more strongly in the 1970s than in the previous decades. The deceleration of female enrolment in relation to male during the 1970s needs urgent investigation and action for improvement.

The total expenditure on education has increased considerably during the last three decades—from Rs. 911 million in 1950–51 to Rs. 21,843 million in 1976–77. One way of assessing the priority actually given to the different sectors of education is to examine the proportion of the educational expenditure that is actually spent in the specific sectors. Table 6 provides some relevant data.

The following statement was made in the Third Five Year Plan covering 1961–66:

> The Constitution envisaged the provision of free, universal and compulsory education for children up to the age of 14 years. In view of the magnitude of the task, it was agreed early in the

Table 6: Percentages of Direct Expenditure on Different Levels of Education in Four Selected Years between 1950-51 and 1976-77

	Total direct Expenditures (Million Rs.)	Primary School (I–V)	Middle School (VI–VIII)	High School (IX–XI–XII)	College/ University	Others
1950–51	911	40	8	25	18	9
1960–61	2,574	29	17	27	20	7
1970–71	9,611	24	18	28	27	3
1976–77	21,843	25	19	28	26	2
1976–77						
Kerala	1,635	27	22	31	18	2
Rajasthan	963	28	24	24	22	2
West Bengal	1,459	34	5	34	24	3
Uttar Pradesh	2,627	28	10	33	26	3

Source: India, CSO, 1982, pp. 517–18.

Second Plan that as a first step facilities should be created for the education of all children in the age group 6–11. This is one of the central aims of the Third Plan, to be followed by extension of education of the entire age group 11–14 during the Fourth and Fifth Plans, (India, Planning Commission, 1961, p. 578).

The expenditure figures in Table 6 indicate, however, that the primary sector of education actually received the least priority in terms of budget allocation during the 1960s, despite the Third Plan's (1960–66) avowed declaration that the creation of all facilities for the primary sectors was one of its central aims. Contrary to all good intentions to increase the priority of primary education, the proportion of expenditure on this sector came down significantly during both the 1950s and the 1960s (from 40 per cent in 1950–51 to 27 per cent in 1970–71). It is all the more disconcerting because the average annual cost per student in India rises quite sharply from one level of education to another. For example, the average annual cost per student in 1974–75 was Rs. 83 at the primary level and Rs. 508 at the general college level (India, Ministry of Education, 1978). Table 6 indicates some stabilization during the 1970s of the proportion spent on different levels of education in India. The proportion spent on the primary level should, however, increase considerably in addition to other necessary changes, if the priorities set forth in the Five Year Plans are to be met.

Obviously, a larger proportion of pupils going through primary schools would require more resources to be allocated to primary school education. This can be done through the allocation of resources within the education system and by allocating a much higher share of additional new resources to primary school education. Reallocation within the education sector is likely to vary between states because 90 per cent of the resources allocated to education are met from the states' own resources. Reallocation within the education sector could be difficult because 85 per cent of the direct expenditure represents fixed costs of salaries of teachers and other personnel. Whether or not reallocation within the education sector is feasible, additional resources allocated to education from the central government should be mainly allocated to primary school education. Some of these resources should be allocated to better understand determinants of admission, repetition, and drop-out rates and to study the effectiveness of specific programs to reduce high magnitudes of repetition and drop-out rates from primary schools. The economic rate of return (social and private) on investment in primary education is estimated to be higher than for secondary education which, in turn, is higher than for general tertiary education in India (Heyneman, 1979). A proportionately higher allocation of additional resources for primary education in India would, therefore, make sense in economic terms. This would help the country to move towards the national objective of universal primary education and would have additional benefits to the society in terms of suppressing the fertility of future generations.

At present, almost all the direct cost of education—at the primary and higher levels—is met from the government's resources. Because of this and the disproportionate political influence of the middle class and elites in both urban and rural areas, there has been an increasing pressure on the government to expand budgetary allocation and expenditure for college and higher education. If the parents' share in the actual cost of education beyond the secondary level is increased, it would reduce pressure for a continuous expansion of colleges and universities. Such a policy would also have a negative feedback effect on the fertility of parents and their peer groups because it would increase the cost of educating children. A policy change in this direction needs, however, adequate precautions. Certain measures, in terms of loans and scholarships for bright students from poor families, would have to be taken so that they have opportunities for better education.

Concluding Remarks

Since the fertility behaviour of women has been shown to be influenced negatively by their level of education, it is important to incorporate this potential effect into educational sector policies and programs in India. Although advancement in female education cannot be used as a primary means to reduce fertility during the next decade, changes in current education policies can substantially contribute to the reduction in fertility in the long run.

From a limited time perspective—for example, during the next decade—the investment in education, perhaps, is not the most cost-effective way to reduce fertility in India. A significant reduction in fertility within the next decade in India cannot be achieved without a significant reduction in the fertility of women who are already in the reproductive age group or who would begin their reproduction shortly. Educational policies cannot change the educational achievement of such women except through adult education. Very little is known about the impact of adult education programs on the improvement in educational achievements of adults and on their subsequent fertility. Advancement in female education, therefore, cannot be used as a primary means to decrease fertility during the next decade.

Since the population problem is not a short-term phenomenon, it is necessary to consider the anti-natalistic effects of education policies from a longer-term perspective. The following recommendations can be made based on the analysis presented in this paper:

1. The educational policy in India, as far as fertility reduction is concerned and perhaps for other aspects of development as well, should give high priority to increasing female primary education.
2. Educational policies can reduce fertility and this effect can be enhanced by allocating disproportionately greater resources to female primary education, emphasizing the reduction of currently prevalent high repetition and drop-out rates from primary schools, and by increasingly sharing the direct cost of education beyond the secondary level with parents rather than by absorbing most of it in the government budgets.

The findings of this paper also lead us to hypothesize that primary education, by providing basic functional literacy and numeracy, enhances women's status within and outside their family and increases their exposure to the information and ideas disseminated through printed material. This brings changes in their general behaviour involving breast-feeding, the use of contraception and fertility. In addition, staying longer in school increases their age at marriage. In other words, advancement in female education can be expected to influence fertility behaviour even without simultaneous changes in other factors, such as, increased opportunities in the paid labour force.

References

ARNOLD, FRED, et al. 1975. *The Value of Children: A Cross-National Study. Volume 1: Introduction and Comparative Analysis*. Honolulu: East-West Population Institute, East-West Center.

BATTACHARJEE, P.J. 1984. 'The Family Planning Programme, Education and Development: A Case Study of Karnataka,' *Journal of Family Welfare*, Vol. 31, pp. 3–13.

BONGAARTS, JOHN. 1978. 'A Framework for Analyzing the Proximate Determinants of Fertility,' *Population and Development Review*, Vol. 4, pp. 105–32.

BUTZ, W.P. and JULIE DAVANZO. 1981. *Determinants of Breastfeeding and Weaning Patterns in Malaysia*. Report No. WD-995-1-AID. Santa Monica, California: Rand Corporation.

CALDWELL, JOHN C. 1979. 'Education as a Factor in Mortality Decline: An Examination of Nigerian Data,' *Population Studies*, Vol. 33; pp. 395–413.

CALDWELL, JOHN C., P.H. REDDY and PAT CALDWELL. 1982. 'The Causes of Demographic Change in Rural South India: A Micro Approach,' *Population and Development Review*, Vol. 8, pp. 689–728.

———. 1985. 'Educational Transition in Rural South India,' *Population and Development Review*, Vol. 11, pp. 29–52.

COCHRANE, SUSAN H. 1979. *Fertility and Education: What Do We Really Know?* Washington, D.C.: The World Bank.

———. 1983. 'Effects of Education and Urbanization on Fertility,' in R.A. Bulatao and R.D. Lee, eds., *Determinants of Fertility in Developing Countries*. Vol. 2. New York: Academic Press, pp. 587–626.

D'SOUZA, S. and A. BHUIYA. 1982. 'Mortality Differentials in Rural Bangladesh,' *Population and Development Review*, Vol. 8, pp. 753–70.

EASTERLIN, RICHARD A. 1978. 'The Economics and Sociology of Fertility,' in C. Tilly, ed., *Historical Guides of Changing Fertility*. Princeton: Princeton University Press, pp. 57–133.

GOPUJKAR, P.V.; et al. 1984. *Infant-feeding Practices with Special Reference to the Use of Commercial Infant Foods*. Scientific Report No. 4. Delhi: Nutrition Foundation of India.

HERMALIN, ALBERT and WILLIAM M. MASON. 1980. *A Strategy for the Comparative Analysis of WFS Data, with Illustrative Examples*. The United Nations Programme for Comparative Analysis of World Fertility Survey Data. New York: UNFPA.

HEYNEMAN, S.P. 1979. *Investment in Indian Education: Uneconomic?* Working Paper No. 327. Washington, D.C.: The World Bank.

INDIA, CS (Cabinet Secretariat). 1967. *Tables with Notes on Family Planning. The National Sample Survey Report No. 116* (Sixteenth Round: July 1960-June 1961). New Delhi: The Cabinet Secretariat, Government of India.

———. 1970. *Tables with Notes on Couple Fertility. The National Sample Survey Report No. 154.* (Seventeenth Round: September 1961-July 1962). New Delhi: The Cabinet Secretariat, Government of India.

INDIA, CSO (Central Statistical Organization). 1982. *Statistical Abstract of India, 1980, New Series, No. 25*. New Delhi: Central Statistical Organization, Government of India.

INDIA, MINISTRY OF EDUCATION. 1978. *Education in India: 1974-1975*. New Delhi: Government of India Press.

INDIA, PLANNING COMMISSION. 1973. *Draft Fifth Five Year Plan*. New Delhi: Planning Commission, Government of India.

———. 1981. *Sixth Five Year Plan, 1980-85*. New Delhi: Planning Commission, Government of India.

INDIA, RG (Office of the Registrar General). 1976. *Fertility Determinants in India, 1972*. New Delhi: Vital Statistics Division, Office of the Registrar General and Census Commission, Ministry of Home Affairs, Government of India.

———. 1982. *Levels, Trends, Differentials in Fertility, 1979*. New Delhi: Ministry of Home Affairs, Office of Registrar General.

JAIN, ANRUDH K. 1981a. 'The Effect of Female Education on Fertility: A Simple Explanation,' *Demography*, Vol. 18, pp. 577-95.

———. 1982. 'Education Sector Policies, Educational Attainment and Fertility: A Case Study for India,' in R. Barlow, ed., *Case Studies in the Demographic Impact of Asian Development Projects*. Ann Arbor (Michigan): Center for Research on Economic Development, University of Michigan, pp. 169-201.

———. 1985. Impact of Public Policies Concerning Development and Population in India,' *Studies in Family Planning*, Vol. 16, No. 4.

JAIN, ANRUDH K. and JOHN BONGAARTS. 1981. 'Breastfeeding: Patterns, Correlates, and Fertility Effects,' *Studies in Family Planning*, Vol. 12, pp. 79-99. Also presented at World Fertility Survey Conference in London, July 1980, and published in its proceedings.

JAIN, ANRUDH K., T.C. HSU, RONALD FREEDMAN, and M.C. CHANG. 1970. 'Demographic Aspects of Lactation and Postpartum Amenorrhea,' *Demography*, Vol. 7, pp. 255-71.

JEJEEBHOY, S.J. 1984. 'The Shift from Natural to Controlled Fertility: A Cross-Sectional Analysis of Ten Indian States,' *Studies in Family Planning*, Vol. 15, pp. 191-98.

KHAN, M.E. and C.V.S. PRASAD. 1983. *Family Planning Practices in India: Second All-India Survey*. Baroda: Operations Research Group (mimeo).

MANDELBAUM, D.G. 1974. *Human Fertility in India: Social Components and Policy Perspectives*. Berkeley: University of California Press.

Nag, Moni. 1980. 'How Modernization Can Also Increase Fertility,' *Current Anthropology*, Vol. 21, pp. 571–87.

———. 1983. 'Impact of Social and Economic Development on Mortality: A Comparative Study of Kerala and West Bengal,' *Economic and Political Weekly* (Bombay), Annual Issue, Vol. 18, pp. 877–900.

Nag, Moni and Neeraj Kak. 1984. 'Demographic Transition in a Punjab Village,' *Population and Development Review*, Vol. 10, pp. 661–78.

Operations Research Group. n.d. *Family Planning Practices in India: The First All-India Survey Report*. Baroda: Operations Research Group.

Preston, S.H. 1975. 'Health Programs and Population Growth,' *Population and Development Review*, Vol. 1, pp. 189–99.

———. 1980. 'Causes and Consequences of Mortality Declines in Less Developed Countries during the Twentieth Century,' in R.A. Easterlin, ed., *Population and Economic Change in Developing Countries*. Chicago: University of Chicago Press.

Rosa, F.W. 1975. 'Breast-feeding and Family Planning,' *Protein Advisory Group* (United Nations) *Bulletin*, Vol. 5, pp. 5–10.

Sarma, D.V.N. and Anrudh K. Jain. 1974. 'Preference about Sex of Children and Use of Contraception among Women Wanting No More Children in India,' *Demography India*, Vol. 3, pp. 81–104.

Sharma, A.K. and B.D. Misra. 1978. 'Fertility Differentials in India: An Analysis of Census Fertility Data,' *Journal of Family Welfare*, Vol. 25, pp. 44–56.

WHO. 1979. *Preliminary Report of the WHO Collaborative Study on Breastfeeding* (MCH/79.3). Geneva: World Health Organization.

Zachariah, K.C. 1984. *The Anomaly of the Fertility Decline in India's Kerala State: A Field Investigation*. World Bank Staff Working Paper No. 700, Population and Development Series No. 25. Washington, D.C.: The World Bank.

9

Child Labour and Education in India— A Perspective

Usha S Naidu

Context of the Child Labour Situation in India

MAGNITUDE OF THE PROBLEM

According to the 1981 Census, there were about 13.6 million child workers. Of this, 8.1 million were boys and 5.5 million girls and about 90 per cent work in rural areas. About 10 per cent of the total child population in the 5 to 14 age group were working children and they constituted as much as 7 per cent of the total work force.

There are considerable variations between the states with respect to child labour. Work participation rates among children are above the national average in Andhra Pradesh, Karnataka, Madhya Pradesh, Orissa and Punjab while they are below the national average in Kerala, West Bengal, Uttar Pradesh, Himachal Pradesh and Maharashtra. These variations can partially be explained by variations in the level of poverty and resource availability.

It will be reasonable to assume that there is no significant change in the situation between 1981 and now.

WHY CHILD LABOUR?

I do not want to get into the debate of definitions of 'child,' 'labour' and 'education'. I am concerned with the age group up to 14 years, although I recognize that there is a variation in the legal and cultural definitions of childhood. I have focused on exploitative work conditions which do not leave any scope for working children to go to school or for any developmental activities for themselves. I have used education in formal school education terms unless specified as non-formal education or vocational training in the text.

Child labour is basically a phenomenon found in developing countries and poverty has generally been accepted as the cause. In the lower income communities of a developing country, like India, it is difficult to run a family on the income of the parents, especially if the parents are daily rated or casual labourers. In such cases, the income of working children, though small in itself assumes far greater value and they are encouraged and persuaded to undertake jobs.

CONCENTRATION OF CHILD LABOUR IN THE UNORGANIZED SECTOR

By and large, there is a decline in the employment of children in registered factories. Thus, child labour is mainly concentrated in the unorganized, semi-organized and the small-scale sectors, the overwhelming majority being in rural India.

OCCUPATION AND CONDITIONS OF WORK

The type of occupation and the working conditions in the urban areas are often such that they impair physical and mental development and reduce or suppress possibilities of upward mobility of the children.

In rural areas, child work is part of the socialization process and a means of acquiring traditional skills; children may benefit from parental supervision, particularly when work is carried out within the household economy.

In the urban and semi-urban areas, children work on daily wages or on a piece-rate basis. The working hours range from 8 to 15 hours a day. They have meagre earnings of about Rs. 100 per month. In the small-scale and cottage industries there is no paid leave for children. Thus, they work all the days of the year. By and large, such is the situation in the glass and bangle factories of Firozabad, garage and repair shops, and cottage units in Bombay, Calcutta, Delhi and Bangalore. The match factories in Sivakasi are well-known for making 45,000 children work for a pittance and in hazardous conditions.

LEGISLATIVE AND OTHER MEASURES

Article 24 of the Constitution provides that 'no child below the age of fourteen years shall be employed in any hazardous employment'. Articles 39 (e) and (f) of the Directive Principles of State Policy require each state to direct its policy towards ensuring that 'health and strength of workers, men and women, and the tender age of children are not abused,' 'that citizens are not forced by economic necessity to enter vocations unsuited to their age or strength,' and 'children are given opportunities and facilities to develop in a healthy manner' and are 'protected against exploitation'.

To this end, a number of legislations (such as, the Factories Act, 1948, the Plantations Labour Act, 1951, the Apprentices Act, 1961, to mention only a few) have been passed. One of the objectives is to restrict the minimum age of entry to employment and regulate the conditions of child employment.

Child labour has also been the specific focus of a number of committees and commissions. Special mention may be made of the Report of the National Commission on Labour (1981) and the Report of the Committee on Child Labour (1979). Following the recommendations of the high level Committee on Child Labour, the government established a special Central Advisory Committee on Child Labour in 1981. The Committee is headed by the Union Labour Minister, with representatives from various allied ministries, persons from public and child welfare agencies and educational institutions. The objectives of the Committee are to review the implementation of existing legislations, suggest legislative and welfare measures for working children, review the progress of such measures and identify industries and areas where there must be a progressive abolition of child labour.

With this background of the existence of legislation, special review committees and seminars were also convened, sponsored, collaborated or attended by the government. Thus, if child labour in India continues to be among the highest in the world, it is certainly not for lack of awareness.

In contrast to the reluctance of several governments elsewhere to even admit that the problem of child labour exists, in India open discussions on the problem of child labour take place in the media, professional journals and official circles. India is one of the few countries in the Third World which publishes statistics on child labour. Indeed, recognizing the problem is the first necessary step for the improvement of the status of working children and, finally, for the abolition of child labour. Thus, India is in a politically advantageous position both for effective national action to deal with the problem of child labour and for learning from its experience.

Educational Status of Working Children

For a detailed assessment of the educational status of working children adequate statistics are unfortunately not available.

The 27th (1972–73) and 32nd (1977–78) rounds of the National Sample Survey (NSS) are devoted to the employment and unemployment aspects. The very complex distribution given in the 27th NSS does not provide comparable educational data while the information from the 32nd round is not yet released.

The 1971 Census gives the educational distribution of workers but not by age. Hence, educational distribution for working children is not available.

According to the 1981 Census, child workers fall into two categories, viz., main workers and marginal workers. The statistics released so far gives the educational distribution for only the main workers and not for the marginal workers. Table 1 gives the educational distribution of working children obtained from the 1981 Census.

Table 1: Distribution of Working Children in India by Education (age 5–14 years)

Area	Illiterate	Literate without Educational Level	Primary	Middle	Total
Rural					
Male	5,322,600	649,410	612,941	96,362	6,681,313
	(79.7)	(9.7)	(9.2)	(1.4)	(100.0)
Female	3,117,993	193,931	173,665	23,943	3,509,532
	(88.8)	(5.5)	(4.9)	(0.8)	(100.0)
Total	8,440,593	843,341	786,606	120,305	10,190,845
	(82.8)	(8.3)	(7.7)	(1.2)	(100.0)
Urban					
Male	461,874	109,036	131,635	30,681	733,226
	(63.1)	(14.9)	(17.9)	(4.1)	(100.0)
Female	189,618	26,787	25,237	4,746	246,388
	(76.9)	(10.9)	(10.3)	(1.9)	(100.0)
Total	651,492	135,823	156,872	35,427	979,614
	(66.5)	(13.9)	(16.0)	(3.6)	(100.0)
Total					
Male	5,784,474	758,446	744,576	127,043	7,414,539
	(78.0)	(10.2)	(10.1)	(1.7)	(100.0)
Female	3,307,611	220,718	198,902	28,689	3,755,920
	(88.1)	(5.9)	(5.3)	(0.8)	(100.0)
Total	9,092,085	979,164	943,478	155,732	11,170,459
	(81.4)	(8.8)	(8.5)	(1.3)	(100.0)

Figures in brackets are percentages.
Source: *Census of India, 1981.*

It is clear from Table 1 that most of the working boys and girls, both in the urban and rural areas, are illiterate. However, their number was smaller in the urban areas than the rural areas. A few working children were found to be literate and fewer could achieve primary level education. Even less could reach the middle level. The situation is serious as only about 18 per cent of the working boys and 10 per cent of the working girls had primary school education in urban India, while these figures were half in the rural areas.

According to a survey conducted on working children in Greater Bombay (Naidu and Parasuraman, 1984), about 29 per cent of the working children never enrolled in school. While about 59 per cent dropped out, only about 11 per cent were found to be working as well as attending school (see Table 2).

Table 2: Schooling Status of Working Children in Greater Bombay

Schooling Status	Number	Percentage
Never enrolled in school	227	29.07
Drop outs	467	59.79
Attending school	87	11.14
Total	781	100.00

The explanations offered by working children for non-enrolment in school are worth noting. About 37 per cent of the working children stated that they were not interested in studies; 31 per cent reported that their families did not send them to school; 24 per cent found themselves working full-time and 9 per cent stated that they could not enrol themselves in school because, before their arrival in Bombay, they were living in villages where there was no school near their residence.

On probing for the major reasons for drop-out, it was found that about 57 per cent of the children left school to work due to poverty at home, 16 per cent dropped out due to repeated failures in examinations and 26 per cent lost interest in studies. One significant factor to note is the level of education at which these children dropped out from school. Out of 467 children who enrolled, 22 per cent completed primary education and the remaining dropped out within the first four standards only.

As regards working-cum-learning children, it was found that most of them (69 per cent) were enrolled in regular day school and a few (31 per cent) went to night school. Children attending day school were generally working in production units after school hours while those who attended night school were mostly employed in repair shops.

When non-schooling working children were asked if they would like to avail of educational facilities without disturbing their work schedule, about 35 per cent said they would while 53 per cent refused.

Out of 418 children who refused proposed educational facilities, 72 per cent clearly said that there was no use in matriculating as it was not likely to improve their job potential. Another 12 per cent felt so tired at the end of the day's work that they could not go to school. 14 per cent had very long working hours which left no time for any recreational activities, leave alone attending school. This was particularly true of the children working in hotels/restaurants

Table 3: Distribution of Children by Occupation and Reasons for the Lack of Interest in Educational Programs

Type of Occupation	Not Interested in Studies	Reason Tired After Work and Not Able to Concentrate	No Time to Attend School	Total
Hotels/Restaurants	136* (68.7)**	19 (9.6)	43 (21.7)	198 (100.0)
Construction Work	31 (58.5)	15 (28.3)	7 (13.2)	53 (100.0)
Domestic Service	15 (46.9)	7 (21.8)	10 (31.3)	32 (100.0)
Repair Shops	93 (87.7)	6 (5.7)	7 (6.6)	106 (100.0)
Production Units	21 (63.6)	5 (15.2)	7 (21.2)	33 (100.0)
Total	296 (70.1)	52 (12.3)	74 (17.5)	422 (100.0)

* Frequency distribution
** Figures in parentheses indicate row percentages.

Table 4: Distribution of Children by Occupation and by their Disposition to Schooling

Type of Occupation	Already Attending School	Eager to Avail the Proposed Educational Facilities	Total
Hotels/Restaurants	3* (25.0)**	9 (75.0)	12 (100.0)
Construction Work	8 (42.1)	11 (57.9)	19 (100.0)
Domestic Service	20 (42.5)	27 (57.5)	47 (100.0)
Repair Shops	69 (52.3)	63 (47.7)	132 (100.0)
Production Units	23 (54.7)	19 (45.3)	42 (100.0)
Total	123 (48.8)	129 (51.1)	252 (100.0)

* Frequency distribution
** Figures in brackets indicate row percentages.

and at construction sites. From Tables 3 and 4 it is clear that more than half of the children employed in domestic service, repair shops and production units were interested in education.

From the foregoing discussion it is clear that we still have to go a long way to improve the educational status of working children.

Services and Educational Programs for Working Children

There are a few small-scale programs that provide supportive welfare services to working children. A brief description is given with a view to highlighting the intentions and attempts of various sectors to improve the status of working children.

GOVERNMENT SPONSORED PROGRAMS

This activity illustrates the genuine concern and desire of the government as well as of voluntary agencies to improve the status of working children. The Ministry of Labour had initiated programs in Ahmedabad, Aurangabad, Bangalore, Calcutta and Delhi.

In Ahmedabad and Delhi, the voluntary organization SEWA (Self-Employed Women's Association) is offering services to girls who help their mothers in economic activities. Three centres have been established for the working daughters of working mothers. These are for:

— wastepaper picking girls at *Khadia*
— patchmakers at *Dariapur*
— Cart-pulling girls at *Chamanpura*

Basic services of nutrition, literacy and vocational training are given at the three centres. Each centre has 15 to 20 girls. SEWA, Delhi, is offering services of health, nutrition and education to rag-pickers as well.

The Indian Institute of Rural Workers, *Khadkeshwar, Aurangabad*, has undertaken a training-cum-relief program for child workers.

Some of the boys and girls are trained in various trades and based on this experience the institute has proposed 'pre-vocational training-cum-relief centres' for child labourers. These aim at (*i*) providing interesting educational and socially-useful work to the children and improving their present working capacity accordingly; (*ii*) providing effective apprenticeship schemes with pleasant occupations to improve their skills in the present occupations; (*iii*) helping to integrate the child into community and social life; and (*iv*) providing residential accommodation to working children to better their conditions.

Bangalore. The program is addressed to a particular occupational group, i.e., rag-pickers. This program is run by a voluntary agency—Indian Council for Child Welfare (Karnataka State branch). The program has been in operation for the past two years. Rag-pickers in the age group of 5 to 14 years are contacted. Their rags are bought by the Council at a price higher than what they were getting from the middle-men.

The Council also extends services by organizing regular medical examinations and, when necessary, medical treatment. Personal hygiene, non-formal education, recreational facilities as well as counselling services are provided. Counselling services are extended to the parents of these young children. The program for these children will be continued beyond the age of 14 years (i.e., up to 18 years).

Calcutta. The program for working children in Calcutta is based on a survey conducted by the Institute of Psychological and Educational Research and is on a larger scale than the programs in Aurangabad, Bangalore and Delhi. The Calcutta program is meant for 10 per cent of the total working children's population of Calcutta. At the initial stage, there was much resistance from the employers which resulted in the under-reporting of working children.

The main areas of the action program are (*i*) improving the level of general education of working children and by doing so improving their vocational efficiency; (*ii*) bettering the vocational skills of those child workers who are engaged in vocation-based work; (*iii*) providing regular medical check-ups and arranging for clinical treatment and the supply of medicine where needed; (*iv*) providing food to supplement nutritional deficiency; (*v*) improving service conditions at the place of work; (*vi*) arranging facilities for cultural participation and social opportunities for their self-image; (*vii*) infusing self-confidence in the working children and helping them develop a more healthy and harmonious personality; and (*viii*) detecting psychological maladjustment and disturbing conflicts in the working children and providing them with proper guidance to overcome personality disorders.

The Centres (popularly known as holiday schools) have timings which are convenient to wage earners, part- as well as full-time household servants and self-employed children. 12 holiday schools have been established in 10 wards of Calcutta. They provide remedial education to improve the educational level of working children in order to bring them into the mainstream of education. For cultural participation and social interaction, several visits are arranged to places which are of interest to children. Regarding 50 per cent of the children under the program who are domestic servants, neither the employers nor the child workers were interested in programs meant for improving children's vocational efficiency.

Garages and manufacturing units have laid down specific tasks to be done by children, hence they are not keen to change their vocation. Only a few working children came forward in the project to learn new trades or improve upon their present one.

Neglect and indifference were the usual reactions when child workers fell sick. Although medical care facilities were available for the children who had joined the holiday schools, the medical officer and social workers felt that the children did not take their medicines regularly and they did not care about their own health. The apathy on the part of parents and the employers to the problem of health care is another factor which adds to the difficulties of the medical staff and the health care program was found to be ineffective.

The proposal to improve the working conditions of children is an extremely difficult one. Persuasive methods are being applied to negotiate with employers. As a result, improved sanitary arrangements have been introduced in a large number of places. In some cases, employers have been induced to adopt protective measures against the use of corrosive or poisonous materials handled by child workers. In sweet shops and large eating houses where child workers are forced to work next to large ovens, the attention of the employers has been drawn to the danger that is caused to the child's health by such exposures to excessive heat.

A new social consciousness and community feeling has dawned on child workers after joining holiday schools. They have overcome their sense of inferiority that perpetually haunted them and weakened their personality. They have now developed a new self-confidence and a sense of worthiness. Employers can play a vital role in bringing about an improvement in the working conditions of child workers.

PROGRAMS UNDERTAKEN BY VOLUNTARY AGENCIES

Some welfare programs have been started by voluntary agencies in rural and urban areas. Since 1979, Apanalaya in Bombay has been providing services (like vocational training, non-formal education and material assistance) for continuing general education. It caters to children employed in hotels, garages and small-scale industries. Ananda Kendra in Bombay offers basic services to improve the situation of destitute children.

PROGRAMS JOINTLY CONDUCTED BY THE GOVERNMENT AND VOLUNTARY AGENCIES

Community Aid and Sponsorship Program (CASP), Bombay, in collaboration with the Maharashtra government, is providing sponsorship aid to children working in bidi-making, stone-breaking, construction sites, and so on. Rs. 60 per month is given to a child as a stipend for education and medical care. The program was started in 1980. So far, approximately 450 children working in different cities like Bombay, Nagpur, Pune and Solapur have benefited from this program.

A unique experiment was started in June 1984 for children working in match factories at Sivakasi, Sattur and Vembakottari Blocks in Tamil Nadu. This is known as the *Social Inputs Under Area Development Program* (Match Factories), Sivakasi. This program differs from the other programs as it has a multi-dimensional approach. This is essential for resolving the problems pertaining to child labour. The salient feature of the Sivakasi program are (*i*) provision for integrated services for working children, i.e., health, education, environmental hygiene and nutrition; (*ii*) provision for macro-level developmental measures, viz., improving the drinking water supply, providing drainage, providing environmental sanitation by toilets and mosquito control measures.

The project is a collaborative effort of the Tamil Nadu state government, UNICEF, and the owners of the match factories. In the government, the Ministry of Social Welfare is the nodal ministry for the project. It coordinates the participation of nine other departments which are under various ministries. The concerned departments are public health and preventive medicine, medical services, water supply and drainage board, education, labour department dealing with the on-going integrated nutrition project, department of applied research, rural development and local bodies. The project has been planned, discussed, revised and continually modified to meet the changing needs. This has been an interesting experiment insofar as all concerned parties have participated. Thus, this well-planned experimental project with a multi-sector approach to provide integrated services to working children.

PROGRAMS UNDERTAKEN BY ACADEMIC INSTITUTIONS

Based on the recently completed survey of the needs of working children in Greater Bombay undertaken by the Unit for Child and Youth Research, Tata Institute of Social Sciences, Bombay, an action plan is being drawn up to provide integrated services of education, recreation, health and nutrition to working children in one of the slums of Bombay. This is being done as an experiment to test the strategy for making developmental services actually reach the working children.

Another effort by academicians, which is of recent origin, is to develop condensed courses for children working and studying in night schools. One such successful experiment in remedial learning in Algebra for the students of Standard IX has been by Jude Henrique. Based on the experiment, a *Manual for Remedial Learning in Algebra for SSC Students* has also been prepared (Henrique, 1984). An experiment on remedial learning in the English Language for middle school level working students is also being conducted in Haryana by a teacher teaching English there (Rai, 1985).

Thus, the interest taken by a few individual academicians and supported by their respective institutions in developing condensed courses for working children is a significant step in the education of working children.

COMMENTS

Most of the programs are limited to parts of a few cities. Apart from expanding these programs, it is also necessary to extend them to small towns and rural areas. Along with a geographical expansion, there is also the need to initiate and popularize such experimental projects to cover all categories of child workers. The pilot projects have so far been limited to very small segments of working children (like domestic servants, rag-pickers and workers in cottage and small-scale units). Fields with high juvenile employment (such as, agriculture and family trades) have not been touched upon as yet.

The few small-scale programs we have are not adequate enough to motivate the children for school education. Education as a means for upward mobility of working children may be in the minds of educationists and policy planners but child workers are not motivated enough to regard school education as an agent of positive change in their lives.

Constraints in Educating Working Children

ECONOMIC PRESSURES

Even if parents wish to school their children, the cost of books, stationery, uniforms and the other needs of school-going children deter them from sending their children to school. While working children who contribute to the family income are considered as asset, school-going children are regarded as liabilities.

PARENTAL ATTITUDES

In most of the cases, parents feel that an apprenticeship, or even a job without pay for a short period, is more beneficial than spending years at school. They believe that four or five years spent on a job at a very small wage has a better pay-off than spending those years in school.

Moreover, beyond functional literacy education is not viewed by the parents as a promise for a job. Realizing that the family environment would not be very conducive to building up academic skills, they fear that the child would simply become a liability. This view is reinforced by their observation that a large number of educated youth remain unemployed.

One of the common beliefs in India ever since the inception of formal education by the British has been that education helps one get a white collar job. Parents feel that if a child does not get a white collar job when he completes high school, he would prefer to remain unemployed and would refuse to take up manual work or a blue collar job. In order to avoid such a situation, they prefer the child to take up a job in childhood. This way neither he nor his parents would have to face any frustration on this account.

India being primarily an agricultural and rural-based country, the majority of the people in the villages are occupied in farming and/or in crafts. Parents in such families prefer not to send their children to school because schooling is not regarded as relevant for vocational skills. They prefer to train the child in the craft in which the members of the family have been engaged traditionally.

Regarding the education of girls, conservative and illiterate parents do not look upon the education of girls as a necessity. The female child's role in the family is perceived mainly as assisting in household chores and looking after the younger siblings. In families where the mother is also working (which is a common feature in low income groups), the role of a female child as one who looks after the other children becomes all the more pronounced.

EMPLOYERS' ATTITUDE

The education of working children is generally discouraged by employers. Employers mostly regard a child worker as a labourer who works for lower wages, who is easily pliable, who does not involve the employer in trade union problems and who, in jobs which require soft hands, is more efficient than an adult worker. Employers in the unorganized sector do not wish to lose juvenile manpower and thus discourage the education of working children. Instead, they impress upon the children the need to work and, at times, may even give false hopes of upward mobility—if children continue in the present job.

WORKING CHILDREN'S OUTLOOK

Another constraint in the schooling of working children comes from the child workers themselves. Like their parents, child workers look upon their job as a training for a skill or an experience for getting better jobs with higher wages.

Schooling is regarded as a drudgery by working children. The curriculum is not job-oriented and does not motivate them or hold any prospects for providing them a job. Besides, once a child gets a job, he does not want to become dependent on his family. Schooling for him implies dependence on the family for about 5 to 7 years.

Adopting an adult attitude, working children often rationalize their employment as a means to educate and support their younger siblings. In a way they consider themselves the financial support of the family (Naidu, 1985).

THE GOVERNMENT'S APPROACH

The government's approach is another constraint in educating working children. This is because most of the programs for providing compulsory elementary education are addressed to dependent children and not working children. Though some night schools/classes and other means of part-time education have been recognized and supported financially by the government, they appear to be an extension of the formal system of education which is not at all suited to working children. The curriculum in these evening schools is similar to the other elementary day schools and the cost, the time needed to study the exhaustive curriculum and the pattern of evaluation frustrate the working children. These, to at least some working children, seem frightening and impossible goals.

Moreover, as the problem of child labour is the divided responsibility of several ministries, each ministry looks upon the educational needs of the working children according to its basic approach to the problem. For instance, for the Ministry of Education it is the problem of providing universal elementary education to all children, and working children are one of the disadvantaged groups; the Ministry of Social and Women's Welfare may look upon the education of working children as a welfare rather than a developmental service; the Ministry of Labour may view the education of working children only in terms of vocational skills to be provided to the working children, and so on.

Strategies for Educating Working Children

Strategies for educating working children in India must be linked to three major aspects of the problem. They are (*i*) the system of education; (*ii*) the quantum of child labour in the country; and (*iii*) the working and living conditions of child workers. These aspects differ from each other but from the perspective of an action policy they should be viewed jointly. Taking these aspects into account some short-term and long-term measures are suggested.

SHORT-TERM MEASURES

Provision and Popularization of Multiple Entries in Schools. Generally, our schools function on a single point entry system and a sequential curriculum which expects a child to rise from one standard to a higher standard at yearly intervals. Grown up children, who missed the point of entry for one reason or another, find it almost impossible to enter school. The provision of multiple points of entry in schools can increase the enrolment of working children and prevent heavy rates of wastage.

Preparation of Condensed Courses. Working children who missed the opportunity to enter school or dropped out after being in the school for a year or two need condensed and quick study courses for their sensitized minds. The preparation and use of condensed courses for all relevant subjects is imperative to popularize education among working children. Translation of such materials into regional languages is also needed to reach the large number of working children who are in various parts of the country.

Developing Vocational Skills and Upgrading Skills. In various surveys, it has been found that parents/guardians of working children and children themselves look for the type of education which would improve the earning prospects of children. We need to examine seriously how to combine formal as well as vocational education and training to prepare them for a vocation, to upgrade their skills and to provide them literacy and general education.

To Regulate Hours of Work and Wages Paid to Working Children to Facilitate their Access to Education. Children work very long hours for pittance. For example, in one study it was found that the average duration of work for a working child in Greater Bombay is about 11 hours a day (Naidu and Parasuraman, 1984). Thus the child does not have the time or energy to attend an educational program. Such children require organized support from adults so that they can be relieved from long hours of work and allowed spare time for growth and development.

It is essential to mobilize employers to help their child employees to educate themselves. This is not an easy task, particularly, when most of the children are employed in the unorganized sector. Many of the children work in establishments which employ less than five individuals. The employers demand hard work from children under close supervision. Reducing the working hours of children has monetary implications both for the children and employers, especially when they are working on a piece-rate basis. In such circumstances, employers, parents and working children themselves have to come to a consensus to allow children to combine education and employment.

To Make Education Relevant for Life. The message is clear from the disadvantaged population that the present system of education is not relevant for their life. To keep child workers out of the educational system is not the answer either. According to Karl Marx and Engels (1969), 'the combination of paid productive labour, mental education, bodily exercise and polytechnic training, will raise the working class far above the level of the higher and middle classes.' But, then, education has to be socially productive and individually meaningful. Gandhian basic education could be a viable alternative to the presently unattractive and meaningless system of school education for the Indian masses, in general, and working children, in particular.

Thus, it is a challenging proposition for educationists and policy planners to make education attractive and relevant enough to the needs of working children so that employers, parents and working children may be mobilized with conviction.

LONG-TERM DEVELOPMENT MEASURES

The problem of the education of working children cannot be tackled in isolation. Child labour is basically a problem of the developing countries. It is generally accepted that poverty is the reason why children work. Their income is essential for the survival of the family.

Though the Government of India has accepted child labour as a 'harsh reality' and has proposed that measures be taken to improve the working conditions of children rather than eradicate child labour, as such, attention should be given to ending the employment of children in hazardous occupations, putting a ceiling on the age of starting employment, improving conditions of work, regulating the hours of work and wages paid, and developing supplementary education programs for employed children. However, this does not mean a change in long-term goals—of ending child labour and implementing compulsory primary education. Hence it is necessary to link all the measures taken to the achievement of these goals.

In this context, not only is the provision of schooling and access to education important but the relevance of education and scholastic achievement should also be examined vis-a-vis the employment and unemployment status and upward mobility of the weaker sections of society. Further, provisions should be made for day-care centres to help in relieving families who depend on older children (particularly girls) to look after the younger siblings. A reduction in the infant mortality rate can lead to a reduction in the incidence of child labour. In consultation with banks, voluntary agencies and community-based organizations, programs should be formulated for adult employment and income generation. The development of backward districts is an essential macro-level measure for controlling the migration flow of rural landless labour to urban areas.

Summary and Conclusions

In spite of the regulatory measures to effect improvements in the conditions of working children and to decrease its incidence, child labour persists, especially in the unorganized and small-scale sectors. In this context, a multi-pronged action program is necessary to tackle the problem of working children in India.

From the foregoing discussion it is clear that educating working children is a complex task. These children differ on several counts, for example, in terms of their level of education and training, the kind of trade they are employed in, the nature of their working conditions, living conditions, and so on. Further, working children are different from non-school-going children who are not working. They are also different from school drop-outs. At the same time, they cannot be equated with adult labourers. By virtue of joining the labour force at a tender age, they have obtained 'education' and 'maturity' of the kind which places them in a distinct social category.

The strategies for educating working children have to be directed by short-term and long-term measures. Considering their economic situation, they are not in a position to abandon their jobs in order to join school. Therefore, presently, any kind of education (i.e., planned for this particular group of children) has to be combined with their job.

The content of education for this group of children, therefore, will be different from what children in regular schools learn. Some of them may require literacy as well as general education, others may need literacy and education combined with vocational training. Careful planning and programming has to be done to cater to the educational needs of the different categories of working children. Some of the working children may like to pursue formal education (including higher education) in order to improve their future prospects. Our formal system of school and college education should be flexible enough to allow such working children to pursue their education.

The need of the hour is to involve all those who are concerned with the education of working children in formulating an action program and implementing it effectively. This is not the task of only parents or employers or educationists or welfare personnel; everybody needs to cooperate and collaborate in this massive task so that they can build a better future for India.

References

GOVERNMENT OF INDIA. 1979. *Report of the Committee on Child Labour.*
———. 1981. *Report of the National Committee on Labour.*
———. 1981. *Census of India.*
HENRIQUE, J. 1984. *Manual for Remedial Learning in Algebra for SSC Students.* Bombay: Tata Institute of Social Sciences (mimeo).
MARX, KARL and F. ENGELS. 1969. *Selected Works*, Volume 2. Moscow: Progress Publishers.
NAIDU, U.S. 1985. 'Health Problems of Working Children: Some Issues for Planning Long Term Care,' in U.S. Naidu and K.R. Kapadia, eds., *Child Labour and Health—Problems and Prospects.* Bombay: Tata Institute of Social Sciences.
NAIDU, U.S. and S. PARASURAMAN. 1984. *Health Situation of Working Children in Greater Bombay.* World Health Organization sponsored study (Interim Report). Bombay: Tata Institute of Social Sciences.(Ms).
RAI, R. 1985. Manual for Remedial Learning in English for VII Standard Students (in progress). Personal communication.

10

Education, Development and Women's Liberation: Contemporary Debates in India

Vina Mazumdar

The role of education in women's liberation is currently the subject of several debates in India. In fact, these debates spring from another general debate on the role of education in the achievement of social justice, which has been going on for a long time. Till 1975, the specific role of education in the attainment of women's equality was not being debated. The concept of education as a pre-requisite for women's equality had been accepted for well over a century and was, in fact, the first demand of the earlier women's movement that developed during the 1920s and 1930s. In the post-Independence period the national policy again accepted education as *the* key instrument to translate the Constitutional guarantee of equal status and opportunities for women into reality. Most national agencies responsible for educational development tended to regard women's educational needs as a special responsibility. The University Grants Commission liberalized its conditions to provide greater assistance to colleges catering exclusively to women. Several state governments made the education of girls free, not only within the school system but even up to the university level. Quite a few teacher-training colleges for women also provided free training to increase the number of women in the teaching profession. The National Committee on Women's Education, appointed by the Government of India (1958–59), identified certain major problems and advised the government to focus its policy and program efforts on reducing the gap between men and women within the educational process and to eliminate any differentiation in curricula between the two sexes.

However, the assessment made by the Committee on the Status of Women in India (1971–74) recorded a major failure of these efforts. Not only had the country failed to eradicate illiteracy among women but the number of women illiterates and their proportion amongst total illiterates had, in fact, increased during the decades after Independence.[1] The major section of children not at school consisted of girls. The most damaging finding of the Committee was that, in the realm of social values and attitudes to women's roles, the educational system had not succeeded in bringing about any major change. On the other hand, it had helped to strengthen and perpetuate traditional ideas of women's subordination.[2]

The debates began after the publication of this report, and have become more vehement with the revitalization of the women's movement. The aim of this paper is to present some of the crucial debates and the contextual setting which gave them birth and to challenge some myths that seek to mystify the education and development scene vis-a-vis the quest for women's liberation.

There are, in fact, three major debates: (a) has education, instead of eliminating women's unequal roles and position in society, widened gender inequality, and added a new one—that between educated and uneducated women? (b) should the education policy, which upheld non-discrimination/non-differentiation on the grounds of sex since Independence, be reversed to provide a special type of education which women would find more valuable? and (c) should education play a more prominent and active role in eliminating gender inequality and, if so, how? Who should be its target?

[1] See Appendix Table.
[2] Govt. of India, *Towards Equality, Report of the Committee on the Status of Women in India*, New Delhi: Ministry of Education & Social Welfare, December 1974, Chapter 6, paras 6.108–111.

Each of these debates, often presented in strictly statistical and educational terms, hides a political controversy. The stand of the women's movement is unequivocal. The Indian freedom struggle adopted gender and social equality as the founding principle of the Indian political system. Four decades later, women activists do not support any attempts to reverse that principle. Education, along with legal reform and equal political and civil rights, was seen as the major instrument to translate this principle into reality. Education's achievement has been mixed, like all other development policies. Goals were not clearly defined, ambiguities and mystification abounded, providing cover for reactionary elements. Social goals inevitably received lower priority before economic ones, unless there was organized pressure to demand otherwise. And, for three decades after Independence, the women's movement was absent from the political arena, so the education system, or the government behind that system, cannot be solely blamed for all the failures and mistakes.

This does not mean that they can be absolved of all responsibility. Apart from the Constitutional directives, there were many policy directions—five year plans, national commissions and committees, parliamentary resolutions—that set goals to eliminate gender differences in the access to education and in the content of education. Courts upheld the right of women to enter any educational institution and, except for the Army, no profession could be debarred to women. The ratio of women to men in higher education[3] today can stand comparison with the most developed countries of the world. Women have held decision-making positions in the educational bureaucracy since Independence, have always received equal pay and have also enjoyed some special privileges on the logic of being a 'weaker section'. These privileges included special weightage or a reserved quota in admissions to some courses, special grants to institutions which cater exclusively to women's educational needs (e.g., training in sciences), for hostels, and so on, free education at school and teacher-training in many states.

However, all these achievements pale into insignificance in the face of the statistics of illiteracy. 75 per cent of women still remain

---

[3] During the decade 1971–81, the number of women for every 1000 men in higher education increased from 294 to 382 (27.64 per cent). sciences, over 40 per cent; medicine. 354 per 1,000; law, 75 per cent; engineering/technology. 47 per cent; agriculture. 36 per cent; vet. science, 45 per cent.

illiterate and during 1971–81, the sex ratio (number of women per 1,000 men) among illiterates changed from 1,330 to 1,427. This ratio becomes still greater in regions with higher educational development. For rural India it is 1,412, but it is 1,523 for urban areas. In Kerala—the most educationally advanced state with a female illiteracy rate of less than 35 per cent—the urban sex ratio among illiterates is 1,930. The nine states recently classified by the Government of India as specially backward in women's education, however, have illiteracy sex ratios lower than the national average in some cases.

Efforts to use illiteracy sex ratios as an indicator of increasing gender differentiation in educational development began only during the last five years. Similar data regarding non-school-goers is being used to demand special programs to increase girls' enrolment in schools. A recently concluded conference organized by NGOs [non-governmental organizations] which cater to the needs of women drew special attention to the fact that 55 per cent of girls in the 6 to 11 age group, 75 per cent in the 11 to 14 age group and 85 per cent in the 14 to 17 age group are still out of school. Comparable figures for boys are 20 per cent, 57 per cent and 71 per cent.

These figures all tell the same story. The gender gap reduces as you go up the education ladder but widens among the entire population, which fails to have access to the educational process. So education has both reduced and widened the gender gap among different levels of the population. The issue is, therefore, primarily of class. The assumption that Indian women are deprived of education because of purdah, or social seclusion, does not hold good any longer because the sections that confined their women to the home have taken the lead in educating them (*a*) because otherwise they could not find a suitable groom; and (*b*) to push them into the labour market when necessary to maintain or improve the family's standard of living.[4]

The classes that have not been included are (*a*) those whose women were always in the labour force (36 per cent of the agricultural work-force are women) either as family labour or as wage labour, as their families could not survive without women's economic contribution; (*b*) aspirants or new entrants into the ranks of the middle class, who tend to emulate the traditional norms of the social elite—of

---

[4] *Towards Equality, op. cit.*, Chapter 6 (Imbalance in Educational Development).

controlling their women by confining them to the home; and (c) downwardly mobile families, among whom women's labour under disguised, exploited conditions is often responsible for the difference between survival and extinction.

When women labour, daughters are needed as helpers, and even the presence of a school nearby cannot bridge the gap without supportive services. A peasant woman's work day has been found to extend from 14 to 18 hours. Against this, men average between 8 and 10 hours. Hence the demand for special programs:

(i) for child-care centres attached to schools;
(ii) for the improved supply of water, fuel and fodder;
(iii) for income generation strategies as entry points for adult and school education for women;
(iv) for increasing the number of women teachers; and
(v) for supplementary nutrition for school children through midday meals, book and uniform grants and retention scholarships.

Pressure for these special programs mounted during the decade 1971–81, resulting eventually in some of them being initiated by the government from 1983. The demand for child-care centres as an extension of schools, however, has been resisted all along by the educational administration, on the ground that this will impose a tremendous burden on teachers. A recently concluded National Seminar on Education for Women's Equality attempted a compromise, by recommending that child-care centres should be located near schools to enable older children to leave their siblings there and undertake only occasional supervision.

Above all, there is a demand for vigilant monitoring of these supports by NGOs, because previous experience indicates that the greatest resistance to the promotion of women's development is at the local level. Rural India, which has accepted the vote as a political right and is familiar with the notion of worker's rights, is still unaware of women's and children's rights. Only pressure from the top, earmarked allocations, and NGO pressure can change this. However, NGO pressure has been lacking so far because women's organizations have been mainly urban, middle class based. Rural women's organizations, which were promoted under the Community Development Program from the fifties, declined because of lack of official support.

The Working Group on Adult Education Programs for Women (1977–78), and many conferences on adult literacy since then, have advocated the use of such programs to raise women's awareness of their legal rights. Amazingly, however, educational authorities have never implemented this. On the other hand, non-formal training programs for women (initiated by the Central Social Welfare Board)—whose syllabus since the sixties had included legal rights—actually omitted this portion in the training.[5]

The problem of women's illiteracy and the ways of eradicating it has also provoked a great deal of debate. The failure or non-implementation of government-sponsored programs for adult literacy were sometimes rationalized by charges of women's lack of motivation. Researchers on women and women activists have retorted by pointing to poor women's lack of time as the primary obstacle to their attending literacy classes. The struggle for survival does make literacy a low priority for these women. Activists promoting organizations of poor women have, however, found that while women give first priority to increasing their earning capacity, they do ask for literacy and other educational inputs fairly soon, when they begin to realize their importance in protecting themselves against exploitation and in obtaining information or assistance. The Working Group on Adult Education Programs for Women had, therefore, recommended combining literacy programs with organization building and income generation. While some voluntary organizations have actually developed this kind of package for their work among poor women, government sponsored programs have found it virtually impossible to integrate these different approaches because income generation is not the responsibility of educational agencies.

The difficulty of coordinating the development assistance offered by different government agencies has created problems for many voluntary organizations engaged in women's development. One of the by-products of the women's movement, however, has been a revival of interest in eradicating women's illiteracy amongst women's organizations. A group of them have now formed a National Committee for Eradication of Female Illiteracy by the year 2000. The Committee has been engaged in dialogues with government agencies to provide a better channel for coordinated assistance so

---

[5] Kumud Sharma *et al.*, *Women in Focus*, New Delhi: Sangam Books (India) Pvt. Ltd., 1984, p. 80.

that literacy and educational inputs can be combined with other services which would enable poor working women to cross the barrier of illiteracy. The recent document of the Government of India to initiate a national debate on a new educational policy indicates that the government has also begun to realize that unless adult literacy programs are coordinated with economic development programs, the target of eradicating illiteracy before the end of the century will not be achieved.

The second debate is still muted because national policy has repeatedly rejected curricular differentiation. The British Raj had followed a policy of differentiated curricula between men and women. Resistance to this came from educated women and from some universities. In the post-Independence period, the controversy was settled by its rejection by an Expert Committee,[6] and the Education Commission.[7] But State Secondary Education Boards continue to advocate home science and fine arts rather than mathematics for girls and get away with it because no one is monitoring such matters. Vigilance from the women's movement has also been slow.

The revival of the movement in the late seventies was so convulsed from the start by issues of growing violence against women and their marginalization in the economy that it could not devote any time to curricular deviations. Demands for vocational training mounted, along with criticism of over-concentration of training in household crafts, tailoring, embroidery, handicrafts, etc. A growing realization of the importance of educated skills for information gathering, project planning and implementation and for dialogues and battles with the bureaucracy, however, is drawing women NGOs closer to understanding some of the subtle ways by which educational institutions can discriminate. At the same time, the value of information from women's studies specialists in academic institutions is drawing them closer to NGOs,[8] for mobilizing pressure on the government for needed policies.

New contacts with women at the grassroots and the articulation of major grassroot organizations are bringing up new demands.

[6] Committee on Differentiation of Curricula for Boys and Girls, Govt. of India, Ministry of Education, 1964.

[7] Govt. of India, *Education and National Development, Report of the Indian Education Commission*, Ministry of Education, 1966.

[8] Many women's studies specialists are activists in the women's movement and have joined, or promoted organizations, to work for a better deal for women.

Women want to know their rights under law—why were they not informed all this time? And would it be enough to teach this only to women? Why have educational authorities not recognized all these years that rural women working in agriculture need and want knowledge about better farming methods, sericulture, pisciculture, animal husbandry, etc., rather than child-care and nutritional techniques which most of them cannot afford?

The basic assumption that has mystified and defeated the policy of non-discrimination in content, or curricula is the view that all women are primarily housewives. This middle class bias vitiated earlier programs for rural women's educational development by loading curricula with things only wealthy women could afford. The efforts of researchers and some NGOs in the last decade and, above all, the Report of the Committee on the Status of Women in India has helped to reduce this myth somewhat. However, it is still an uphill task to teach educators that they must adopt a participatory approach, that adult women cannot be treated as irresponsible children, that one can teach them only if one accepts their priorities and is willing to learn from them as well.

What the educators have failed to learn, however, is that a small section of the bureaucracy responsible for agriculture or rural development is being forced to learn through other sources. The National Commission on Agriculture (1976), and the National Committee on Women's Role in Agriculture and Rural Development agreed that the non-recognition of women's major role in agriculture, and the failure to teach better knowledge, techniques and tools to women is one of the factors responsible for the slow progress in improving agricultural productivity. Simultaneously, groups analysing population policy successes or failures reached the conclusion that the answer lay in changing women's role and status. They began to press for policies for women's development through employment, health and education to arrest their 'devaluation to mere reproductive machines'.[9]

About the same time (i.e., in the seventies), rural women in the Himalayan region precipitated a protest movement against the denudation of their forests for industrial development shattering another myth that women, in general, and rural women, in particular, are just passive spectators of events who need to be motivated by

---

[9] ICSSR, Advisory Committee on Women's Studies, *Critical Issues on the Status of Women: Priorities for Action*, 1977.

those who know better as to what is good for them. New research studies have also discovered women's active role in peasant and workers struggles during contemporary periods or in the past.

In 1975, the Report of the Committee on the Status of Women in India documented, with official data, the process of marginalization of women in the economy and society that had started earlier but had actually accelerated during the period of planned development since Independence. The Committee's critique of the government's policies raised several fundamental questions. Why had the Constitutional guarantees of equality made so little impact on planners, administrators and local governments? Why had the entire community of social scientists, busy analysing different aspects of social change, failed to examine what was happening to the majority of women, even though census after census was reporting very disturbing things—the declining sex ratio in population and economic participation, the rapid rise in female migration, the widening gender gap in mortality and life expectancy, and the rising number of women illiterates? Why had the efforts to bridge the enrolment gap between boys and girls, speeded up in the sixties after the Report of the National Committee on Women's Education, been allowed to slow down from the late sixties? Above all, why were there so many manifestations of 'regression from the norms developed during the freedom struggle'—escalation of dowry, greater resistance to the idea of gender equality among many sections of the population and total apathy among planners and administrators? Why had political parties, trade unions, elected representatives of the people and voluntary organizations taken no note of these trends?

The trends were glaringly visible, not only from the available data but from the Committee's conversations with nearly 10,000 women from different classes, occupations, communities and regions across the country. It was obvious to the Committee that no one had, in fact, ever asked women about their problems, needs, priorities or views. Political and legal rights had failed to reach them; most women did not know their rights or were unable to exercise them effectively.

As for education, it has failed in terms of reach and impact, quantity and quality, method and in content. Opposing the current approaches that seek to reduce education to a mere skill-generating process, the Committee on the Status of Women in India fell back on the classical theory of the role of education:

The deep foundations of the inequality of the sexes are built in the minds of men and women through a socialization process which continues to be extremely powerful. Right from their earliest years, boys and girls are brought up to know that they are different from each other and this difference is strengthened in every way possible—through language forms, modes of behaviour of labour, etc. The only institution which can counteract the effect of this process is the educational system. If education is to promote equality for women, it must make a deliberate, planned and sustained effort so that the new value of equality of the sexes can replace the traditional value system of inequality. The educational system today has not even attempted to undertake this responsibility.[10]

This challenge provides the basis for the third debate. The women's movement and a section of people in academic institutions—men and women—are questioning the actual contribution of education to social development. Dowry was supposed to disappear with the spread of education. Instead, dowry escalation has followed educational development. The higher the education and its labour market value, the higher is the groom's price in the marriage market. From the ill-treatment of brides who carried small dowries, we have moved to dowry murders and dowry suicides. Domestic violence has reared its ugly head among the educated classes, eve-teasing is becoming a significant phenomenon in university campuses in metropolitan cities and it is the educated middle class which is now accused of using women, not excluding women, from their own families, as commodities to assist the family's climb up the social ladder.

It is in this context that the revival of the women's movement is taking place, spearheaded by educated middle class women—young and old, from affluent and hard up families, with or without a general political ideology. It is, at present, a confused mass of various groups but certain trends are significant. Class interests are being bridged on occasions. The first major explosion in 1979–80 took place because two policemen raped a young Scheduled Caste agricultural labourer. New organizations for poor working women (like SEWA[11] and WWF[12]) have demonstrated that with a little

[10] *Towards Equality, op. cit.*, Chapter 6.
[11] Self-Employed Women's Association, Ahmedabad.
[12] Working Women's Forum, Madras.

support from educated women—as correspondents, accountants, trainers; basically support groups—such organizations can even upset established power balances. The partial success in bringing about policy change or legislative reform is making many women's groups realize that they can exercise more political power than they had thought before. And some of them are beginning to acknowledge that they have potential allies within the government, media, judiciary, academia, political parties, trade unions, student groups, and so on.

Women's studies or an investigation of the women's situation at the grassroots has played a major role in feeding this ferment and pressurizing the government for better policies. This movement began with the research commissioned by the Indian Council of Social Science Research for the Committee on the Status of Women in India. It was sustained through the ICSSR's decision to initiate a sponsored program for research on women, focusing on the impact of economic development, social change and population dynamics on hitherto neglected groups of 'invisible' working women in the informal sector (including agriculture), with a view to suggesting policy corrections, and re-examining the theoretical perspectives and analytical tools of the social sciences. Another objective of the ICSSR's program was to stimulate the reopening of the social debate on the women's question 'which had faded out of the public arena in the period after Independence'.[13]

Increasing interest in women's issues among the academic community resulted in the formation of an Association for Women's Studies and the holding of national/regional conferences. The close interrelationship between the growth of women's studies or research on women, the revitalization of the women's movement and the growth of a pressure lobby to struggle for policy changes has led to it being described

> as the intellectual arm of the women's movement, as a powerful instrument which is not value neutral but works actively to transform values in favour of women, as the essential instrument to provide needed information for policy change, as an instrument that transforms women's perceptions about themselves and tries to transform perspectives about women.[14]

[13] ICSSR, *Policy Statement of the Program on Women's Studies.*
[14] *Samya Shakti,* Vol. 2, No. 1, CWDS, 1985 (Editorial).

The ICSSR had suggested a re-examination of social science theories and analytical tools in the light of the findings of research on women, with a view to explain the previous neglect of women in research (e.g., on the economics and sociology of agriculture, studies on the informal sector and studies on poverty, unemployment and equality). The first National Conference on Women's Studies in 1981 challenged the non-inclusion of data on women and women's issues and concerns in most of the university courses, and suggested a revision of the university curriculum. This trend in the women's studies movement has been aptly described as women's 'growing involvement with the politics of knowledge,' forcing scholars to assault the 'sacred cows of learning'

> the long entrenched Social Darwinists, whose hierarchical view of the universe has served mainly the patriarchs, racists and captains of industry; the historians who for far too long have been permitted to reconstruct a past devoid of women; the economists with their myopic view of labour, or whose theory of growth proclaiming the magic of the market-place for decades has so disastrously deluded so much of the Third World.[15]

As an outcome of this pressure, the University Grants Commission requested universities to consider ways of incorporating women's problems, issues and concerns in teaching, research and extension-type activities of various disciplines. The continued dialogue within the academic community has now produced a set of aims and objectives for incorporating women's studies within the university system.

1. To change the present attitudes/values in society regarding women's roles and rights to one of equal participation in all social, economic and political processes and national and international development.
2. To promote awareness among women and men of the need to develop and utilize women's full potential as resources for national development in its economic, political and socio-cultural aspects on the need to question existing values and of their social responsibilities so as to participate equally.

[15] Lucille Mair, *International Women's Decade: A Balance Sheet*, Third JP Naik Memorial Lecture, CWDS, 1984.

3. To counter the reactionary forces emanating from certain sections of the media, economic, social and political institutions that encourage the demotion of women from productive to mere reproductive roles.
4. To revitalize university education, bringing it closer to burning social issues, to work towards their solution and to produce sensitive persons able to play more committed and meaningful roles in development activities for women in all sectors.
5. To fulfil a special responsibility—to produce for all levels of the educational system teachers who are aware of the need for non-sexist education and who would actively pick up the challenge to promote values of social equality, including gender equality, secularism, socialism and democracy.
6. To up-date university curricula by incorporating the results of new scholarship and the issues raised by the latter as they challenge some of the established theories, analytical concepts and methodologies of various disciplines.
7. To promote increased collaboration between different disciplines in teaching, curriculum designing, research and extension activities since women's studies are interdisciplinary by nature.
8. To generate new and organic knowledge through intensive field-work. This would help the generation of data essential for the evaluation and correction of development policies and programs and in extending the areas for academic analysis into hitherto neglected sectors. For a better understanding and investigation of the problems being experienced by women at the grassroots, a closer contact between institutions of higher education and groups directly involved in action; to assist women enjoy their rights within the family, the community and at work, would be very valuable. Such contacts would also help universities and colleges to design their extension activities in a more meaningful manner.
9. To contribute to the global debate on the women's question through a rediscovery of the debate in India—from ancient to contemporary periods, through research and translation from Indian literature, including folk literature.[16]

---

[16] *Report of the Seminar on Perspectives and Organisation of Women's Studies Units in Indian Universities*, Department of Political Science, Delhi University, April 1985, pp. 3–4.

Since the beginning of 1985, there has been a national debate to develop a new education policy. The Ministry of Human Resource Development, Department of Education, Government of India, sponsored a National Seminar on Education for Women's Equality in early November 1985. The seminar discussions focused on two basic issues—women's access to all levels of education and the role of education in transforming values and attitudes. The report of the seminar articulates very clearly that 'incorporation of women's lives, problems and perspectives as a legitimate area of concern, scientific enquiry and understanding within various disciplines, courses and faculty offers a method and an instrument for transforming the role of the educational system to one of active promotion of new values'.[17]

This debate has shifted the perception of the women's issue in education from one of discrimination against a deprived group to recognizing it as an instrument for educational reform, to make education a vital instrument for national development and for the creation of a new kind of social order. What the national policy will ultimately contain is still to be seen. The most significant aspect of this debate, however, is the challenge that the women's movement is putting before education as an institutionalized process. It is no longer a demand for women to be allowed entry into the system as it stands today but a demand to change the nature, objectives and organizational structure of the system. Women's studies activists are well aware that it is not going to be an easy or a short-term process. Academia is as reluctant to change as any other established system but it cannot remain indifferent for long to such challenges, if only for its own survival.

Appendix Table 1: Number of Illiterate Females in India and their Proportion to Total Illiterate Population

Year	Female Illiterates (in millions)	Per Cent to Total Illiterates
1951	156	53.24
1961	185	55.55
1971	215	55.44
1981	242	56.97

[17] *Report of the National Seminar on Education for Women's Equality*, CWDS, November 1985 (mimeo).

11

Participatory Research, Educational Experience and the Empowerment of Adults

Rajesh Tandon

Introduction

The last three decades have seen an increasingly diverse range of models and theories of social change. The implementation of these models in developing countries, like India, have brought mixed results. While some improvements—for example, in overall agricultural production—have taken place, the situation of more than half the rural population has not improved, and may even have worsened. Starting from community development in the 1950s as the basic program for changing the situation in rural India, we now have people-centred models of development. These models emphasize the principle of people's participation in developing themselves. This concept of people's participation in development has gained currency in the last ten years. Various definitions and meanings are attached to people's participation.

It is perhaps useful to clarify, at the very outset, that people's participation in this paper is seen both as a means as well as an end in itself (Fernandes, 1981). Participatory research is a concept, approach and movement which developed over the last decade. It refers to 'an integrated activity that combines social investigation, educational work and action' (Hall, 1981, p. 7). The educational aspect of social investigation is central to the concept. Participatory research differs significantly from traditional research methods because of its emphasis on 'people as experts' and its commitment to the empowerment of learning for all those engaged in the process. Even the development of its theory and practice has been a collective process (Hall, 1981). Social change is that process where people actively define their desired goals and collectively work towards them. It also assumes that the present society, in a country like India, is comprised of a large mass of 'have-nots' who have so far been left out from this process of social change. These are landless labourers and marginal farmers, tribals and Harijans, women, workers in the unorganized sectors, urban slum-dwellers, etc. These persons are generally characterized by lower levels of education and lack of consciousness and organization, besides a very weak economic base (Tandon and Brown, 1981).

Thus, social change implies collective and organized efforts on the part of these 'have-nots' to transform their situation in their common interests. It is only through organized, informed and collective action that the 'have-nots' can influence the direction of social change to their common benefit.

Viewed in this way, the role of education in promoting social change becomes critical. In particular, the role of adult and non-formal education acquires major significance in the persuit of this model of social change. The educational process in informing, mobilizing and organizing the 'have-nots' has been demonstrably effective (Tandon, 1983).

In this paper, this role of adult and non-formal education is examined and the contribution of participatory research in this educational process is elaborated. The paper also presents some recent illustrations of the use of participatory research as an educational process in India and ends with some implications of this approach.

Knowledge as Power

In the early period of this century, the bulk of the control exercised by the 'haves' over the 'have-nots' was a direct one. The 'haves' controlled land and other resources and the 'have-nots' were landless. They were able to manipulate the 'have-nots' largely because they exercised this direct power which was often reinforced with physical force. While this form of control still continues in a country like India, a more subtle form of control has also emerged since World War II. This is the form of control that is exercised through knowledge.

Knowledge has increasingly become a major source of power and control. The very thinking and valuing process of the ordinary people is being indirectly influenced through the control and use of knowledge (Gaventa, 1980). This also allows for indirect and remote control, such that New Delhi can control the destiny of those living in far-flung villages.

This exercise of power through control over knowledge has been further consolidated with the help of more organized research enterprise. Ordinary persons and the 'have-nots' have been facing two forms of assault in this regard. First, their own knowledge, the popular knowledge, has been completely devalued with the rise of modern knowledge producing enterprises. This is most evident in the case of health-care, for example, where traditional health-care practices have been made to appear meaningless with the rise of modern medicine. This devaluation starts from the experts who, in the process of establishing the reign of modern knowledge producing enterprises, have done so at the cost of popular knowledge. The 'cult of expertise' has acquired much more significance in recent years and this has been supported by the institutions of research. Over a period of time, the 'have-nots' themselves began to devalue their own knowledge and the mechanisms of producing that knowledge, which has been relevant for their survival and development throughout the history of humankind

Secondly, ordinary people have been systematically deprived from having an access to either the knowledge produced by experts or the means of production of that knowledge. In fact, the research enterprise has created such an elite stance that ordinary persons are not considered capable of creating their own knowledge. This is further fortified with degrees, scholarships, institutions, etc. Unless one has been 'properly' trained through long schooling, one is not considered capable of producing any knowledge (Tandon, 1981).

If social change implies people's collective participation in determining their own destiny, as mentioned earlier, then knowledge is a necessary ingredient in that process. If people can learn to value their own knowledge, and produce as well as use new knowledge, then it will be a contribution to the process of their empowerment. Participatory research is based on this basic philosophy of empowering the 'have-nots' through their involvement in both valuing their existing knowledge and producing and using new knowledge.

Participatory Research as an Education Process

Participatory research has been shown to act as a powerful educational experience for those involved in it. This educational experience takes place in several ways:

1. **Recognition and Value of Existing Popular Knowledge.** Participatory research starts from the assumption that ordinary people already possess some knowledge. Some elements of this knowledge may be distorted while some may be authentic. This, in fact, is also the starting point of adult education. Adults already have some understanding and information. They do not start with a clean slate. This recognition is reinforced in participatory research and its significance to their on-going survival and development underscored. It is this existing knowledge which is used daily by the people in their on-going struggle for survival. And this existing knowledge is examined to identify the elements that are distorted and the elements that are authentic. In participatory research, the synthesis of popular knowledge, with existing scientific knowledge, strengthens the educational experience of the people (Vio Grossi et. al., 1983).

2. **The Building of New Knowledge on Existing Knowledge.** The starting point for creating new knowledge is the existing knowledge of the people, particularly the authentic elements of it. As people begin to appreciate what they already know, they are more open to seek new information. This desire to seek new knowledge is enhanced if it is done in the context of concrete problems which the people are facing. People will be motivated to create and use new knowledge if they see its relevance in solving some concrete problems that they face.

3. **Control by the People.** The process of participatory research places emphasis on the active participation of ordinary people in generating their own knowledge. This encourages them to take responsibility for their own learning. It is this active posture which constitutes a powerful impetus for learning to exercise control over their own lives. This is particularly so since participatory research explicitly calls for and promotes the exercise of control by the people themselves (Brown and Tandon, 1983).

4. **A Collective Process.** One of the elements of participatory research is the promotion of collective responsibility for seeking new knowledge. Unlike classical research, it does not encourage the individual production of knowledge. As a result, people learn to get together, collectively seeking and analysing information. Often, this forms the seed of a rudimentary organization of people. This has been the particular experience in those situations where 'have-nots' are not yet organized (Fernandes and Tandon, 1981).

5. **Creation of Informed Options.** The very process of collectively analysing a given situation throws up various alternatives. As part of the process of analysis, options are debated on the basis of concrete information. As a result, people are able to accept and reject options on an informed basis. This creates a sense of empowerment which is based on the confidence that information has been understood and interpreted.

6. **Analysis Emerging to Action.** The very act of involvement in the process of analysing a given reality creates a sense of ownership of that knowledge and willingness to transform that situation. Those people are able to take concrete actions as a part of their involvement in participatory research. In fact, participatory research is normatively linked to the transformation of the situation of the 'have-nots'. As a result, acting as a legitimate form of knowing and learning is emphasized.

From the educational aspect, participatory research is essentially a self-initiated and collective process of inquiry. It builds expertise and awareness among the 'have-nots'; it encourages action and experimentation by them to transform their reality; and, it creates a sense of empowerment and organization among them.

Some Illustrations

It may be useful to provide some illustrations of the foregoing from our experiences in the Indian context. If we examine these illustrations, then we will note how the educational process in participatory research occurs:

(a) A group of bonded labourers in Thane district of Maharashtra wanted to get out of the bondage they had been in for years. With the assistance of some activists, they analysed their own history of bondage and prepared a documentation on it. In the light of this documentation, they examined the provisions of the Act. As new information became necessary, they re-investigated the historical process of their bondage in relation to the provisions of the Act to establish their case. Based on this, they approached the Block Development Officer and Sub-Divisional Magistrate with applications to release them from bondage. When the government officials visited them to confirm their applications, they found that the labourers had collected authentic information. The process of documenting their bondage had also brought them close together as a group. They continued to pressurize the government officials till they were released. This group of freed labourers has since taken on new issues, like education of children and agriculture.

(b) Several tribals in the Ganjam district of Orissa were concerned about their almost landless situation as it was becoming difficult for them to make both ends meet. When they sat down to discuss this one night, one of them described the loss of his father's land due to the construction of a small irrigation dam nearby. The group became motivated to investigate this problem further. They started talking to the elder in the villages and meeting the Patwari, only to discover that many of their fathers had lost their land in the process of the construction of this dam. Their investigation also revealed that they had not received any compensation for it. They began examining the necessary legal provisions for compensation in cash or kind. With the help of some activists, they discovered that cash compensation does not last long (as was seen in other cases in the nearby state). So they formulated a demand for land as compensation. They have collectively taken up this issue to the Revenue Commissioner and are still continuing their struggle.

(c) Bombay has several thousands of people living on its pavements. Many of these families are headed by women who perform meagre jobs to feed their family. When some activists started working with these women, they began to explore the possibility of alternative economic activities. After further analysis, they realized that all the economic activities they were considering required some capital. They found out that nationalized banks were extending loans to women like them. They visited the bank officials to collect more information on loan schemes. Simultaneously, they collected information on the economic viability of the various activities they had identified. Now, many of these women have received bank loans and are involved in new economic activities. Moreover, these women have become a strong cohesive group and are meeting regularly to share their experiences and solve other problems which concern them.

(d) The workers in a textile factory in Kanpur, UP, recently became concerned about the impact of their work on their health. They invited some experts on occupational health to share some information with them. This prompted them to investigate the problems of ill-health arising from their work, in general, and *byssinosis* [a pulmonary condition caused by the inhalation of cotton dust], in particular. They are presently carrying out a sample study of 300 workers. In this study they will document the health status and medical records of each worker. They will also critically examine the management's attitude towards health and safety as well as government legislation and machinery in this area. In the course of their involvement, they have already conducted group discussions with a large number of fellow workers. Thus, there appears to be a growing consciousness among these workers about the problems of occupational health.

In these examples, participatory research is demonstrated in micro-perspective, concerned with oppressed people. While these efforts have helped to counter the direct mechanism of exploitation, an important role of participatory research is to give the 'have-nots' the power of knowledge.

Steps in Participatory Research

As seen in the foregoing, this paradigm provides access to knowledge for the oppressed by creating a knowledge that comes from the people and is understood by them. A series of simple steps are taken in conducting participatory research. The process begins with a few basic questions.

(*i*) **What is the Problem?** The group of people first agree on a common statement of a problem. Some common problems are, for example, landlessness, low income, indebtedness, sickness of children, etc. The problem should be stated clearly and concretely.

(*ii*) **Do We Need a Solution?** The group must express interest in solving the problem. Sometimes problems are identified only when people are asked about their problems. This step should ensure that there is a willingness to understand the underlying causes and the problem in its entirety as well as an attempt to solve it. Questions like 'Why do we want to solve the problem?' and 'How will we benefit if the problem is solved?' may help in clarifying this step.

(*iii*) **What do We Know About the Problem?** The group records all that they already know about the problem. For example, if the problem is sickness among children, then they can each describe the sickness, its characteristics, intensity and duration in the case of their own children. This helps in focusing on the problem in a personal and concrete way.

(*iv*) **What Else do We Need to Know About the Problem?** Having articulated and recorded what they already know about the problem, the group can then begin to identify what else they need to know about the problem. For example, how widespread is the problem? Why does it occur in this form? Continuing with the example of sickness among children, the group may need to know how many children in the hamlet (or village) are affected by these diseases, why the sickness occurs, what are the ways to prevent and cure the sickness, etc.

(*v*) **How are We Going to Collect Additional Information?** This is the step of data collection. The group has to decide how to get the information, whose assistance is needed, when to get the information and what responsibilities group members have.

(*vi*) **What do We Learn from this Information?** Having obtained the information, the group collectively analyses that information. It is important that analysis and reflection is undertaken as a collective process, and not done individually. This will help the group understand the causes of the problem and provide clues for possible solutions.

(*vii*) **What Solutions are Possible? What Actions are Needed?** Various solutions to the problem are generated, their workability is assessed and the choice of solution is made. Then, in order to solve the problem, what actions are to be taken by whom, when, where, and how, are also discussed and decided. Then these actions are taken.

(*viii*) **What do We Learn from these Actions?** In this step, the impact of the actions taken is systematically assessed to see if the problem is fully or partially solved. The actions taken may sometimes create new problems. So, this step is once again the beginning of another problem in the process of participatory research. Thus, participatory research becomes an on-going process in the group, as a part of its normal activity and not something separate.

Implications

Participatory research thus promotes the capacity of adults to seek and utilize knowledge in their interest, thereby promoting their collective empowerment (Hall, 1981). It is this aspect of participatory research that makes it a potent tool in the context of empowering people and transforming reality. What

are the implications of the foregoing for adult and non-formal education?
Some of the important implications are briefly mentioned here:

(a) Participatory research as an educational process reiterates our commitment in the ability of ordinary people. As in adult education, we need to continue to strengthen our faith in people as self-initiating adults. It is this faith which provides the starting point for the educational process. In essence, our involvement in participatory research justifies that faith in the capacity of the ordinary people.

(b) It shows that those of us working with adults can strengthen our work if we acquire a greater degree of competence in the process rather than content. Adult educators, like participatory researchers, need to have process expertise and orientation and need not be competent in all the various contents. This is because the educational content in participatory research gets determined by the concrete situation. But the educational process can be generalized.

(c) It also brings out the need for developing an orientation of inquiry among adult educators. Many of us do not approach our work with the 'have-nots' with an orientation of learning. Often, adult educators themselves lack a questioning and research orientation which, if they develop, can help them in their work. Training of adult educators in participatory research acquires importance in this context.

This paper has argued that participatory research acts as a powerful educational and empowering experience for the 'have-nots'. It has been effectively used in India, other parts of Asia and throughout the world as a tool for conscientization and liberation, as an alternate approach to development. The recent illustrations from India exemplify this. Some steps of participatory research have been briefly enumerated in the hope that adult educators committed to social change will be able to use it as a process of knowledge and action.

References

Brown, David L. and Rajesh Tandon. 1983. 'Ideology and Political Economy in Inquiry: Action Research and Participatory Research,' *Journal of Applied Behavioural Science*, Vol. 19, pp. 277–94.

Fernandes, Walter. 1981. *People's Participation in Development*. New Delhi: Indian Social Institute.

Fernandes, Walter and Rajesh Tandon. 1981. *Participatory Research and Evaluation*. New Delhi: Indian Social Institute.

Gaventa, John. 1980. *Power and Powerlessness*. Oxford: Clarendon Press.

Hall, Budd. 1981. 'Participatory Research, Popular Knowledge and Power: A Personal Reflection,' *Convergence*, Vol. 14, pp. 6–17.

Tandon, Rajesh. 1981. 'Participatory Research in the Empowerment of People,' *Convergence*, Vol. 14, No. 3.

———. 1983. *Our Own Health*. Toronto: International Council for Adult Education.

Tandon, Rajesh, and David L. Brown. 1981. 'Organization-Building for Rural Development: An Experiment in India,' *Journal of Applied Behavioural Science*, Vol. 17, pp. 172–89.

Vio Grossi, Francisco, Sergio Martinic, Gonzalo Tapia and Ines Pascal. 1983. *Participatory Research: Theoretical Frame, Methods and Techniques*. Paris: UNESCO.

Social Change for Cultural Revitalization

12

Modernity of Tradition in Indian Education: The Revival of Indian Languages and Indigenous Systems of Education

Joseph Di Bona and R P Singh

Introduction

Discussion of education in South Asia have long been hobbled by an unhealthy repetition of perennial topics inherited from the nineteenth century and uninformed by modern critical scholarship. More important, perhaps, is the use of a paradigm that focuses on the state as the central agency of action and people as passive victims of administration. Beginning with the East India Company in the early nineteenth century and through the colonial government to Independence and until today, we predicated our work on the assumption that education was a creation of the government, subservient and dependent.

Nor have orthodox Marxists been helpful in providing a new theoretical understanding of the relationship between education and society. Samuel Bowles and Herbert Gintis, for example, see schools as largely reflective of the social and economic system which they serve. In capitalist countries, schools prepare workers for subordinate positions of employment where values (such as, docility and loyalty) are fostered rather than creativity and compassion. The children of the privileged, according to this analysis, go to better schools where they are encouraged to think, to understand and to become future leaders. Analysts as diverse as Althusser and Braverman each reiterate a similar theme in which schools form a part of a repressive state apparatus designed to maintain the status quo. Needless to say, such a tight, mechanistic and simplistic formulation has not found favour with the large number of educators who strive daily to create a better world. In addition to these, there are the radicalized teachers, both in the West and in the developing world, who see themselves as being in the forefront of social change as they work through professional organizations and political parties to bring justice and understanding to a larger clientele.

What makes this issue still more complicated is when we have clear evidence of the role of education in creating conditions of change, it is usually from cases in the Third World rather than the West. Unfortunately, these intellectual traditions of Africa and Asia have not had an impact on the thinking of the West. A number of examples come readily to mind. Bruce McCully, in his still seminal volume on English education and the rise of Indian nationalism, sees English-medium schools as enabling a class of men to form themselves into a powerful political force that formed the Indian National Congress in the late nineteenth century and later brought about Indian independence. Figures associated with similar developments in Africa (such as, Nkrumah, Azekewe and Kenyatta) were all Western trained men who led their respective anti-colonial struggles and brought their nations to freedom. And Paolo Freire in Brazil has made a similar point in *The Pedagogy of the Oppressed*. A few words spoken and patiently explained to the dispossessed and landless labourers of north-east Brazil can create a revolution. So much so that in his case, he was forced to flee Brazil for his work in adult literacy.

What we have as a result of this peculiar situation in educational theory in the Third World is theory without any practical applicability and, on the other hand, numerous common sense examples of the revolutionary nature of schooling but without a theoretical understanding of what is happening or what is the agency of change.

What we have done in this paper is to shift the focus of discourse away from administrative agencies towards the people, who are themselves the objects of attention.[1] In the Indian case, we have to deal with a widening gulf between the English speaking elite that controls the government, economy and highest educational apparatuses, on the one hand, and, on the other, a much larger population with inadequate facilities, vernacular knowledge and no prospects of economic or social mobility. The latter are locked into a frozen social structure in which the cement of oppression is the school. But this is not the entire story or what we would have to say would be only what has already been repeated by orthodox Marxists. We see schooling as playing a dynamic role in the lives of these largely rural, poor or backward masses because it gives them the justification for rebellion. Without any education, the villager remains docile in his misery; but enhanced with minimal schooling, we see struggle and discontent that may reach epic proportions.

This view, as we have said, requires us to see problems through the eyes of India rather than through the eyes of the government or an English elite. This, admittedly, is only inadequately possible under the present circumstances. The struggle between these two contending giants—one the dominant force in Indian society, the other the mute colossus banging on the walls of the examination hall and country classroom seeking redress for the injustice—is only dimly but powerfully felt. In addition, there is a cultural chasm between this elite class in India and the rural masses who grow up knowing only their mother-tongue. Though they aspire to government and commercial employment, they are condemned by poverty and tradition to relive subordinate roles in society. One of the questions suggested by our earlier outline is how can these people create their own opportunities without waiting upon the sufferance or authority of the government? Put another way, can we look to indigenous elites or organic intellectuals to challenge the entrenched English-medium elite that dominates cultural life in India today?

Two objections may arise from this approach to the problem of Indian education. The first is practical and stems from the obvious difficulty of trying to discuss a subject without reference to the

---

[1] In 1982, the Australian National University hosted a conference organized by Ranajit Guha on the Subaltern in South Asian History, using a dominant-subordinate frame of reference but seeking to place the subordinate group on centre stage. See *Economic and Political Weekly*, Vol. 18, No. 9, 26 February 1983, p. 299.

accepted source of information, namely, the excellent accounts available in English and interpreted by Indian intellectuals in English. Further, it could be argued, these same Indians are closer to the scene and Westerners have no recourse but to defer to their more immediate familiarity with the dynamics of cultural change. The second objection is more political and may arise from a sense that unorthodox criticism may be appropriate from indigenous sources but is unacceptable coming from abroad. This last kind of chauvinism may be quickly rejected by reiterating what is obvious to most sincere scholars that inquiry has no political or special limits. Science is fortunately independent of such restrictions. But, to the initial objection, it must be said there is no intention to disregard the important work on Indian education that already exists in English nor to ignore the talented men and women who now write on this subject in whatever language. No writer can do without the insights of colleagues in India today. The attempt to separate the English-speaking elite from the vernacular masses is intended to accomplish a conceptual break with the past. The degree to which this effort succeeds is an evaluation the authors must leave to the reader.

The Theoretical Conceptualization of the Problem

It was Antonio Gramsci who originally propounded the view that intellectual leadership is not a single class of men who serve society in a general sense but can arise 'organically' from any class to lead indigenous groups. He assumed that the working class, like the bourgeois, is capable of developing from within its ranks a class of men capable of giving direction to the needs and aspirations of that group. As Gramsci puts it:

> Every social group, coming into existence on the original terrain of an essential function in the world of economic production, creates together with itself, organically one or more strata of intellectuals which give it homogeneity and an awareness of its own function not only in the economic but also in the social and political fields.[2]

[2] Antonio Gramsci. *Selections from the Prison Notebooks*, New York: International Publishers, 1971, p. 5.

This type of formulation draws our attention away from a more structural emphasis found within Marxism towards an explicit concern with forms of consciousness. It is the divide that separates structuralists and cultural Marxists, between talking about modes of production and everyday life. Particularly in developing countries (such as, India) where 'class' analyses even for avowed Marxists[3] is difficult, attention to cultural consciousness and struggle promises to be a more fruitful approach.

E.P. Thompson, in his article on 'Class Struggle Without Class' puts it in terms that elevate struggle above class.

> People identify points of antagonistic interest, they commence to struggle around these issues and in the process of struggling they discover themselves as classes. They come to know this discovery as class consciousness. Class consciousness and class are always the last, not the first stage in the real historical process.[4]

In his earlier book on the making of the English working class, Thompson found that in the first half of the nineteenth century when the formal education of most working people was little more than rudimentary, this did not stop them from articulating their needs and desires for equity and justice. The times were not devoid of curiosity and intellectual excitement for men of humble circumstances. Given the elementary techniques of literacy, labourers, artisans, shopkeepers, clerks and schoolmasters proceeded to instruct themselves. Even illiteracy did not exclude men from political discourse.[5]

In this view, the working class of England 'madè itself as much as it was made'. As Perry Anderson puts this formulation,

> . . . the criterion of consciousness as the touchstone of class: namely, the contention that class happens when some men, as a result of common experience, feel and articulate the identity of their interests as between themselves and as against other men whose interests are different from and usually opposed to theirs.[6]

[3] Bipan Chandra, for example, in his *Nationalism and Colonialism in Modern India*, deals extensively with the capitalist class but is silent on the proletariat.
[4] E.P. Thompson, Eighteenth-Century English Society: Class Struggle without Class?, *Social History*, Vol. 3, No. 2, 1978, p. 151.
[5] E.P. Thompson, *The Making of the English Working Class*, New York: Vintage Books, 1963, p. 711.
[6] Perry Anderson, *Arguments Within English Marxism*, London: NLB, 1980, p. 31.

What remains problematic is the relation between consciousness and social being. For Marx, it was 'not the consciousness of men that determines their being, but on the contrary, their social being that determines their consciousness.' In India, this awareness of who you are stems more from the identity derived from an educational experience rather than an occupational role. This is not to deny the importance of 'classes' as economic associations but rather to indicate that in India, for millions of young men and women, education is a lived experience whereas *work* is an uncertainty but derived from and closely associated with educational status. It is this educational status which does not change despite the vagaries of the market, which might see highly educated individuals reduced to menial labour. The educational certificate or degree is the single firm anchor on which a person can attach his hope for a better life and, as such, is infinitely more contested than a mere employment opportunity. For this reason, the struggle for academic success is more intense than the demand for food or higher wages and gives to the participants an identity more intense than any other.

The Indian Evidence

To deal with these issues, we must now turn to more historically specific examples of the Indian condition and the central role of education in creating the opposing forces in society. But this evidence should ring true to the people in India and, as such, the evidence is practical or commonsensical. It is the way the man-in-the-street views the dichotomy between those who have English education and those who don't. Subsequently, we shall return to our central theoretical concerns. There is no doubt that as a nation India has modernized and advanced to 'high levels of literacy and urbanization with vertical and horizontal mobility, a high per capita income and a sophisticated economy that has gone beyond the takeoff state.'[7] Literacy is around 40 per cent and India is industrializing with the most advanced technology available in the world. The English language has been accepted throughout the country as the *lingua franca* of business, administration and the military forces. The old nationalistic slogans of 'back to the villages'

[7] A.B. Shah and C.R.M. Rao, *Tradition and Modernity in India*, Bombay: Manaktales, 1961, p. 15.

or 'adopt the village handicraft and attain freedom' are forgotten if not buried.

In 1947, when India achieved Independence, the zeal for protecting indigenous languages and culture was weakened. The bitterness shown by Indian political leadership against the British and their language—English—lost its relevance. Not only were the days of Anglo-Oriental controversy buried in the dustbin of history but the contempt with which Macaulay viewed India's classical literature was forgiven. India retained English as an Associate Language by the Act of Parliament in 1963 despite opposition from a small, highly vocal section. What was regarded by Jawaharlal Nehru and others as a 'window on the world' at one time, slowly became the 'link language' in the country of its occupation and finally acquired the status of a passport 'to governmental positions which control the economy'.[8] The English script was adopted in the eastern part of the country for many tribal languages. The resultant mushrooming of English-medium schools, 'rapidex courses or English-in-one month' became a near craze and the more affluent classes insisted that children be educated from infancy exposed to the language. With this emphasis on language, there was a parallel adoption of Western culture, especially for the young, that included pop music, faded jeans and a denigration of things Indian as *desi* or backward.

There was a positive aspect to this emphasis on English and Western culture. A new breed of doctors and engineers trained in the best institutions of the country constantly seek opportunities abroad. The days of exporting indentured labour and unskilled workers are back in a transformed form with the exodus of qualified, competent professionals abroad leading to a long, unending debate on the question of the 'brain-drain'. The patriotic fervour that once attracted a large number of foreign-trained professionals back to India during the freedom struggle against Britain has now faded, leaving no trace of bitterness against their erstwhile rulers.

Even the most heated debates on regional versus official language/languages have given way to other matters. Regional languages flourish as mediums of instruction to the highest level and literary efforts in those languages are supported by the centre as well as stage governments. The linguistic basis of carving out states has

---

[8] D.P. Patanayak, *Multilingualism and Mothertongue Education*, OUP, 1981, p. xvii.

already been accepted so that no Ramalu[9] has to sacrifice his life. The sporadic riots on language issues are no longer taken seriously and are regarded more basically as economic fights rather than linguistic issues. The reason for all this is not because Hindi has been accepted as the *lingua franca* or because the superiority of one language over the other has been conceded but because jobs are available to only English-knowing scholars while the rest find themselves at a loss when the question of all-India jobs comes up. The apparent sanity on the Indian scene about the language issue should be ascribed largely to the recognition of an economic reality and not to any degree of maturity which Indians may have attained over a period of time.

The position of English in India has been considerably strengthened. There are several indicators of this phenomenon. First, although all official documents are produced in both Hindi and English, very few prefer the Hindi version. Not only are telephone directories in Hindi not acceptable to English-knowing people; even those who are completely innocent of English would want to pass off as English-knowing persons and, therefore, queue up for English directories. More books in English sell even as the editions of English dailies are multiplying in sizeable numbers. Buyers of Hindi text-books published by the National Book Trust and the National Council of Educational Research and Training are hard to find. The Children's Book Trust publishes more comic books in English than in Hindi. Second, writing of official notes in Hindi is rewarded and the Government of India shoulders the responsibility of teaching all its officials Hindi. However, the result of all this is far from satisfactory. The fact is that Indian people are a pragmatic lot. They go in for what pays socially and economically. Third, India's dependence on a world language for its research information and international contacts is too well-known to be repeated. More and more sponsored programs in English produced in Great Britain, USA and Australia are being telecast everyday than a decade back and the demand seems to be inexhaustible.

The best indicator for this is that the Government of India is now beginning to open public schools (a private, elite fee-charging school)—once a preserve of the very rich. Besides, more than 300 central schools have been opened which are regarded as the second

---

[9] The first man in the country to immolate himself for the cause of Telugu as a state language (present-day Andhra Pradesh).

best in the country. There are many reasons why these schools are necessary but why they are rated the best is because they provide an excellent grounding in English.

What we must note at this juncture are a few important facts about India's new *class structures*. Caste-ridden and regionally-biased though India may be, in order to describe a social reality we also must use the well-known term Lord C.P. Snow used two decades ago to describe British society. India has now two parallel societies with the minimum possible communication. The English-speaking/knowing urban elite knows nothing or very little about the majority of non-English-knowing Indians. Thanks to the oil boom, non-English knowing unskilled workers have hit a gold mine. They have built huge mansions in remote villages and are willing to invest in education for their children. The results of this investment are not available as yet. But the urban elite has a vested interest in the preservation of the once discredited 'British heritage'. Therefore, they read, speak and think in English and attend the same clubs as their erstwhile rulers did. They have their exclusive schools which charge heavy fees just 'to maintain standards'. Their children go to Mission colleges and join the all-India services or the multinationals. They marry within their class; if the caste also matches, they have the best of both worlds.

The majority of the non-elites join government-run/grants-in-aid/charity schools. These schools may teach the same curriculum but teaching is conducted in Hindi or a regional language. And from here onwards starts the discriminatory process, eventually leading these children to a future of second-grade citizens.

The great urban-rural divide has become glaring in certain parts of the country. Villages have schools—a vast majority of them being single-teacher schools. The village school retains, by and large, their 'community centre character' where, ranging from political meetings and gram panchayat sessions, all varieties of social functions are held. During summer and winter breaks, its buildings serve as a *barat ghar* (wedding hall) and when the teacher is away, which is fairly frequent, the students indulge in free-for-all-games. The seriousness with which the government issues fiats for running these schools turns into a mockery where even the barest minimum facilities and climate for teaching are found to be non-existent.

All Indian cities are facing population explosion, a large chunk of which consists of migrant, unskilled labour, adding a shanty township each month. Since they serve as vote-banks for the ruling party, before every municipal or parliamentary election, they are regularized. The inhuman conditions in which these people live are seasonally improved and gradually municipal schools start appearing as pleasant oases in an otherwise bleak surrounding. However, what is surprising is that even villages are gradually becoming slums—where the landless labour and the old cobbler or blacksmith find it difficult to survive. With the arrival of technology in Indian farming and the formation of cooperatives in states like Maharashtra, Gujarat, etc., rural life has become quite comfortable for the landowners, even when their land holdings are not very large. With television covering 70 per cent of the country's population and pocket radios available almost universally, the complexion of social life is gradually becoming urbanized even in remote corners of the country. While banking services are now available in a majority of rural pockets, hordes of urban entrepreneurs have landed in rural areas in search of cheap labour and land for their industries. Once again, the politician has helped in these in-roads because backward regions of the country are being developed economically as a part of their election-time promises. The consequence of all this is that large, planned townships have come up in the most backward parts of the country equipped with schools, hospitals and other facilities. India's backwardness lives cheek by jowl with her biggest technological advancements. If the village school has no teaching facilities, the nearby cousin institution has the best equipment that technology can create. The planned efforts, therefore, can have only a limited impact.

With the introduction of non-formal education, yet another class of socially deprived is being brought into existence. The non-formal education programs have few takers and even fewer admirers. Despite the best efforts the Government of India is making to accord respectability to them, somehow people view this program as an alternative to education and not an alternative to the formal system; the latter in any case stands questioned. Survival in a complex, technologically advanced age is not easy and with no skills to eke out a living it is extremely difficult.

What is the position of regional languages in schools and colleges and what steps have the state and central governments taken to help improve this position? According to the Census in 1961, 1,652 mother-tongues were reported. Professor M.G. Chaturvedi and his associate, B.V. Mohale, did a status survey of language instruction in the country.[10] They have argued that there are variations in the reporting of mother-tongues and 1,652 cannot be accepted as a correct statement of fact. The VIII Schedule of the Indian Constitution recognizes 15 major Indian languages but, in reality, they are 51 languages which are spoken by more than 1,00,000 people each. There are 35 languages in which daily newspapers appear. Others, out of 51, have no scripts. All of these 35 languages are accepted as mediums of instruction in schools.

Following the Kothari Commission's recommendations, a three-language formula was adopted as a national policy in 1968. Since then, mother-tongue, regional language and a foreign language are taught in schools. The distortions of the formula do not concern us but the official status remains the same. In order to buttress this position, the government has put into operation several schemes in which the state governments are also helping. For example, out of the 22 institutions being run by the government under the Education ministry, nine following subordinate offices also contribute to the promotion of language policy. In one way or the other, these departments produce education material in regional languages as well as in English and Hindi. They are:

1. The National Council of Educational Research and Training, New Delhi
2. Kendriya Vidyalaya Sangathan, New Delhi
3. Central Institute of Indian Languages, Mysore
4. Central Institute of Hindi, Agra
5. Central Institute of English and Foreign Languages, Hyderabad
6. Central Hindi Directorate, New Delhi
7. Rashtriya Sanskrit Sansthan, New Delhi
8. National Book Trust, New Delhi
9. Commission for Scientific and Technical Terminology, New Delhi

For its language policy support, the central government alone spends Rs. 3,74,00,000 annually (1985 figures). This does not include establishment expenditure. Proposals are being made to set up an International Sanskrit University, besides one for Hindi, and a

---

[10] *Position of Languages in School Curriculum in India*, NCERT, 1976.

Board for the promotion of Sindhi. The fact that the government is serious in its attempt should be obvious. Almost all major languages have support from their state governments. In brief, efforts are being made to develop all regional languages. However, the impact of this policy cannot be seen very concretely nor gauged accurately.

The indigenous system of Adam's report died more than a hundred years ago as it could not face its contemporary competitors. If the indigenous system means the basic schools [a term introduced in the 1930s for a revitalized, village-oriented, craft-centred reformed elementary school based on Gandhi's principles] of the Gandhian variety, they were still-born.

The Indian Constitution guaranteed that all Indians were entitled to compulsory, free elementary education up to the age of 14 + by the year of 1965. Somehow this kind of education mobilization of resources in men and material has not been possible to date. The target of 100 per cent literacy is now fixed to be achieved by the end of 1990 by extending non-formal education to all those who are not being covered by the formal school system. A massive adult literacy program has already been undertaken. In other words, India is determined to become a modern, liberal, educated democracy within the next five to ten years. To support this program several schemes for industrial training, vocational education, etc., have also been put into operation. The effort this time matches the goals. With the youngest Prime Minister in India's history, the expectations of the people are high.

The draft Seventh Five Year Plan has acknowledged the dependence of economic development on education. It is a big change from the earlier attitude when education was seen merely as an instrument of social change. Besides social change, education has a close connection with development and modernization. This official confirmation of the obvious is significant for all.

The goals of education set by the Indian National Congress in their first manifesto in 1947 emanated from the Gandhian philosophy of craft-centred basic education. In the course of the last thirty years, the ideas of Gandhi have been thrown overboard and the new name given to craft-teaching is SUPW (socially useful productive work) which really only serves as a reminder to many that it has had a Gandhian past. Beyond that it means nothing to teachers or educational administrators.[11] Computer education was introduced

---

[11] For details, see John Kurrien, *Elementary Education in India*, New Delhi: Vikas Publishing House, 1984.

in 1984 in 300 government schools on a trial basis. This is a clear indication that Indian education is trying to meet future demands as far as they can be anticipated. The distance we have travelled in these past thirty-eight years would equal the journey undertaken in the previous 380 years.

Education as an Arena of Struggle

Despite government's efforts to promote general welfare, the clear perception of the man-in-the-street is that an English-medium education entitles the bearer to a life of superior status. Not only is the medium of instruction important but the course of study, especially professional study, can ensure social success. Unfortunately, as we have discussed in the earlier section, this type of education is not available to the Indian masses. As a result, education in India has become the chief arena of conflict between the English speaking minority and the larger vernacular population of village youth and the urban poor who aspire to enter preferred occupations in commerce and government. We have previously alluded to the difficulty of identifying this as a 'class' conflict although it is through conflict and struggle that a common identity can develop. This struggle takes place in the examination hall, in the entrance and exit of academic institutions and in the acquisition of marks and degrees. From the standpoint of the elite establishment, any attempt to circumvent the stringent rules and regulations that work primarily to the advantage of the dominant group are considered 'unfair' or stigmatized as 'cheating,' etc. However, from the standpoint of those who seek advancement by any means available to them, the goal is worth the effort. To this extent, they are already aware of the advantages of superior credentials and sensitive to the lack of these benefits to themselves. This awareness is already the beginning of consciousness and their overt efforts to do something about it evidence of struggle on the part of the dispossessed against those with privilege and power.

However, education may be seen as working in very different ways to arouse people to action when they use schooling to identify who they are and to develop the means of expressing a corporate character. In the case of some tribal communities, education has led a few individuals to insist that their language or script be used in their own primary schools. Rather than studying in 'foreign' schools, they may now have their own schools—presumably permitting them to succeed without the disadvantages of the other language. In other cases, rural schools have sought to give disadvantaged youth a chance to become literate by providing them with non-threatening environments where they could attain some semblance of literacy. But in all these cases, though the results are laudable, the attainment of success in that vernacular idiom does not threaten the hold of the English elite on the preferred positions in government and industry.

Some of these localized educational movements designed to benefit the depressed communities have developed anti-capitalist and anti-caste tendencies (such as that of Karmaveer Bhaurao Patil's rural education movement in western Maharashtra). Started in the early twentieth century, the Ryat Shikshan Sanstha created hostels for Scheduled Caste students, Muslims and women, who together could receive education in their mother-tongue. By 1979–80, the organization was responsible for primary schools, over 300 secondary schools and colleges in the rural areas, and seven teacher training colleges.[12] Like Gandhi's basic education movement, it emphasized manual labour and self-reliance and, to this extent, like Gandhi's educational system, was opposed to the urban English schools that came to dominate entrance to the highest echelons of power.

This phenomena was repeated in other parts of India as well. In the nineteenth century, the Bengali language was imposed on the Assamese because Bengali was considered merely a *patois* of Bengali. After twenty years, the injustice of this imposition was recognized and the Asamiya Bhasha Sabha was formed in 1888 to foster the language and literature of the province.[13]

In Orissa, though Oriya was used in schools in the nineteenth century, the people agitated over the presence of 'foreigners' taking away jobs that should have gone to the natives of Orissa. Among the tribals today, there is similarly a link between schooling and a consciousness of who they are. Santhals in Chotanagpur invented a

[12] See S.A. Kakrambe, 'Politics and Education in India: A Study of Karmaveer Bhaurao Patil's Rural Mass Education Movement,' in Bishwanath Prasad and Sakendra Prasad Singh, eds., *Aspects of Education and Politics in India*, Patna: Swarna Prakashan, 1983.

[13] Sudhir Chandra, 'Regional Consciousness in 19th Century India,' *Economic and Political Weekly*, Vol. 17, No. 32, 7 August 1982, pp. 1278–85.

script *Ol Chiki* based on ancient symbols. Text-books are written in this script, teachers are trained in it and schools established. In March 1981, the *Ol Chiki* was recognized by the West Bengal government who announced that primary schools would use the script in areas where there were enough students to warrant its use.[14] In Bihar, a Ho leader reportedly 'found' the *Varana Kshiti*, the shining letters of the Ho people, and sought to popularize the script in schools. Tribals in Tripura have demanded recognition of the *Kak Barok*—originally an unwritten language but now, after considerable agitation, has a grammar and a literature. A *Kak Barok* Sahitya Sabha has been formed to work for a Roman rather than a Bengali script.

In these and many other cases, schooling has helped develop an awareness of who the people are and how they are different from their neighbours. It has not led to a revolutionary consciousness nor challenged the established order. In fact, to the extent that attention is diverted from the English language avenue of mobility and prestige,[15] it may be an essential but not a sufficient step towards success in Indian society.

The most dramatic challenge to the English speaking elite comes from the struggle of those who have access only to inferior, largely vernacular schooling and who are alert to the crucial role that schooling and degrees play in achieving prosperity. Indiscipline, cheating, and unfair means are considered deviant behaviour, but at the same time function in the context of social conflict. If a student has had some schooling and realizes to be successful he must have more education or higher marks or an advanced degree or some other indication of his experience, he will exert every effort to compete with the many others who benefit either from family background or family influence in realizing their goals. This is not easy and individual efforts to circumvent the rules are dangerous but corporate efforts on the part of student or teachers' organizations may not succeed either. The safest path is to find allies among politicians who can themselves benefit from successful assistance to select individuals. In 1981 a Bombay homeopathic college refused

---

[14] K.S. Singh, 'Transformation of Tribal Society,' *Economic and Political Weekly*, Vol. 17, No. 34, 21 August 1982.

[15] It has been likened to the government of South Africa's efforts to foster the use of indigenous vernaculars for the black population so they will not aspire to compete with whites.

to admit the daughter of a former State Minister because of her low marks. There were 601 applications for 30 seats at the time and, according to a writ petition admitted by the High Court,[16] the college was threatened by the Health Minister of the State who stated that unless the young lady was admitted the college would have its allotment of seats cut in half. From 1967 to 1972, 64 per cent of the legislators in Maharashtra were associated with educational institutions.[17] And that whole lower level of politics from the panchayat to the district level where schools are spawned and nurtured are affiliated with lower and middle castes.[18] It is here at the lower administrative levels that political and educational careers work in tandem.[19] It is still shocking, but not surprising, when 'unfair' means take place with the collusion of educational and state officials.

A well-advertised example was when the Vice-Principal of a West Delhi public school was arrested for passing examination papers to students before the All India Senior School Certificate examinations.[20] Another instance came to public attention when the Vice-Chancellor of a Bihar University was removed from his post after he altered the answer books and mark sheets of his daughter-in-law 'who topped the graduate and post graduate examinations with astoundingly high marks.'[21] An IAS officer was arrested for falsifying his son's marks in a medical college examination. In this case, the son gained admission to college with altered grades and after twelve years still had not graduated.[22] Other students find ways to gain admission to selective courses, such as, medicine or engineering, with only minimal marks. There was a case brought to light by the Kerala High Court looking at random samples of student examinations

---

[16] *Patriot* (New Delhi), 24 September 1981, p. 5.

[17] P.L. Joshi and N.R. Khekale, 'Politics of Education in Maharashtra,', in Bishwanath Prasad and Sakendra Prasad Singh, eds., *Aspects of Education and Politics in India*, Patna: Swarna Prakashan, 1983, p. 64.

[18] A.R. Kamat, *Education After Independence: A Social Analysis*, Bombay: Lala Lajpatrai Institute, 1975.

[19] Joseph Di Bona, 'Gurus and Graduates: The Ruralization of Higher Education in the Punjab,' in J. Di Bona, ed., *The Context of Education in Indian Development*, Program in Comparative Studies on Southern Asia, Duke University, Durham, NC, 1974.

[20] *The Hindustan Times*, 24 April 1982, p. 1.

[21] *Indian Express*, 28 April 1982, p. 5.

[22] *Times of India*, 28 March 1982, p. 11.

where one student who received zero marks in botany, physics and chemistry was admitted to medical school and another who received only 85 out of 450 in his exams was also admitted.[23] In Varanasi, more than 80 per cent of the 1,000-odd students who appeared in the examination for an education degree had secured admission on the basis of forged marks.[24] Forged degrees are just as common. In fact, one talented artist prepared thousands of Ayurvedic medical practitioners certificates.[25]

These are hardly isolated examples and can be repeated all over India. Medical students have employed 'writers' who are outside the examination hall and pass the answers in after they are completed.[26] When the grades of Kerala students were questioned and they were threatened with reprisals, the students became violent and demanded the resignation of the Registrar and the Controller of Examinations. As a result, in 1981, all educational institutions in Trivandrum remained closed.[27] The Delhi newspapers reported that 'mass copying' was taking place on an unprecedented scale in the resettlement colonies and rural areas. Reports said that candidates came to the examination hall with text-books and slips of paper with answers scribbled on them 'but were also being helped by scores of friends lurking in the vicinity of the centres'.[28] When efforts are made to control such practices, the result is likely to be violence. In Delhi, when six cases of cheating were detected, 200 students suddenly turned violent. The police refused to intervene and the invigilators informed the authorities that they would not return in view of the 'insecure conditions'.[29]

The reaction of the country's established order to this mass ferment has been to reiterate its own values. The *Indian Express* editorialized that the condition of education was a matter of shame after the state of Bihar had to derecognize five of its nine medical colleges.[30] There have also been attempts to shift education from local control and put it more under the central authority. In 1982, Madhuri Shah, Chairman of the University Grants Commission,

[23] *Times of India*, 10 December 1981, p. 1.
[24] *Hindustan Times*, 15 September 1981, p. 4.
[25] *Times of India*, 28 September 1981, p. 3.
[26] *Times of India*, 22 October 1981, p. 1
[27] *Times of India*, 17 December 1981.
[28] *Times of India*, 20 March 1982, p. 1.
[29] *Times of India*, 24 March 1982, p. 3.
[30] *Indian Express*, New Delhi, 14 April 1982, p. 6.

called for placing education on the concurrent list.[31] And Jawaharlal Nehru University accepted a suggestion to reduce the admission advantage granted for socially disadvantaged youth. The Indian Education Minister asked that no new colleges be opened because 30 per cent of those currently in operation were not viable.[32] The Director of the Indian Institute of Management, Bangalore, has called for admission on the basis of the ability to pay for preferred education.[33] This is already taking place in many parts of India. Sheila Kaul reported to the Lok Sabha in 1982 that 13 colleges in Andhra Pradesh, 10 in Bihar and 33 in Karnataka offer engineering education to those who could pay between Rs. 5,000 and Rs. 25,000 as capitation fees. There is a sense of frustration and helplessness in India when schooling is considered; where opportunities are clearly available to those who can pay for them and there is violence or the threat of violence from those who cannot. The implication of such practice is that India will become a more clearly stratified society, the lines drawn primarily on the basis of education. The widespread acceptance of the importance of education leads inevitably to a general consciousness that where failure occurs, it is not due to individual failings but to the general manner in which schooling is structured.

Conclusion

Since this paper deals with consciousness and struggle over education and language, it is appropriate to reiterate some of the material that has been presented here. In a developing country like India, where clear class divisions have not yet materialized, the formation of consciousness takes place as a result of education and not on the basis of a mode of production. This is not to say that education acts as an independent agent of change but, rather, that it serves as the central agency in a context of social and cultural polarization. What makes the picture more complicated still is that it serves different strata of society in different ways. For the upper castes and wealthy sections of society, prestigious education associated with engineering, medicine, technology and

---

[31] This would place it more under central control. *Indian Express*, 1 May 1982, p. 5.
[32] *Times of India*, 19 March 1982, p. 6.
[33] *The Hindu*, 25 August 1981, p. 17.

management are a means of reinforcing their hegemony over the subaltern classes by recourse to a so-called objective standard of selection.

For the backward classes, the rural and urban poor, Scheduled Castes and tribals receiving vernacular schooling, education serves as a means of giving them hope to achieve a modicum of prosperity. Education, as we have seen, can serve to unite small groups, help them to identify their common interests and then to act in limited ways to achieve more security through united action. More often, schools rouse the poorer classes to look beyond the articulation of their own parochialism and dare to scale the forbidding walls of the entrenched English elite. To do this they must penetrate the intricacies of the complex bureaucratic schooling apparatus and find ways to gain access to the keys that unlock the doors to competetive success. This means to enter the most desirable courses of study, to do well in examinations and to acquire the highest degrees. Naturally, these treasures are well guarded by the elite establishment and every effort is made (including recourse to the police power of the state to fend off such outrageous attacks) as are represented in 'cheating,' 'unfair means' and 'indiscipline'. To counter what would otherwise be a formidable task, the poorer sections of society seek alliances with political powers at the local level, even down to the panchayat [a village-level council for local self-government] and taluka [sub-division or district] administrators and wherever else help may be found. The result is a dramatic and daily confrontation between the haves and the have-nots on the academic battlefield.

If there is yet an important theoretical issue to be resolved, it is the connection between action (as taken by those who are seeking to improve their position at any cost through education) and the circumstances that give rise to these actions. It must be admitted that this consciousness is not yet a revolutionary consciousness except insofar as it challenges state power but usually in only a limited and local sphere. Through this struggle we can expect that the awareness of differences becomes sharper by those who are successful in circumventing the system (for they realize how empty are these standards) as well as by those who fail—for the latter become frustrated and hostile to a system that victimizes them at the expense of the unworthy children of the privileged. These classes then are not the classic result of a materialist conception of history, nor the inevitable advance of complex industrial social organization.

But, for developing countries like India where education is the most important emotional catalyst that anyone will ever know, it will serve.

Indian education is rapidly changing and even as these words are written there is debate concerning the extent that indigenous elites are replacing the English-speaking minority in ever-widening arenas of action. This development has been clear in the political area for some time but has not been documented for business, government and the professions. As this movement becomes more evident, it will require renewed analysis and revision of the thesis presently put forward.

13

Religious Traditions in Modern Indian Educational Policy and Practice

Arvind Sharma

Introduction

Whether religious education should be imparted or not as a part of educational policy has been an issue since the inception of modern education and the decision, hitherto, has been (*a*) not to impart it in state-run educational institutions, and (*b*) to allow it to be imparted in state-aided schools. This paper surveys the historical evolution of this position and the ideological convolutions involved in the process and in the present situation.

It offers the conclusion that religious education of a comparative character should be imparted in state-run educational institutions and that state-aided educational institutions should be allowed to impart religious education specific to a particular religion. Such a step would preserve religious freedom in India and, at the same time, preserve it from religious fanaticism.

The relationship of religious traditions or, broadly, of religious education to educational policy and practice has been a contentious one since the very inception of modern education in India with the establishment of the British Raj. This paper, therefore, will be divided into two parts. In the first part the changing contours of the controversy regarding the nature of the relationship through different historical periods (e.g., Smith, 1963) will be surveyed. In the second part, the ideological issues underlying the controversy will be analysed (e.g., Sinha, 1968).

I

The major important historical periods involved in the survey are (a) 1813–54; (b) 1854–1902; (c) 1902–47, and (d) 1947–85.

1813–54

The year 1813 has been selected as the starting point of the discussion because the Charter Act of 1813

> forms a turning point in the history of Indian education. With it, the agitation which Grant and Wilberforce carried on for nearly twenty years came to a successful conclusion; the education of the Indian people was definitely included within the duties of the Company; a comparatively large amount was annually secured for educational activities; and missionaries began to land in India in large numbers and establish English schools, thereby laying the foundation of the modern educational system. (Nurullah and Naik, 1951, p. 82; hereafter cited as Nurullah.)

The role of religious education in educational policy became an issue right from the very beginning. Grant had argued for the spread of English education in the hope that this would secure mass conversions to Christianity. The same Charter Act also permitted Christian missionaries to operate within the areas controlled by the East India Company. This led to some confusion because although 'in 1854 the largest part of educational enterprise in India (indigenous schools apart) was provided not by the Company but by the missionaries,' the missionaries resented the fact that the intention and implementation of Section 43 of the Charter Act of 1813 was *not* to secure financial assistance to the missionary educational institutions (as some missionaries seemed to think), but to create a rival set of institutions conducted by the Company or by the Indian people in order that there may be 'a reliable counterpoise, a protecting break-water against the threatened deluge of missionary enterprise'. This object was generally kept in view between 1813 and 1853. (Nurullah 1951, p. 179.)

A clear distinction was thus established right from the beginning between:

(*a*) educational institutions run entirely by Christian missionaries where religious education, in this case Christian, could be imparted;
(*b*) educational institutions run by the Company which were exclusively secular.[1]

These two types of schools 'grew up independently of each other between 1813 and 1853' (Nurullah, 1951, p. 179). In other words, religious education did not affect government (i.e., Company) educational policy except insofar as it was excluded.

As a result of this competition between Missionary and Company schools, the missionaries launched a campaign to take over the educational system wholesale, i.e., to receive grants-in-aid for their schools. It is striking, though, that even after the introduction of English in 1835 as the medium of education in Company schools as a result of the advocacy of Macaulay, and despite increasing willingness on the part of the Company to ignore native sentiment as evidenced by the abolition of Sati (1829), the policy of keeping education in the Company schools secular was not reversed. Although this may be in part due to the overconfidence of Macaulay in the efficacy of secular education in securing conversion to Christianity (Sharma 1973, 1982a, b), it was also due to the position taken by Lord William Bentinck that 'all interference and injudicious tampering with the religious beliefs of the students, all mingling of direct or indirect teaching of Christianity with the system of instruction ought to be positively forbidden' (Smith, 1963, p. 340).

[1] Grants-in-aid from Company to mission schools were rare during this period (out of its annual grant of a lakh of rupees, later raised to 10 lakh from 1833 onwards) (Nurullah, 1951, p. 179). Private Indian enterprise in education was not assisted (*ibid.*, p. 190).

This situation was resented by the missionaries who thought that 'the ideal state of affairs in India would be one in which the Company would withdraw completely from direct educational enterprise and *all* the institutions required by the country would be provided by the missions on a grant-in-aid basis' (Nurullah, 1951, p. 180). In contrast with what the Christian missionaries thought of as the ideal state of affairs, the real state of affairs was that 'strange as it might first appear, India became one of the very first countries in the world to develop a system of secular public schools' (Smith, 1963, p. 340).

1854–1902

The Despatch of 1854, like the Charter Act of 1813 earlier, constitutes another landmark in the history of modern Indian education. The Despatch actually admitted the contention of the missionaries in principle (Nurullah, 1951, p. 121) and aroused hopes that the missionaries would be able to take over the whole field of education (*ibid.*, 141; see also Smith, 1963, pp. 341–42). However, the Mutiny of 1857–58 made the authorities cautious in this respect, and led to the proclamation of the principle of religious neutrality (Majumdar, 1963, p. 745; Nurullah, 1951, p. 240). It was because the missionaries felt thwarted in this respect that they started 'an agitation, both in England and India, to the effect that the educational administration of India was not carried on in accordance with the Despatch of 1854 which had recommended the closure or transfer of Government schools' (Nurullah, 1951, p. 243). This led to the appointment of the Indian Education Commission in 1882 which was called upon to decide the following specific issues in this respect (*ibid.*):

(a) Should government withdraw from direct educational enterprise in favour of missionaries, as the Despatch of 1854 had led some of them to hope?
(b) What should be the policy of Government in religious education? Should it be imparted in schools or not? If it was to be imparted, in what form and subject to what conditions was it to be allowed?

The answer to question (a) was given in the negative; there was to be no governmental retreat. The answer to (b) had two aspects to it, relating to (i) the imparting of religious education in government schools, and (ii) the imparting of religious education in aided schools. As for (i), the idea of imparting religious education in government schools was rejected. As for (ii), it was decided

> (a) that private schools should be permitted to impart such instruction as they chose; (b) that government should just ignore such religious education; and (c) that it should pay grants-in-aid on the basis of the secular education imparted in them. This view had already been propounded by the Despatch of 1854 and the Commission, in deference chiefly to missionary opinion, reiterated it with almost equal firmness. (Nurullah, 1951, p. 248.)

The question of religious education had thus affected the government educational policy in two ways in two spheres. The principle of religious neutrality had been upheld *directly* in the case of government schools but the dice had been loaded in favour of religious education *indirectly* in the case of aided schools. The Commission, however, made certain recommendations which were never implemented but are of interest in the present context. It 'recommended the preparation of a text-book on morality based on the principles of "natural religion" '; it also recommended the gradual transfer of governmental educational institutions 'to responsible local bodies composed chiefly of Indians. The Commission explicitly excluded missionary societies from this role' but curiously enough 'envisaged the imparting of religious instruction in the institutions to be taken over by local Indian communities,' citing it as one of the advantages of the recommendation (Smith, 1963, p. 344). Syed Nurullah and J.P. Naik (1951, p. 251) remark thus on the significance of these decisions:

> The enquiries held by the Indian Education Commission marked the last great occasion when the government policy in religious education was discussed in India. Ever since 1813 when the Company accepted responsibility for the education of the Indian people, the subject of religious education was almost continuously debated upon and no final decision could be reached. The credit of having laid down a definite and final policy on the subject, therefore, belongs to the Indian Education Commission. Its rulings were perhaps none too happy. They did not satisfy *any* section of public opinion in *full*; but they had to be accepted as the only practicable solutions of the problem under Indian conditions.

1902-47

The viceroyalty of Lord Curzon (1898–1905) was a turning point in the history of British India in several ways. Here we are concerned with his reforms in the field of education which drew fire at the time but are now appreciated (Nurullah, 1951, p. 497). The year 1902 has been selected because of the appointment of the Indian Universities Commission, which 'while it considered the inadequacy of a purely secular education' 'had no definite suggestions to offer' (Biswas, 1971, p. 439). The Indian Education Commission had already virtually relegated that question into the background.

Another aspect, however, came into the foreground during this period. The Calcutta University Commission (1917–19) recommended that 'having regard to the comparatively backward condition of the Muslim community in regard to education, every reasonable means should be taken to encourage Muslim students and to safeguard their interests' (Nurullah, 1951, p. 503).[2]

This was a development of some importance for, although it is not directly connected with religious education, it is connected with the education of a religious community. Similar developments were represented by the establishment of the Benaras Hindu University in 1917, and the Aligarh Muslim University in 1920, even though both of them were open to students of all castes and creeds.

Early during this period, the recognition of secondary schools was transferred to provincial departments of education (Sargent, 1968, p. 43). As has been pointed out earlier,

> the common schools were secular since their inception and although missionaries and others had agitated for the provision of religious education, the momentous decision of the Indian Education Commission had closed the controversy and prohibited all religious instruction in publicly managed schools. The issue was not opened for about four decades. (Nurullah, 1951, p. 724.)

---

[2] Biswas and Agrawal (1971, p. 439) remark that the Calcutta University Commission was silent on the subject of religious and moral education. This is true, as such, but should not lead us to ignore the significance of the recommendation just cited in our context.

In 1911, however, the situation began to change. In certain provinces, religious education was provided at the desire of the parents, when imparted outside school hours by outside staff without extra cost. In 1921, the Government of India became

> 'of the opinion that the embargo which hitherto has been placed on the introduction of religious instruction in publicly managed schools may be removed'. Certain conditions to be attached to its introduction were indicated, viz., no preference to any particular religion to the exclusion of others, no charge on public funds and the instruction to be given outside regular school hours. (Nurullah, 1951, p. 724.)

Such experiments and precedents led Hartog to conclude that 'after all, the concept of "secular education" was not an inescapable concomitant of the Indian school system and that it ought not to be difficult to provide for the religious education which the Muslims demanded even in a system of common schools for all' (*ibid*).

This politicization of religious education was destined to have major implications for the formulation of government policy, for when the 'government announced its intention to aid the Hindu University of Benaras and the Muslim University of Aligarh' it was 'giving countenance in education to the communal issue, which had already been accorded official recognition in the Morley-Minto reforms' (Sargent, 1968, p. 43). How these relations affected the issue of religious education in the formulation of government policy directly can be seen in the reports of the Central Advisory Board of Education (CABE) published since 1944. On the question of religious education,

> the Board first appointed a committee with a neutral chairman, on which Hindus and Muslims had equal representation. After several meetings, the committee reported to the Board that it had failed to arrive at any agreed recommendation. The Board reconstituted the committee with a few changes of personnel and asked it to try again. After several further meetings the committee had to tell the Board that the only suggestion, upon which it could agree, was that colleges and schools should start the day with a brief period of silent meditation. When this came up at the next meeting of the Board, an amendment was moved and

carried that during this period there should be no obligation upon any pupil or student to meditate upon religion! (Sargent, 1968, p. 94)[3]

This is the backdrop of the next period under review.

1947-85

Account must be taken of the Partition of the country into India and Pakistan in assessing the role of religious education in Indian educational policy and practice during this period. Four facts need to be clearly borne in mind in this connection. The first is that while Gandhi was a deeply religious man, he worked for a secular India, while Jinnah, secular in outlook, campaigned for a theocracy (Smith, 1963, pp. 154-55; see also Tinker, 1963, p. 72). The second is that the division of the sub-continent into India and Pakistan was not a division between a Hindu India and a Muslim Pakistan as might appear on the surface but, in terms of political ideology, it was a division between a *secular* India and a *theocratic* Pakistan (Organ, 1974, p. 272). The third is that the blood bath which accompanied this division may have reinforced the Indian commitment to a secular state (Smith, 1963, p. 351). And, finally, unlike the secularism of the West, secularity in India has not been equated so much with the negation of religion as with exclusive identification with only one religious tradition, usually referred to as communalism (Saran, 1979).

It is, therefore, not as surprising as John Sargent thinks that in view of the communal bickerings of the pre-Partition days in the field of religious education, the 'first recommendation of the University Commission reads: "all educational institutions should start work with a few minutes of silent meditation" ' (Education

---

[3] Biswas and Agrawal (1971, pp. 439-40) report: 'In 1944, the Central Advisory Board appointed a committee under the chairmanship of Rt. Rev. G.D. Barne, the Bishop of Lahore, to examine the desirability and practicability of providing religious instruction in schools and colleges. After considering the report of the committee, the Board resolved that "while they recognize the fundamental importance of spiritual and moral instruction in the building of character, the provision for such teaching, excepting insofar as it can be provided in the normal course of secular instruction should be the responsibility of the home and the community to which the pupils belong".'

Commission, 1966, p. 20). In fact, it would be worthwhile, at this point, to draw full attention to the recommendations of the University Education Commission (1948-49) in this respect.

I—*University Education Commission (1948-49) and Religious Education.* The Chairman of the Commission was S. Radhakrishnan, a leading scholar of religion (Mahadevan, 1971, pp. 284-85). His views on the matter seem to have left their impress on Chapter 8 of the Report which deals with religious education. The argument on which its recommendations are based may be presented syllogistically thus: '(*i*) dogmatic religion leads to conflict; (*ii*) religious conflict leads to the secular state; (*iii*) the secular state bans only dogmatic religious instruction in state schools; (*iv*) the state can and should provide for the teaching of universal religion' (Smith, 1963, p. 351). The report made four recommendations, which will recur in future reports, in the light of this conclusion (*ibid.*, pp. 352-53).

> The first is that all educational institutions begin each day with a few minutes of silent meditation. Second, that the lives of great religious leaders like Gautama Buddha, Confucius, Socrates, Jesus, Ramanuja, Mohammed, Gandhi, etc., should be studied in the first year of the degree course. Third, that selections 'of a universalist character' from the scriptures of all religions be studied in the next year. 'We should not prescribe books which feel an obligation to prove that their religion is true and often that it alone is true'. Finally, that various problems of the philosophy of religion be considered in the third year.

The universalist orientation of the recommendation was criticized as being neo-Hindu in orientation (Smith, 1963, pp. 351-54). This idea of a universal religion was also criticized as lacking in emotional appeal (*ibid.*, p. 355) in contrast to Gandhi's ideas which 'combine equal respect for all religions with wholehearted adherence to one's own faith' (*ibid.*, p. 355; see also Rao, 1978).

II—*The Indian Constitution (1950) and Religious Education.* The relevant sections of the Constitution are reproduced here in the end-note.[4] Its salient features are that (*a*) private religious institutions can be established and administered, and (*b*) government educational institutions can fall into any of the following categories: (*i*) institutions wholly maintained out of state funds; (*ii*) institutions recognized by the state; (*iii*) institutions receiving aid out of state funds; (*iv*) institutions that are administered by the state but are established under any endowment or trust which requires religious instruction to be imparted therein. In the case of (*i*) no religious instruction can be provided. In the case of (*ii*) and (*iii*) attendance at such institutions is optional. In the case of (*iv*) "there is no restriction on such instructions" (Bhatt and Aggarwal, 1969, p. 131).[5]

It is clear from the foregoing that although India has 'accepted the principle of secularism in educational matters with the imprint of Constitutional sanction,' 'this principle does not imply so much a separation between state and religion as states' involvement in religion provided it is non-discriminate as between different religions' (Sinha, 1968, p. 104). It should also be noted that as Article 27 forbids the use of tax revenues 'for the promotion or maintenance of any particular religion' presumably the state 'is not prohibited from non-discriminatory financial support of religion' (*ibid.*, p. 167, note 13).

---

[4] Bhatt and Aggarwal (1969, pp. 130–31): Article 28(1) provides, 'No religious instruction shall be provided in any educational institution wholly maintained out of State funds.' Article 28(2) provides, 'Nothing in clause (1) shall apply to an educational institution which is administered by the state but has been established under any endowment or trust which requires that religious instruction shall be imparted in such an institution.' Article 28(3) states, 'No person attending any educational institution recognized by the State or receiving aid out of State funds shall be required to take part in any religious instruction that may be imparted in such institutions or to attend any religious worship that may be conducted in such institutions or in any premises attached thereto unless such person or, if which person is a minor, his guardian has given his consent thereto.' Article 29(1) states, 'No citizen shall be denied admission into any educational institution maintained by the State or receiving aid out of State funds on grounds only of religion, race, caste, language or any of them.' Article 30(1) states, 'All minorities whether based on religion or language, shall have the right to establish and administer educational institutions of their choice.' Article 30(2) provides, 'The State shall not, in granting aid to educational institutions, discriminate against any educational institution on the ground that it is under the management of a minority, whether based on religion or language.'

[5] Article 15(1) which forbids discrimination based on religion may also be noted.

III—Secondary Education Commission (1952–53). This commission suggested about religious instruction that 'if at all such instruction could be done, it must be privately organized' (Sinha, 1968, p. 104). It recommended that 'religious instruction may be given in schools only on a voluntary basis and outside the regular school hours, such instruction being confined to the children of the particular faith concerned and given with the consent of the parents and the managements' (Biswas and Agrawal, 1971, p. 312). Another relevant recommendation ran: 'No book prescribed as a text-book or as a book for general study should contain any passage or statement which might offend the religious or social susceptibilities of any section of the community or might indoctrinate the minds of the young students with particular political or religious ideologies' (*ibid.*, p. 311).

IV—Committee on Religious and Moral Instruction (1959). The Chairman of this Committee was Sri Prakash. It was appointed by the 'Government of India to make a detailed study of the entire question of religious and moral education in educational institutions'. Its recommendations, therefore, have a direct bearing on the issue under discussion (Report, 1960).

The Committee emphasized the cultivation of moral and spiritual values, pointing out that 'just as moral values affect the relation between man and man, so do spiritual values affect the individual in his relations with himself' (Biswas and Agrawal, 1971, p. 443). It is these values which it sought to emphasize in its advocacy of 'an objective, comparative and sympathetic study of all the important religions of India' (*ibid.*). Its major recommendations are summarized below (*ibid.*, pp. 444–45):

MAJOR RECOMMENDATIONS

1. *Elementary Stage*: (*a*) The school Assembly should be held for a few minutes in the morning for group singing.

   (*b*) Simple and interesting stories about the lives and teachings of prophets, saints and religious leaders should be included in the syllabus for language teaching.

   (*c*) In the school program, two periods a week should be set aside for moral instruction.

   (*d*) Through the school program, the attitude of 'service' and the realization that 'work is worship' should be developed in the child.

2. *Secondary Stage*: (*a*) The morning Assembly should observe two minutes' silence followed by readings from the scriptures or great literature of the world or an appropriate address.

(*b*) The essential teachings of the great world religions should be studied.

(*c*) An hour a week should be assigned to moral instruction. Apart from this regular class instruction, suitable speakers may be invited to address the students on moral and spiritual values. Joint celebrations may be organized on the occasion of important festivals of all religions.

(*d*) Organized social service during holidays and outside class hours should be an essential part of extra-curricular activities.

3. *University Stage*: (*a*) Students should be encouraged to meet in groups for silent meditation in the morning.

(*b*) The following recommendations of the University Education Commission (Radhakrishnan Commission) are commended:
- (*i*) that in the first year of the degree course, the lives of great religious and spiritual leaders be taught;
- (*ii*) that in the second year, some selections of a universalist character from the scriptures of the world be studied;
- (*iii*) that in the third year, the central problems of philosophy of religion be considered.

(*c*) A fairly long period of social service should be introduced by all universities.

It is interesting to compare the approaches of the University Education Commission (1949) and the Committee on Religious and Moral Instruction (1959). Donald Eugene Smith offers the following interesting comparative assessment:

While the Committee on Religious and Moral Instruction was strongly influenced by the specific curriculum recommendations made by the Radhakrishnan Commission, it did not attempt to base these on a Vedantic 'Indian view of religion'. In this sense, its report marked a definite advance over that of the earlier Commission. The recommendations are simply founded on the sound observation that religious diversity is one of the most important features of Indian life and that every educated citizen should understand the basic principles and values of religions other than his own. The objective is to promote the spirit of tolerance through the understanding of differences, not to prove the unity of all religions by syncretistic harmonization. Of course, it could be expected that many Hindu teachers would take the latter approach in actually presenting this material in the classroom. (Smith, 1963, pp. 355–56.)

This Report was also felt to be closer to Gandhian concepts (Sinha, 1968, p. 105).

V—Committee on Emotional Integration (1961–62). This Committee (Report, 1962) touched on the question of the role of religion in emotional integration (Sinha, 1968, p. 39, note 78) and concluded that

although it is not possible to provide religious education as a part of the curriculum for schools in a secular state, education will be incomplete if students are not helped to appreciate the spiritual values which the various religions present to the people. Talks, open to all, on the teachings of various religions by able and competent persons may be arranged in the schools. (Biswas and Agrawal, p. 449.)

VI—The Education Commission (1964–66). The Education Commission noted that the recommendation of neither the University Education Commission (1948) nor of the Committee on Religious and Moral Instruction (1959) had made any appreciable impact and recommended their whole-hearted adoption (Report, 1966). Its own contribution lay in further elaborating the recommendation of religious instruction by explaining the importance of the text-books used and their manner of preparation for degree courses (*ibid.*, p. 21):

We suggest that a syllabus giving well-chosen information about each of the major religions should be included as a part of the course in citizenship or as part of general education to be introduced in schools and colleges up to the first degree. It should highlight the fundamental similarities in the great religions of the world and the emphasis they place on the cultivation of certain broadly comparable and moral and spiritual values. It would be a great advantage to have a common course on this subject in all parts of the country and common text-books which should be prepared at the national level by competent and suitable experts available on each religion. When these courses have been prepared, it would be worthwhile to have them scrutinized by a small committee of eminent persons belonging to different religions to ensure that nothing is included in them to which any religious group could take legitimate objection.

II

The current situation, and the historical developments preceding it, were briefly reviewed in the previous section (Rudolph, 1972, pp. 13–24). In this section, ideological rather than historical issues connected with the role of religious education in the formulation of governmental educational policy and practice will be discussed. The discussion will be organized around the following questions: (a) should religious education be imparted at all, in governmental educational institutions, and (b) if so, in what form?

Before these questions are addressed, however, it will be useful to summarize the views expressed in the past since the introduction of modern education on this point. The opinions have varied. One view was that no religious education should be countenanced, a view which by and large prevailed for a long time. But eddies of different if not opposing views can be detected in this general current. Thus the Woods Despatch of 1854, while it did not countenance the introduction of religious education, does seem to suggest that its existence be overlooked, consistently with its pro-missionary stance. The Despatch noted that

considerable misapprehension appears to exist as to our views with respect to religious instruction in the government institutions. Those institutions were founded for the benefit of the whole population of India; and in order to effect their object it was, and is, indispensable that the education conveyed in them should be exclusively secular. The Bible is, we understand, placed in the libraries of the colleges and schools and the pupils are able freely to consult it. This is as it should be; and, moreover, we have no desire to prevent or discourage any explanations which the pupils may, of their own free will, ask from the masters upon the subject of the Christian religion provided that such information be given out of school hours. Such instruction being entirely voluntary on both sides, it is necessary, in order to prevent the slightest suspicion of an intention on our part to make use of the influence of government for the purpose of proselytism, that no notice shall be taken of it by the inspectors in their periodical visits. (Nurullah, 1951, p. 211.)

Another stance of a somewhat similar colour but a deeper hue may be identified as the missionary view; for the issue of 'religious education,' namely, education in Christianity in this context, was

dear to the heart of the missionaries. They had always put forward the view (*a*) that the Company's policy of religious neutrality was not in the spiritual interests of the Indian people; (*b*) that, as all true education is inseparable from religion, every school and college conducted by the Company must impart instruction in religion (which, however, they interpreted narrowly as instruction in Christianity); and (*c*) that the missionaries should have full freedom, in spite of their being in receipt of State grants, to teach the Bible compulsorily to all students who may join their schools. (Nurullah, 1951, p. 245.)

We have so far encountered three opinions on the point: (*i*) no religious education; (*ii*) condoned Christian education; and (*iii*) active Christian education. With the emergence of the Hindu religious movements in modern India (Majumdar, 1963, IV), the third position yielded to a fourth; (*iv*) general religious education for members of each religious community, a position which was placed before the Education Commission of 1882. Thus

insofar as the general demand for religious education was concerned, the ranks of the missionaries were soon strengthened by other groups. The Brahmo Samajists, the Prarthana Samajists and the Arya Samajists, the new sects among the Hindus, also demanded religious education in schools on the lines of their own faith; the orthodox Hindus who, in the earlier period, had fought against the new education altogether now gave up that fight and began to demand that the new schools should combine instruction in the principles of Hindu religion with Western science and literature, in the case of all Hindu children; and the Muslims who were now coming under the modern system of education insisted that the Koran should necessarily be taught to Muslim children. In short, there was, by 1882, a general feeling among several sections of the people that the policy of secular education should be abandoned and that religious education should be provided to each child in the principles of his own faith. Such a proposal could not obviously be accepted by the Commission on administrative and financial grounds. The Commission, therefore, reiterated the necessity of keeping all government schools secular. The missionaries, therefore, lost their demand that Christianity should be taught in all government schools; even the modified demand that each child should be taught his own religion was rejected. The policy of secular education in government schools was upheld once more, and in spite of all attacks, continues to hold the field even today (Nurullah, 1951, p. 246).

There have been dissenting views, such as those expressed by Hartog before Independence and by several Commissions after. It is interesting to note that although the Report of the Education Commission of 1882

> was in consonance with the declared religious neutrality of the state in not connecting the institutions with any *one form* of faith it recommended 'that an attempt be made to prepare a *moral text-book*, based upon the fundamental principles of national religion, such as may be taught in all government and non-government colleges,' and 'a series of lectures on the duties of a man and a citizen' to be delivered to each of the college classes. The government, however, doubted 'whether such a moral text-book as is proposed could be introduced without raising a variety of burning questions'. (Biswas and Agrawal, 1971, p. 439, emphasis added.)

The purpose of this historical review was to show that the historical choices discussed also cover the range of logical choices available. For it is not enough to ask: should religious education be imparted at all? The question is capable of a three-fold break-down:

1. Should no education in any religion be imparted?
2. Should education in only one religion be imparted?
3. Should education of a generally religious and moral nature be imparted which does justice to all the religions?

Most modern Indian thinking is concerned with debating the first and third questions. But before any of these can be answered, the basic question must be tackled: should religious education in any form be imparted at all?[6]

A question like this cannot be answered without reference to the goals a nation sets for itself. It will be generally agreed that India has set out to be a modern, socially just, democratic, economically progressive nation determined to occupy its own special place in the comity of nations. We now need to ask ourselves the question: are these ends better promoted by having no religious education in government institutions at all, or by incorporating general education of a religious and moral character in the educational system?

Those who hold the view that the system of education should be entirely secular argue that the study of religion will unleash medieval, regressive and undemocratic forces in Indian polity. S. Alam Khundmiri, for instance, provides in an appendix the following description of a 'Textbook on Indian History for Third Standard Students prescribed at Andhra Pradesh schools' (Sinha, 1968, p. 98):

1. Ramayana; 2. Mahabharata; 3. Buddha; 4. Asoka the Great; 5. Vikramaditya; 6. Harsha; 7. Pulakesin II; 8. Pratapa Rudra . . . Pratapa saved the Hindu religion by bravely facing the Mohammadan invaders of North India. He defeated Mohammad-Bin-Tuglak in the first attack . . .; 9. Padmini of Chittor; 10. Krishna Deva Raya; 11. Shivaji . . . Shivaji was a brave soldier and a strict Hindu. He started a new Hindu kingdom amidst the

---

[6] A distinction can be and was sometimes drawn between moral and religious education (see T.N. Siqueria, 1967, p. 11). However, not much use has been made of this distinction, and the view that moral instruction can take the place of religious instruction was rejected by the University Education Commission (Smith, 1963, p. 352), though its viability is asserted by others (Siqueria, 1967, pp. 182ff.). It is interesting to observe in this context that proposals of an educational nature emanating from some of the neo-Hindu movements do not emphasize religious education so much as building of character, even when the proposals are cast in the philosophical mould of the movement (see Ernest Wood, 1917, Sri Aurobindo Ghose 1924).

many Mohammadan kingdoms. He worried Aurangazeb much . . .; 12. Story of Jhansi Lakshmi Bai; 13. Mahatma Gandhi.

He notes that the 'presence of two great historical religions having separate histories and representing two entirely different attitudes towards life, morality and social obligation offer a great challenge to the modern spirit of secularism'. He goes on to say:

> Some of our educationists talk of making moral or religious instruction compulsory in our schools and universities to raise the moral consciousness of the young. I do not doubt their sincerity and their concern for the future of the young, but the type of moral and religious education which is recommended will further encourage the divisive forces. It is scientific education which should be made obligatory for each student from the early stages, with an emphasis on the scientific method. In this connection complete separation of education from religion seems to be the first step. (Sinha, 1968, p. 92.)

Rather than the promotion of religious education, the 'evolution of secular scientific education seems' to him to be 'more important than even a common civil code which can transcend the existing personal laws of the different groups' (*ibid.*, p. 95). He concludes: 'The marriage between religion and politics has spoiled them both; there is a strong case for divorce' (*ibid.*, p. 97).

Those who argue for the incorporation of spiritual and moral education of a general nature in the curriculum maintain that such a step will promote the emergence of a (*a*) modern, (*b*) scientific, (*c*) socially just, (*d*) democratic, and (*e*) economically progressive, (*f*) nation and help it occupy its proper place in the comity of nations. They argue as follows:

(*a*) *Modern*: Religious education of the kind the proponents of this view have in mind can be connected positively with modernity in at least three ways: (*i*) modern knowledge 'with a lack of essential values can be dangerous' (Education Commission, p. 19). Religious education will overcome this lack; (*ii*) modernity and tradition are not always at odds. 'There are strands within Indian thought itself which can lead to a new outlook appropriate to a modern society' (Rudolph and Rudolph, 1967), and (*iii*) instead of the conservatism of religion overwhelming modernity, it is equally if not more likely that the 'liberalizing forces which have arisen in Western nations' will have a positive effect on the religious tradition themselves when the two are brought in apposition rather than opposition (Education Commission, p. 20).

(b) Scientific: On the one hand, the view that religion is opposed to science has become outdated, especially from the point of view of Eastern thought (Capra, 1975; LeShan, 1974; Kapleau, 1965, Foreword; Bowes, 1977, p. 49). On the other hand, science has come so close to facing the religious questions that the antagonistic divide between them may become nothing more than a cliché.

(c) Socially Just: It is generally recognized that a 'major weakness of the Indian and particularly of the Hindu, society in the past has been a lack of equality and social justice' (Education Commission, p. 20). The *Comparative* dimension of religious education acquires special significance here (*ibid.*), which will generate balancing forces, as also an emphasis on the egalitarian elements within the Hindu world-view (Radhakrishnan, 1939, pp. 373ff.; 1974, pp. 85–86).

(c) Democratic: India is a multi-religious society which can only remain democratic if it remains religiously tolerant. Is such tolerance promoted by a neglect of the religions altogether or by their sympathetic study? The issue is a moot one[7] but it is more likely that a sympathetic study of religions will promote the kind of harmony being sought (Rao, 1978). The Report of the Education Commission (1964–66, pp. 20–21) has noted with consternation that

> children are now growing up without any clear ideas of their own religion and no chance of learning about others. In fact, the general ignorance and misunderstanding in these matters are so widespread in the younger generation as to be fraught with great danger for the development of a democracy in which tolerance is rated as a high value. (See also Shukla, 1976, p. 20.)

---

[7] There is considerable impatience with religion shown by Indian Marxists which may be shortsighted. It should be noted that 'Marxist principles and values have also widely infiltrated Indian life and thinking and are gaining increasing acceptance by all classes of the Indian population' (Fuchs, 1984, p. 10).

It is worth noting here, as the example of Turkey under Kemal Ataturk suggests, that a 'close link' 'can be forged between secularism and dictatorship' (Sinha, 1968, p. 25) and democracy and secularism are not necessarily compatible or correlated (*ibid.*, pp. 109, 189).

(e) Economically Progressive: The role of religion in India's economic development, generally assumed to be negative, has not been critically analysed (Misra, 1962; Sharma, 1980). It is easy to see how some of the religious values (such as, those of work ethic or selfless endeavour) can spur economic development on. The issue of the role of religious factors in economic development is receiving increased attention (Bellah, 1965; *World Development*, 1980 [8: 7/8]), and it has even been argued that the work ethic of the Gita provides an adequate analogue to the Protestant work ethic (Subramaniam, 1983: Appendix I).

(f) India and the World: If India has a contribution to make to world civilization, which realm is it going to be in? It is widely felt by many thoughtful Indians that India's contributions will lie in the field of (*i*) harmonizing science and religion; the secular and the spiritual, and (*ii*) combining morality with technology. The Report of the Education Commission (1964–66) expresses these views eloquently. On the point of India's possible role in harmonizing science and religion, the secular and the spiritual, it remarks:

> A vitalized study of science with its emphasis on open-mindedness, tolerance and objectivity would inevitably lead to the development of a more secular outlook, in the sense in which we use the word, amongst those who profess different religions. This process needs to be carefully and wisely encouraged. Simultaneously, there is a sense in which the walls between the secular and the spiritual are tending to break down and what is secular is seen to have spiritual roots. In the words of Dr. Iqbal, 'The spirit finds its opportunity in the material, the natural and the secular. All that is secular is, therefore, sacred in the roots of its being.' This is what we envisage as the direction of our future development. We believe that India should strive to bring science and the values of the spirit together and in harmony, and thereby pave the way for the eventual emergence of a society which would cater to the needs of the whole man and not only to a particular fragment of his personality. (Education Commission, p. 21.)

On the possibility of India taking the initiative in combining morality with technology it remarks:

> Atom and *ahimsa*, or, to put it differently, man's knowledge and mastery of outer space and the space within his skull, are out of balance. It is this imbalance which mankind must seek to redress. Man now faces himself. He faces the choice of rolling down a nuclear abyss to ruin and annihilation or of raising himself to new heights of glory and fulfilment yet unimagined. India has made many glorious contributions to world culture, and perhaps the grandest of them all is the concept and ideal of non-violence and compassion sought, expounded and lived by Buddha and Mahavira; Nanak and Kabir; Vivekananda, Ramana Maharishi and Gandhi in our own times, and which millions have striven to follow after them. The greatest contribution of Europe doubtlessly is the scientific revolution. If science and *ahimsa* join together in creative synthesis of belief and action, mankind will attain to a new level of purposefulness, prosperity and spiritual insight. Can India do something in adding a new dimension to the scientific achievement of the West? This poses a great challenge and also offers a unique opportunity to the men and women of India, and especially to the young people who are the makers of the future. (*ibid.*, p. 22.)

But how will these young men mould the future if they do not know who Kabir was and what Ramana Maharishi taught? Thus the University Education Commission (1948–49) seems justified in stating that 'if we exclude spiritual training in our institutions, we would be untrue to our whole historical development' (Mahadevan, 1971, p. 283). This is the choice we face: are we going to remain true to the historical development of modern education which has been narrowly secular (Education Commission, p. 20) or are we going to be true to the general historical development of India which has been broadly religious and multi-religious. It all boils down to the question: will the following 'concrete recommendations' of the Commission be implemented (Mahadevan, 1971, p. 283):

1. that all educational institutions start work with a few minutes for silent meditation;
2. that in the first year of the degree course, lives of great religious leaders like Gautama Buddha, Confucius, Zoroaster, Socrates,

Jesus, Shankara, **Ramanuja**, Madhva, Mohammad, Kabir, Nanak, Gandhi, be taught;

3. that in the second year some selections of a universalist character from the scriptures of the world be studied;
4. that in the third year, the central problems of the philosophy of religion be considered.[8]

Donald Eugene Smith (1963, pp. 347, 358) identifies two broad problem areas in the matter of religious education and government policy: (*a*) educational policy in relation to religion in government-run schools, and (*b*) educational policy in relation to religion in state-aided private schools.

The first area was discussed earlier and the discussion may be summarized. The principle of religious neutrality could be interpreted severally: (*i*) religious instruction in no religion; (*ii*) in all religions;[9] and (*iii*) religious instruction in general rather than in a particular religion. Religious instruction, in general, could either promote the concept of a 'universal religion' or stop at an empathic and comparative study of several religions, and be universalistic in this sense.

The other broad area of state-aided schools remains to be discussed. A controversy has arisen in the relevant literature whether state aid to private schools managed by religious bodies 'violates the basic principle of secularism' or not (Sinha, 1968, pp. 165–67, 200–1). Inasmuch as these 'grants are given on the condition that there is no religious discrimination in admissions; that no student is required to participate in any religious service, that similar subsidies are given to non-religious schools' and that religious minorities may not be able to avail of the Constitutional provision to run their own schools without such aid, the situation does not seem to be unfair. It should be noted that the recommendation of the University Education Commission regarding silent meditation is directed at *all* educational institutions.

The question of whether the Indian government should have any

---

[8] A question will naturally arise at this point: how are the books for these courses to be prepared? The tremendous success of Prof. Huston Smith's *The Religions of Man* (New York: Harper & Row, 1965 [first published 1958]) may serve to show that the task may be difficult but not as difficult as might have been imagined. The suggestion of the *Report of the Education Commission (1964–66)* is worth considering on this point (1966, p. 21).

[9] Lest this possibility be considered bizarre see Smith, 1963, p. 348; the views of Gandhi on this point are also not without interest, see Siqueria (1967, pp. 177–78).

role to play in the imparting of religious education is one on which opinions might well differ. In my opinion, one of the most significant statements on the point was made by Maulana Abul Kalam Azad in January 1948 when, while addressing the Central Advisory Board on Education, he declared that India's difficulties are due to religious fanaticism and (Smith, 1963, pp. 348–49):

> If we want to safeguard the intellectual life of our country against this danger, it becomes all the more necessary for us not to leave the imparting of early religious education to private sources. We should rather take it under our direct care and supervision. No doubt, a foreign government had to keep itself away from religious education. But a national government cannot divest itself of undertaking this responsibility.[10]

The issue hinges on the understanding of the word secular, which the Indian government has declared itself to be. An understanding of secularism can move in two directions: one according to which the state has no role, or only a minimal role to play in the religious arena and another according to which the state plays an active role in promoting religious harmony. The popular understanding of secularism is virtually confined to the first sense, on account of the heavy association of the concept with the historical context in which secularization occurred in the west. But if Indian history is taken

---

[10] This view is opposed to two standpoints: that the issue is not an important one or that it is too important for the government to meddle with. For the former view see Sinha, 1968, p. 111; for the latter see Donald E. Smith, 1963, p. 358. It should also be noted that Maulana Azad's position need not necessarily be described as non-secular, as under the term secularism: 'we can assume two theoretical models—one in which the secular institution refrains totally from any deliberate intervention in religious matters excepting on absolutely secular grounds, and another in which it pursues a policy of active intervention in the activities of religious groups but does so indiscriminately as between one religious group and another. There are doctrinal purists like Dr. Ved Prakash Luthra who would accept the terminological legitimacy of applying the term 'secularism' only to the first model. There are more generous scholars like Dr. D.E. Smith who are prepared to consider the second model as a special case of the general principle of secularism.' Maulana Azad's position seems consistent with the second model which allows 'an institution to adopt a positive policy towards religious groups provided it treats them all on a footing of equality' (Sinha, 1968, p. 100). The University Education Commission also saw its recommendations as consistent with the principle of secularism in the sense of religious neutrality (Smith, 1963, p. 352): 'The absolute religious neutrality of the state can be preserved if in state institutions, what is good and great in every religion is presented, and what is more essential, the unity of all religions.'

into account, then the word could and should be extended to cover the second sense which possesses far greater relevance in the Indian context (as exemplified by the figures of Asoka, Harsha, Akbar and Mahatma Gandhi).

Since Independence, the Indian government has essentially followed a secular policy in the first sense. The continuing Hindu-Muslim tension in India and, more significantly, the post-Independence development of Hindu-Sikh tensions seems to indicate that the policy has not succeeded in eliminating or even controlling religious strife. Hence, the time has come to suggest that the Indian government should now apply the second understanding of secularism on the Indian scene according to which the state intervenes in the religious arena to promote religious harmony, through a program of religious education designed for this purpose.

References

BELLAH, R.N., ed. 1965. *Religion and Progress in Modern Asia.* New York: The Free Press.

BHATT, B.D. and J.C. AGGARWAL, eds. 1969. *Educational Documents in India (1813–1968).* New Delhi: Arya Book Depot.

BISWAS, ARABINDA and SUREN AGRAWAL, eds. 1971. *Indian Educational Documents Since Independence.* New Delhi: The Academic Publishers (India).

BOWES, PRATIMA. 1977. *The Hindu Religious Tradition: A Philosophical Approach.* London: Routledge & Kegan Paul.

CAPRA, FRITJOF. 1975. *The Tao of Physics.* London: Wildwood House.

COMMITTEE ON EMOTIONAL INTEGRATION. 1962. *Report of the Committee on Emotional Integration.* Ministry of Education: Government of India.

COMMITTEE ON RELIGIOUS AND MORAL INSTRUCTION. 1960. *Report of the Committee on Religious and Moral Instruction.* Ministry of Education: Government of India.

EDUCATION COMMISSION. 1966. *Report of the Education Commission (1964–66).* Ministry of Education: Government of India.

FUCHS, STEPHEN. 1984. 'The Cultural and Religious Dimensions of Neo-Hinduism. *Update,* Vol. 8, No. 1, pp. 9–15.

GHOSE, SRI AUROBINDO. 1924. *A System of National Education: Some Introductory Essays.* Calcutta: Arya Publishing House.

KAPLEAU, PHILIP. 1965. *The Three Pillars of Zen.* Boston: Beacon Press.

LESHAN, LAWRENCE. 1974. *The Medium, the Mystic and the Physicist.* New York: The Viking Press.

MAHADEVAN, T.M.P. 1971. *Outlines of Hinduism.* Bombay: Chetana Ltd.

MAJUMDAR, R.C., ed. 1963. *British Paramountcy and Indian Renaissance.* Part I. Bombay: Bharatiya Vidya Bhavan.

Misra, Vikas. 1962. *Hinduism and Economic Growth*. Bombay: Oxford University Press.
Nurullah, Syed and J.P. Naik. 1951. *A History of Education in India*. Delhi: Macmillan Company of India Limited.
Organ, Troy Wilson. 1974. *Hinduism: Its Historical Development*. Woodbury, New York: Barron's Educational Series, Inc.
Radhakrishnan, S. 1939. *Eastern Religions and Western Thought*. Oxford: Clarendon Press.
———. 1974. *The Hindu View of Life*. London: Unwin Books (first published 1927).
Rao, K.L. Seshagiri. 1978. *Mahatma Gandhi and Comparative Religion*. Delhi: Motilal Banarsidass.
Rudolph, Susanne Hoeber and Lloyd I. Rudolph. 1967. *The Modernity of Tradition*. Chicago: Chicago University Press.
———. eds. 1972. *Education and Politics in India*. Cambridge, Massachusetts: Harvard University Press.
Sargent, John. 1968. *Society, Schools and Progress in India*. Oxford: Pergamon Press.
Saran, A.K. 1979. 'The Meaning and Forms of Secularism: A Note, *Religious Traditions*, Vol. 2, No. 1, pp. 38–51.
Sharma, Arvind. 1973. 'Hinduism and Christian Missionary Activity: A Case Study of the Nineteenth Century—The Ramakrishna Mission,' *Indian Church History Review*, Vol. 7, No. 2, pp. 151–58.
———. 1980. *The Hindu Scriptural Value System and India's Economic Development*. Delhi: Heritage Publishers.
———. 1982a. 'English Education and Hinduism: The Contrasting Visions of Roy and Macaulay.' *The Educational Review*, Vol. 88, No. 6, pp. 90–92.
———. 1982b. 'Hinduism: The Macaulay Effect,' *Hinduism*, Vol. 95, No. 1, pp. 10–11.
Shukla, P.D. 1976. *Towards the New Pattern of Education in India*. New Delhi: Sterling Publishers Pvt. Ltd.
Sinha, V.K., ed. 1968. *Secularism in India*. Bombay: Lalvani Publishing House.
Siqueira, T.N. 1967. *Modern Indian Education*. London: Oxford University Press.
Smith, Donald Eugene. 1963. *India as a Secular State*. Princeton, New Jersey: Princeton University Press.
Subramaniam, V., ed. 1983. *Cultural Integration in India: A Socio-Historical Analysis*. Columbia, MO: South Asia Books.
Tinker, Hugh. 1963. *India and Pakistan: A Political Analysis*. New York: Praeger.
University Education Commission. 1950. *Report of the University Education Commission*. Simla: Government of India Press.
Wood, Ernest. 1917. *Selected Articles on National Education*. Hyderabad, Sind: The Sind Publishing House.
The World Bank. 1980. *World Development*, 8(7/8).

14

Conclusion: Theses, Antitheses and Syntheses

Mathew Zachariah

The introductory chapter mentioned the major questions raised in Chapters 2 to 13. These twelve chapters have discussed the problems of education and social change in India from several theoretical, policy and practical standpoints. What benefits the spread of formal education gives to individual children and illiterate adults is a question from the diffusionist perspective. When the question is asked in the context not of individuals but of groups or of an entire society, it is changed into a question about cultural transformation and revitalization. The question of which identifiable groups or classes in society benefit disproportionately from the existence and expansion of formal education reveals at least some sympathy with the dependency perspective.

One might transform these questions into the language of empirical social science: Is formal education an intervening, independent or dependent variable in the process described neutrally as social change, often positively identified as development and negatively evaluated as oppression? If by ideology we mean a system of values, beliefs and attitudes that shape our perceptions and choices, our ideological positions tend to shape the questions we ask and the answers we arrive at. Trying to understand arguments from different ideological origins compels us to defend and sometimes re-evaluate our own perspectives. It would not be difficult to identify the authors of most of the papers as diffusionists, developmentalists or dependency theorists. In the conference which preceded this publication, one almost felt that the ghosts of Marx and Weber were engaged in pugilism in the seminar room; but one keenly missed the spirit of Gandhi. With some effort, we might locate all of the authors, whether or not they are nationalists, on a left to right continuum of political ideology. For example, a reformist would assume that the structures of the state can be bent to bring about significant reform whereas a radical socialist would see the state itself as an important part of the problem.

Apart from differences in theoretical and ideological origin, the papers reveal several other differences in treatment and approach. Most have adopted a macro perspective in contrast to the micro perspective of some; some have looked to agencies outside the formal educational system to bring about significant progress whereas others have pointed to the liberative potential of education. The papers remind us also that we must be careful to distinguish between *informal education* that takes place mostly in the context of home and peer group, *formal education* (or schooling) that leads to certification for potential employment in the wage sector (as well as a certain measure of prestige), and *non-formal education* activities, depending on their nature and sponsorship, that *either* take the place of (in some cases supplement to enrich) formal education *or* oppose the propaganda and indoctrination in formal education. The major themes Ratna Ghosh phrased in the form of questions in Chapter 1 are not just intellectual exercises in an academic game; they are issues that create acute dilemmas for the policy-maker, the practitioner and radical persons and groups engaged in praxis.

In the balance of this paper, I shall, for the most part, quote directly from the comments of discussants who had prepared formal responses to the papers. I have depended on my own, the discussants' and the chairperson's notes to present the points of view of those who did not have prepared statements. For the sake of brevity, I have had to omit several relevant comments made by the discussants in the ensuing 'free-for-all'. The following paragraphs will not necessarily resolve theoretical or practical problems but, let us hope, will help sharpen the dialogue initiated at the Conference.

Formal Education and the Reproduction of Elites

Krishna Kumar's paper described in some detail the colourful mosaic of institutions and practices that we call the *system* of Indian education. His arguments that the latent function of the massive school and college examination system is to give the appearance of 'contest' mobility to a system characterized by rampant 'sponsored' mobility is very insightful. While the thrust of his thesis is very persuasive, several questions can be raised about details. Except in the case of the Indian Foreign Service, the fact that some 60 per cent of the total recruits to the highest civil service ranks are from 'government service parents' does not provide *prima facie* evidence of the reproduction of elite roles. 'The government'—which includes the state and federal levels—is the principal employer in India and government employees constitute a huge part of India's regular wage earners. Most of them receive poor wages and can be classified as belonging to the lower and lower-middle classes. We need more discriminating analyses before we can confidently reach the conclusions of Kumar regarding the reproduction of elite roles. Kumar sees as regressive the attempts of some Indian educators to relate modern Indian education to India's glorious past. The dangers of excessive, narrow-minded nationalism are certainly many. Yet, it is now very clear that modern values can be *effectively* propagated only if the people can make sense of them in the context of a system of values they already hold. In that sense, it is necessary to view development, not as a wholesale Westernization, but as creative, selective, cultural revitalization.

Administration of Higher Education in India

Claude Deblois began his comments on Iqbal Narain's paper with a joke:

> If an expatriate spends a week in Africa, he is anxious to write a book about that continent. If he spends a year in one African country, he might be tempted to write an article; if he spends five years there, he does not dare to write anything about it.

The issue of the validity and reliability of what we claim to know about other groups surfaced several times in the Conference. Some asked: Are Canadian and American specialists capable of tearing away their own cultural blinkers and ideological predilections? Others countered: Are Indian academics who mostly belong to the middle and upper-middle classes capable of genuinely understanding the poor and their cultures in India? Another issue added further fuel to the debate: while India's record in the collection and publication of statistics is laudable in comparison to many other Asian, African and Latin American countries, they are useful mainly to indicate orders of magnitude and are not entirely reliable. Poromesh Acharya, for example, referred to the way head teachers in West Bengal do not keep proper records and inflate enrolment figures by 15 to 20 per cent, especially in the rural areas. The controversy reminds us of the need for two attitudes—humility in our scholarly endeavours and resistance to the temptation to consider matters we do not understand as a magician's black box.

Deblois referred to Narian's assertion: 'the basic issue is whether educational administration, or better still, university administration is akin to administration in general or is qualitatively different from it.' Said Deblois:

> The implications of such a proposition are enormous indeed. If there is no specific difference, the appointment of a civil servant or a non-academic person as the head of institutions of higher learning is normal or even preferable from a strict administrative viewpoint. This is not Prof. Narain's view. Higher centres of learnings have to remain committed to the ideal of excellence ...
>
> This mission requires vision and courage on the part of those who have the responsibility of leading these institutions. Administrative theories and principles developed within the field of industries or general administration have limited validity for the administration of universities or educational institutions as a whole. Could it be that the *preoccupation* for 'law and order,' for holding the examinations in time, or the fear of the political involvement of students stems from a narrow understanding of the concept of 'organizational effectiveness' on the part of too many university administrators and members of the academic community? Not that these are unimportant. But, from an educational point of view, these events could be seen as occasions

for growth, for personal development, for discovering a sense of responsibility if they are allowed to be examined in the larger concept of administration that takes into account the ultimate mission of the universities. This presupposes a concept of administration which includes, as an essential component, the educational dimension in a broad sense. Unfortunately, the theoreticians of educational administration have not yet tackled that problem adequately. Therefore, school administrators cannot find much help in the different theories of administration to guide them in those difficult paths. They are left to develop their own praxis without the support of a well-articulated theory. In reading Prof. Narain's paper I sensed that, too often, university administrators are forced to spend a great deal of their energies on trivial administrative duties when leadership and high order reflection and decision should be called for in a time of uncertainties with regard to the future of these institutions and of the constant interference on the part of the various government funding agencies. University administrators are forced to invest in trivia because the community at large evaluates their performance in terms of their ability to deal with such questions rather than on their long term insightful policy decisions.

In the ensuing discussion, Narain acknowledged that the systemic approach of his paper perhaps puts too much faith in good leadership at the top to make matters better. Some Conference participants pointed out that the systems approach, unlike dialectical analysis, would have difficulty seeing political unrest among college and university students as not dysfunctional but valuable.

Caste and Class in West Bengal Education

Paulos Milkias presented a very detailed critique of Poromesh Acharya's paper. Pointing to Acharya's use of broad caste and class categories to describe the socio-economic structure, he said:

> Marx himself was forced to suggest the unique existence of the 'Asiatic mode of production,' which he considered to be inherently

static and as needing an injection of an exogenous class-oriented European style of mode of production through colonialism. But, even today, India remains a mosaic of social structures where there are huge regional disparities and uneven development leading to the coexistence of an industrial life-style together with an archaic feudal order; this results in the difficulty of producing a precise picture of the social structure in West Bengal, let alone in the whole of the India.

Milkias took issue with the omission of the role of the Communist Party of India (Marxist) in Acharya's paper:

The CPI(M) has so far succeeded in making tremendous inroads into the countryside, by-passing the landlords and mobilizing the sharecroppers for reform. It has organized rural labour unions and has championed tenancy reforms. Its Food For Work Program has not only given employment and a decent livelihood to tens of thousands of people; it has helped in expanding the basic infrastructures of road construction as well as the clean-up and drainage of irrigation canals. The local government's structure has been revamped and made more amenable to administrative efficiency. Employment opportunities have increased and wages for labourers have been raised. And, most importantly, working within a bourgeoisie democratic capitalist system, as its Eurocommunist counterparts have shown, it has succeeded in bringing into operation a clean local government that is not entangled in a web of corruption and nepotism. With all these socio-economic changes, educational reforms channelled through what have already been dubbed 'Red Panchayats' could not be underestimated.

Milkias raised the issue of India's place in the international division of labour within a capitalist world system.

Within the framework of the global system, therefore, India in general and West Bengal in particular have a dependent capitalist formation. But, on the level of social formation, India and West Bengal have semi-colonial and semi-feudal modes of production. The relationship between the international system and this particular mode of production has direct spillovers into the educational and socio-economic development or underdevelopment of West Bengal. To consider the problem as being merely endogenous would, therefore, be to miss a crucial variable. Indeed, it would be accepting the modernization theories of Rostow, Smelser and Parsons who tend to see the low-paid, informal and often rural sectors within underdeveloped countries as requiring more technology, knowledge, skills and structured work-related attitudes if these areas were to acquire the necessary productive efficiency to enable development to occur. They assume that traditional values and ways of life should be replaced with attitudes and behaviours appropriate to an industrialized and modern society.

But underdevelopment is a function of dependency, not of historical backwardness. As Baran, Dos Santos, Amin, Wallerstein and Frank have shown, the internal structure of traditional societies is not the main impediment to their development. Rather, underdevelopment is merely the obverse of development in the global system of capitalist accumulation. While the so-called traditional societies (such as, India) were indeed undeveloped, the syphoning off of the hinterland's surplus to the capitalist metropolis transformed those societies into underdeveloped countries. The theory, in both its Marxist and non-Marxist forms, is an approach based on a centre (metropolis)/periphery (hinterland) model of the capitalist system.

Social Class and Schooling in Bombay

J.C. Jacob, in his response to Suma Chitnis's paper, also raised the question of the place of children of poor people in the world system.

The sub-proletariat live and work in the marginal sector of the urban economy where credentials, and consequently schools, are irrelevant. The marginal sector is characterized by chronic insecurity in employment and often subsistence income. Are there reasons to believe that the modern or industrial sectors of a metropolitan economy like Bombay can or will expand to provide sufficient jobs to make school attendance reasonable for the sub-proletarian children? The best place to begin to answer the question about the future of jobs for the poor is an examination of Third World metropolitan economies, specifically focusing on their insertion in the world economic system.

It has been very difficult for countries like India, whether through reform or revolution, to develop an indigenous economy to provide work for its citizens. Third World nations have historically been one link in a metropole-satellite structure that 'serves as an instrument to suck capital or economic surplus out of its own satellites and to channel part of this surplus to the world of metropolis of which all are satellites'. This outflow of capital was connected almost exclusively to basic commodity production. Transnational corporations, along or through their national trading partners, extracted primary products (tea, bananas, cotton, etc.) at low cost and then dumped manufactured goods at above world market prices. The low wages paid to workers who, on a seasonal basis provided the labour for this extraction process, placed them at the margin of the economy and effectively precluded their purchase of imported products.

In the historical and contemporary world of this stereo-typical rural-based economic dependency, school and education made little sense for the poor. One does not need to be a school graduate to cut sugar-cane or pick coffee berries—virtually the only kind of work open to a rural proletariat. School-linked jobs are to be found in the large cities where streams of peasants have been pushed by rural unemployment.

Jacobs' analysis leads him to assert that it makes no sense to provide more and better schools without greatly expanded opportunities for gainful employment and that such opportunities will not expand 'as long as Bombay is physically *and spiritually* (emphasis in original) part of the world system'. He further suggests a solution: ' "delink" from the world system through a thorough-going social and political revolution'.

If we decide not to dismiss such a suggestion as that of an 'armchair revolutionary,' we are faced with several problems. Do we do nothing until the forces of history, whatever they are, bring forth the appropriate revolution? Given that even the most intractable long-term problem compels us to look for short-term solutions (because human beings are only capable of acting in the present and the forseeable future), what can academics and other intellectuals do? We have, it seems to me, only two major options: conscientize the poor so that they become aware of their right to dignity and a decent standard of living; work with those who create policy to make decisions that will advance the welfare of oppressed people. In real life, these are not easy choices.

Baldev Raj Nayar, whose response to another paper I shall discuss later, makes a salient point. The costs of total 'delinking' may be so great that, 'countries may have to adopt alternating phases of partial delinking and relinking with the developed world.' Whether one does what one can in a given set of circumstances or waits for an optimum moment has, again, no easy answers for all occasions.

Education and Economic Growth

George Psacharapoulous fully agreed with Nalla Gounden's paper which, with concepts and tools of economic analysis, reviewed and interpreted quantitative relationships between educational and socio-economic parameters in India. He lamented that 'in a country of the size of India, with so many quality institutions of higher learning and research, it is shocking that there do not exist more recent estimates on vital issues of educational policy.' He suggested four priority research areas:

We need an update on the returns to investment in education by level of schooling. To what extent has the profitability of education declined following the expansion of schooling in the last 20 years?

We need some evidence on the vocational versus general education issue touched upon in Dr. Nalla Gounden's paper. How do the unit costs of the two types of education compare, and what are the approximate benefits the two types of graduates bring to society?

We need some objective measures of the 'quality' of education and how quality has changed over time. What factors contribute to student achievement at the primary and secondary school level? Which policy-alterable factors are most cost-effective in raising achievement?

We need more evidence on how education is currently financed, not only by the federal and state government, but also by the families. What are the financing possibilities for further expansion of the educational system and/or improvements of its quality?

Science and Technology Policy

Baldev Nayar's comments on the 'science and technology (SAT) policy in India' paper chastised the author for not establishing first 'systematically what he understands SAT policy to be or have been and then drawing out rigorously the implications of it for the quality of education.' Nayar also notes the lack of attention in the paper to 'politics and the political process for the quality of education'. He went on to make several salient points:

> Professor Mohan exhibits a strong grievance against spectacular science, such as, nuclear and space science. But he fails to recognize that this is necessary for strategic reasons. Here, a narrow science perspective misleads. One should recognize that, despite all the talk about the interest of the West led by the United States in India's development, the West, but particularly the US, does not wish India well; in the last four decades, it has had the policy of converting India into a satellite either directly or indirectly through neutralizing it by building up Pakistan militarily. Indian scientists have to open their eyes to the policy of containment that the US has pursued, and continues to pursue, in relation to India. So, a larger geo-political perspective would suggest a different interpretation of the importance of what Mohan calls spectacular science.
>
> While the SAT system in India deserves criticism, and Mohan is quite merciless in this regard, I believe such criticism has to be placed in context. And here I wish to make four points. First, if India's SAT system is so bad, why is it a source of envy for other Third World countries, as the author himself acknowledges? And why do so many less developed countries (LDCs) send delegations to India to work out cooperation arrangements in SAT? Or why is India able to send out engineering goods as exports? Again, why has India been able to establish joint

ventures in LDCs? Still again, why do other LDCs want bigger quotas for their students in India's SAT institutions?

Second, the level of research and development (R&D) investment in India, no matter how high, can never be sufficient for a country like India with such a tremendous technological gap. India spends less than many multi-national companies, and its investment is spread thinly in so many areas. Leaving aside the superpowers and the major powers of Great Britain and France, the order in R&D expenditures was as follows in 1975 in one analysis: Germany, Italy, Sweden, General Motors, IBM, Belgium, Ford Motor Company, American Telephone and Telegraph, India, Spain, International Telephone and Telegraph, South Korea. One should note that India's R&D expenditure was less than half that of IBM and almost one-third of General Motors; even Ford Motor Company spent 75 per cent more and American Telephone and Telegraph (AT&T) almost 50 per cent more than did India. One should thus not have exaggerated expectations about local technology generation.

Third, for that reason, one has to make use of what is available in the international technology market rather than incur punishment by denying oneself this opportunity. Mohan recommends technological disengagement or insulation in order to have local technological development, but the likely result would be a technological ghettoization. There is a terrible inclination in India to avoid confronting the technological challenge from the outside by withdrawing from it, but there is no escaping the challenge; withdrawal will only make its vulnerability even more dangerous. Rather than trying to create what has already been invented, the country should attempt to import the best and improve it, like Japan has done and continues to do. In the SAT literature, corresponding to the general schools of dependency and diffusion, there are advocates of disengagement and autarky, on the one hand, and of Open Door on the other. While this is not the place to elaborate further on the notion, the appropriate policy should be one of selective interdependence—a policy that India has, in fact, followed. Indeed, even this policy has to be seen in a subtle rather than mechanical way. India would seem to be now in the phase of relinkage again because its earlier more restrictive posture on technology import in the 1970s placed the industrial system in a technological freeze necessitating technological upgradation and modernization now. Here, as in so many other things, there is a strange rhythmic parallel between China and India in their development policies, despite the many differences between their two social and political systems.

Fourth, India should recognize its own achievements no less than its inadequacies. Without recognizing its inadequacies, there can be no improvement and here Mohan's exercise is of considerable value. But without recognizing its achievements there can be no confidence to meet the inadequacies. Here one spectacular example of success is agriculture. One has only to look at Africa today to recognize what a success story Indian agriculture has been. I do not want to underrate the problems of maldistribution and malnutrition in India, but does one believe that Africa is without them? That achievement in agriculture is a result not of accident but of government policy, commitment and investment, and one should not sell it short. Basic to that achievement has been the linkage between research and the productive system, which has been lacking in relation to industry.... Indeed, India's SAT investment in agriculture alone has given such a high rate of return that it suffices as a return for all SAT investment in India.

Again, in terms of achievements, through its R&D in nuclear and space science, India has built an essentially autonomous scientific establishment in these areas of scientific endeavour. This is intimately linked to national security and it is difficult to put a price tag on it. Indeed, noting the output of this system, a Libyan delegate proclaimed at an UNCTAD meeting in the Philippines in 1979 that 'You Indians can do anything.' Rather than run it down, India ought to recognize what it has accomplished. Similar achievements are also available in small scale industry; you have only to see the activities of the Central Leather Research Institute (CLRI) in Madras in relation to the leather industry. The transformation in that industry from exporting hides and skins to finished leather and even leather manufactures is intimately tied up with the work of CLRI. Nor has private industry completely lagged behind in this regard. One has only to look at IDL Chemicals in Hyderabad and Hero-Majestic mopeds in Ludhiana to recognize local technology generation that has taken place.

Female Primary Education and Fertility Reduction

The paper by Anrudh K. Jain and Moni Nag as well as Mary Jean Bowman's comments on it did not engage in philosophical and ideological debates. Rather, their discussion was within the confines of conventional empirical social science and was similar to the Nalla Gounden and Psacharapoulous papers. Part of Bowman's comments are reproduced here:

> The most unsatisfactory box in Figure 1 in Jain and Nag's paper is that of **Demand for Children**. It is not that any one item in that box is misplaced. The problem is the ad hoc untidiness of the treatment and the tendency to speak in absolute instead of relative terms. Essentially, what is entailed here is a benefit-cost analysis. It may help if we start out distinguishing between situations in which children are seen primarily as 'consumer goods' and those in which they are seen primarily as 'producer goods,' although I strongly suspect that at least up to some point in family size children would almost universally be seen, in part at least, as 'consumer goods'—sources of direct satisfaction to their parents. Another way of stating the consumer versus producer-good orientation to children involved in a demographic transition is to refer to the reversal in intergeneration flows of income or wealth. In the pre-transition situation, the predominant flow may be from children to parents (children as producer goods), whereas in the post-transition phase the flow is predominantly from parents to children. This reversal of intergeneration flows has been a central theme in recent works.
>
> In analyzing the fertility decision, one can start from either approach. Jain and Nag start from a view of children as 'producer goods' in the pre-transition period, which is appropriate enough. But one can begin from the other direction, in a post-transition perspective. To bring these approaches together in the investigation of a demographic transition, it becomes necessary to consider at least the following: (*i*) constraints on the quantity-quality combination in children (here interpreted in terms of numbers of children versus education per child), (*ii*) the relative value of women's and of children's time in the labour market, (*iii*) the compatibility of women's work and child-care (or the 'time

intensity' of child-care), and (*iv*) income from sources other than labour of women and children.

Let us consider income first. If children are regarded as what economists call 'superior' consumer goods, the higher the husband's income and the higher non-labour sources of income, the greater, other things being equal, will be the number of children desired. But there is the question of how much the family would wish to invest in a child. On the simplifying assumption that they would want to treat all children equally, whatever the forms of investments in them, a higher 'quality' of children so defined would raise the cost of adding another child over the cost with lower child 'quality'. Turning this around, the greater the number of children, the greater the cost of raising the 'quality' level per child. This is the basis of the much-cited theory of 'quality-quantity' trade-off. Even if we do not accept the assumption of equal investment per child (note that in anticipation sex is not known), it is clear enough that more spent on a child means less of something else—whether fewer children or less consumption (or investment) in other forms. But, thus far, education of the parental population has entered into the analysis only through the effects of husband's education on his earnings. The 'direct costs' of more children will reflect the preference for better educated children together with the ability to support them—thus indirectly reflecting also mother's education.

What now of the costs of children and the relationship of those costs to parental education? Here it is the mother's education that is most important, and in two ways. First, the higher her education, the greater is the value of a woman's time in the market. If child-rearing is a time intensive good and cannot be readily combined with other productive work, an 'optimizing' decision with respect to desired family size will lean toward small child numbers. The higher a woman's education, the higher, other things being equal, would be the wife's foregone earnings if her time is allocated to child-rearing. But second, better educated women (and men) may contribute efficiently and significantly to the 'quality' of children at a relatively low cost per hour of their time. Even setting 'taste' aside, optimal decisions will then put the greater emphasis on quality relative to numbers.

But notice that higher child 'quality' as defined here entails more time for children in school, and this means foregoing the potential earnings from child labour. The cost of child quality, in a full accounting, must include the foregone earnings of the children themselves. How *important* will those foregone earnings be? In *absolute* terms, it is quite likely that foregone earnings of children will be higher when their parents are well educated than otherwise, and this can also be the case when, in the aggregate, there are higher levels of schooling in the adult population—as appears to have been the situation in Mexico, whether or not in one or another part of India.

What may then be important is (*a*) the *relative* value of children's versus women's time in the labour markets mentioned earlier, (*b*) the returns to investments in children's education net of their foregone earnings, and (*c*) how immediately pressing are the family's needs for the economic contributions of children. The potential earnings of children can come to exceed the costs of their rearing. When incomes are very low (parental education is low), we are back to the situation associated with high fertility in the Indian data.

Let us look once more at the **Demand for Children** box. It must be apparent that what is important in the 'labour value' component of that box is *relative* to levels of non-labour income in the family, adult male earnings and the earning potentials of women. It is at low income levels, with low social provision for security in old age and high levels of risk that the demand for children as 'producer goods' becomes the dominant element in fertility decisions. Education of parents enters into this situation primarily, it would seem, through effects on incomes and the need for supplementary earners.

Within a society as complex and diverse as that of India, one can observe families that are in various situations with respect to the balance of factors relevant to fertility decisions—situations that differ both for individual families in given localities and across localities. A number of studies that have been undertaken using Indian data illustrate these variations and seem to support the theoretical framework just discussed. Indeed, the only well-specified test of a quantity-quality trade-off effect in family planning made use of data on twin and non-twin families in India. This enabled the authors of this test to identify the quantity-quality relationship by making quantity an exogenous variable.

Most interesting, however, may be the results of research by

Indra Makhija (1985) on relationships between the Green Revolution and fertility and schooling in India. She found that the introduction of high-yielding varieties of wheat and rice had sustained effects on family size and the schooling of children, with a significant decline in births among young women and significant increases in the schooling of children from farm families. Each of an array of factors that increase returns to schooling lead to an increase in the proportion of children going to school. But the results attested also to the importance of work done by children. Higher wages for children lead to larger families and less schooling. She found also clear evidence of quantity-quality substitution. For example, when economic change increased the desire for schooling, families with fewer children (where the cost of increasing the average level of schooling is lower) chose higher levels of schooling for their children.

So far as policy is concerned, perhaps we are in the relatively fortunate position that what seems best on other grounds—notably continuing agricultural research and encouragement of primary schooling of girls—will also contribute to fertility decline. The big problem is *how* to bring about the developments in primary education that Jain and Nag would seek. Other papers in this Conference demonstrate something of the extent and complexity of that problem.

Child Labour and Education

Carolyn Elliott commended Usha Naidu for approaching the question of child labour with new questions. For example, child labour is so widely practised—especially in the unorganized and semi-organized wage sectors—in India that condemning it without considering the context is not very helpful.

Several points arose in the ensuing discussion. The Government of India and other official, semi-official and voluntary agencies are to be commended for acknowledging that the problem of the exploitation of children (pitifully low wages and inhuman working conditions) does exist. The fact that the central and state governments are not able to enforce existing legislative measures to protect children from exploitation reinforces Gunnar Myrdal's assertion in *Asian Drama* that India is a soft state. The approach of governmental and other agencies that accepts 'the harsh reality' of child labour and works *in situ* to improve wages and working conditions, on the one hand, and, on the other, provides vocationally-oriented basic skills is understandable. But, such activities should not detract from long-term efforts to improve the opportunities for poor children to enjoy their childhood.

Naidu and Parasuraman's 1985 finding that nearly three-quarters of the working children of Greater Bombay consider schooling useless and not enhancing chances for employment provides empirical support for Jacob's views in his response to Chitnis' paper. One participant pointed out that if Mahatma Gandhi's proposal for basic education—which included socially useful productive work at least at the primary level—was universally implemented, all children would have become part-time workers without becoming exploited and oppressed beings. Another participant pointed out that child labour is widely used inside the home (e.g., chores, cleaning tasks) and outside (e.g., babysitting) in Canada and the United States. Thus, it can have redeeming features if instituted with due regard for the rights of children. All participants recognized that even with the best efforts of committed individuals such as Naidu, the problem will continue to exist into the forseeable future.

The Education of Women

Gail Kelly, in her comments on Vina Mazumdar's rather extemporaneous remarks, made several points. In India, as in other parts of the world, women have been more successful in gaining access to formal education than in having their educated talents put to productive use. Mazumdar was right in emphasizing the importance of women's movement to bring about significant change. Such movements, by their very nature, would rightly develop analyses of local problems and local strategies. (There cannot be international or even national strategies and tactics for women's liberation.) Such analyses should take account of the nature of schooling and the specific obstacles women face in their locales. Kelly concluded by insisting that stratification based on gender should not be subsumed for analysis or policy formulation under socio-economic stratification or class oppression. Women, unlike men, do give birth to children; their problems should be addressed not by promoting schooling for domesticity but by providing day-care facilities. She asked: in order to have equality of outcome, do we need a different process of teaching and learning?

The Empowerment of Adults

Pramod Parajuli and Madhuri Mathema commented on Rajesh Tandon's discussion of how the powerlessness of oppressed people is related to the devaluation of their knowledge as well as the elitist production and utilization of knowledge. They, however, took the analysis much further. The following excerpts are from different parts of their paper.

A deeper analysis of the dialectics of knowledge and power would, however, reveal that knowledge not only reflects power but that power and knowledge directly imply each other. There is no power relation without the correlative of a field of knowledge, nor any knowledge, that does not at the same time presuppose and constitute power relations. In this sense, dispossession of knowledge by the oppressed groups is not so much a post-Second World War phenomenon as implied in the paper as much as the inherent structure of power relations in the communities where the oppressed are situated. Although there is a tendency and a great leap towards the transnationalization of the politics of research and knowledge creation in the last three decades as argued in Tandon's paper, it seems to be the existence of the inequitable hierarchies of power and knowledge creation in the so-called traditional communities themselves that the contemporary hierarchies of power and knowledge are rooted and perpetuated.

The caste-ridden Hindu society and the power and privilege of the Brahmin priest exemplify this point. In western Nepal, a village priest (who also holds the economic and political power) has control over the dynamics of the life processes of the other caste groups. The priest not only gives names, purifies pollution, sends the alive and the deceased to heaven or to hell but also advises people on who and who not to marry, what and what not to sell and buy. Under such a hegemonic situation, the lower castes can only create and legitimate their own knowledge in the process of altering the power relations itself.

It is because of such an interplay of knowledge and power in the rural communities that we see the state as a crucial element in the creation of knowledge. The modern state in the centre as well as the periphery is involved in the control over the reproduction of labour power not only through the organization of economic processes but also through other cultural and educational means: the subordination of manual labour to mental labour; the state's monopoly over intellectual activities, and the process of qualification and deskilling inscribed in the educational systems and training programs. Moreover, the state defines what knowledge is desirable, who should produce it, how much and for what purpose. Tandon's paper is unexpectedly silent on this aspect of knowledge creation and disposition.

Utilizing Gramsci's notion of 'hegemony and counter-hegemony' and Poulantzas' notion of 'popular struggle over the state,' we argue that the side of the struggle is, however, not clear unless we identify the class struggle going on in the society. It is important for participatory researchers to realize that their work is and should be a part of the overall struggle of the oppressed sections of the population and it is against the hegemony of the modern state (assuming relative autonomy of the state over the bourgeoisie class) that the struggle is going on. We view state hegemony not only in the economic and political arena but also in the arena of ideology, knowledge, technology and other forms of power relations within and beyond the state. The role of participatory research in the empowerment of the oppressed thus seems to be twofold: on the one hand, it produces and elaborates the peoples' own day-to-day practices and contributes to the authenticity and the quality of the socio-political movements. On the other hand, it brings back to the grassroots many experiences from the wider socio-political movements. The absence of this dialectic or the assigning of only theoretical or practical roles to participatory research limits the potential of the research for empowering the people.

The author abserves that the success stories of participatory research among the oppressed groups have three important implications for adult and non-formal education. First, they give adults faith in themselves as self-initiating and active people. Second, they give a central importance to process rather than content in the education of adults. Third, they imply that the training of adult educators be participative.

These are crucial implications indeed. However, we think that there are, in addition, other implications which are broader and very important in the field of adult and non-formal education.

First, they demonstrate the lack of neutrality in the production of knowledge. All knowledge is political, not because it may have political consequences or be politically useful but because knowledge has its conditions of possibility in power relations.

This implies that adult and non-formal education for the oppressed groups can either serve the hegemonic purposes of the dominant classes or the interests of the oppressed classes. It requires us as adult educators to make our orientations, choices and objectives explicit.

Second, we as adult educators need a critique of the existing ways in which knowledge is produced and distributed. The creation of a new mode of knowledge also requires an *a priori* critique of the existing form and nature of knowledge. For the oppressed mind is not a blank page but a mixture of good sense and bad sense and filled with elements of attitudes and beliefs perpetuating the status quo.

Third, there is a necessity to associate adult and non-formal education of the oppressed groups with the wider on-going class struggles and socio-political movements. The participatory process of adult learning has tremendous pedagogical advantages. But, in the absence of linkages with alternative organizations and movements, our highly cherished empowerment of the oppressed might not be realized. In fact, it is not conscientization which is a precondition for political action but probably the reverse. Freire shows how his literacy work evolved in response to worker and peasant struggles in northeast Brazil and not that the conscientization program triggered off the peasant and workers' struggle. Thus, conscientization became an additional tool for deepening class consciousness, sharpening the perception of the contradictions in the social relations of production and heightening workers' struggle.

Tradition and Stability in Education

Philip G. Altbach's response to the Joseph Di Bona and R.P. Singh paper was titled 'What Can We Learn From Contemporary Indian Education?' He said:

Indian education shows a remarkable basic stability over time, and it might be more instructive to analyze the reasons for this stability than to bemoan the current (and historical) inequalities in the education system. The education system has grown impressively during the past three decades at all levels. As Di Bona and Singh point out, schooling has become available to many rural Indians. However, the literacy rate, while having modestly gone up, has also shown a depressing stability over the decades. Of course, there are many more literate Indians but the proportion of literates has not improved dramatically. The muddle over language policy remains, with a range of linguistic policies in operation over a short period of time. English, contrary to the wishes of many politicians and educators, remains the key language of higher education and remains important for entry into the elite sector of society. It is not surprising, therefore, that the demand for education in English remains very strong.

The basic curriculum of Indian education has remained remarkably stable over time. Of course, there have been changes. At the post-secondary level, the establishment of the non-university Institutes of Technology and of Management have proved that India can have as good quality higher education as any country in the world. Yet, the universities remain in their basic monolithic structure, with the centralized examination system and the affiliating colleges that have been criticized for a century. The basic structure of the schools remains virtually unchanged. Gandhian educational ideas had virtually no impact. More contemporary educational philosophies of Paulo Freire and others have also barely touched the educational system. Again, some changes are evident—a modest increase in the science component of the school curriculum, upgrading of many text-books, etc. But the basic teaching-learning process, the examination-orientation of the system, the hierarchical nature of the schools, and the like, remain unchanged.

There are, no doubt, many reasons for this. Educational systems everywhere change slowly but India is remarkable in comparative terms for its stability and inertia. Indian educational planners have been so much concerned with expanding educational opportunity and with meeting massive demands for access to schooling that there has been little time and fewer resources available to consider basic changes. And, of course, change is expensive in many cases, and resources have been scarce. The fact that education is the basic responsibility of the states has meant that coordination of effort has been limited as state policies frequently differ. The states have placed differing emphases on education and there are, of course, quite different resource bases available. The professional education community, while in many ways critical of current educational policies and practices, is slow to change since alteration may be threatening to teachers, administrators, and policy-makers alike. And, as Di Bona and Singh would argue, the established elites find the status quo useful to maintaining their own positions of power in society.

A theme of the Di Bona and Singh paper is the revival of Indian languages in education and of indigenous systems of education. Some broad arguments are made but few facts are generated to support these arguments. Just as strong an argument could be made in the opposite direction—that the basic pattern of education inherited from the British remains the dominant mode and that efforts to reform educational systems, whether to return to indigenous roots or to adapt contemporary concepts have not taken hold to any significant degree and show no sign of threatening the dominance of the traditional system. There has been more success in the language area—the use of the regional languages as the main medium of instruction for most Indians has been instituted at the primary and generally at the secondary levels. Hindi, as a national language, however, has not made major inroads outside the Hindi-speaking areas. And English remains the language of choice for those who aspire to elite status. Thus, one might question the 'revival' of traditional educational practices and of Indian languages. Yes, there has been the increased use of Indian languages but not necessarily because of any revival. Indeed, prior to the establishment of British-style education, much of the Indian educational system used Persian as the major medium of instruction and the regional languages had little role in education. There are even more questions to be raised about the 'revival' of indigenous educational practices. While a few changes might be noted at the peripheries of the Indian educational monolith, the basic structure and orientation of the system remains unchanged—and there is little cause for optimism about the prospects for a quick change within the system.

What one has seen in the past three decades is expansion and an increasing sophistication of the educational system, particularly at the top. The accomplishments of Indian education and science have been impressive. Training of skilled personnel has been a necessary component of the building of one of the world's major industrial systems. India now exports technical personnel to many other Third World nations—and of course staffs a significant segment of the British medical service. Educational development has been in two rather contradictory directions. At the top, as indicated, there has been much growth in the size, scope and quality of the educational establishment. But, even here, one can notice a dual system in higher education. The mass of the colleges, many of which have been established in semi-rural areas, have fairly low academic standards and continue to focus on the traditional arts and science subjects, taught in the traditional way and examined through the much-criticized examination system of the affiliating universities. A much smaller, high quality segment of the post-secondary system has appeared in the metropolitan areas, frequently separate from the universities altogether. These institutions are often permitted to set their own examinations and offer their own degrees. The top tier of the post-secondary system have high international standards, usually in English, and feeds its graduates into the Indian elite or abroad.

At the level of primary and secondary education, expansion has not ended the significant inequalities within the school system. Again, the urban-based, frequently English-medium schools are generally the conduits to the prestige sector of the post-secondary educational system. The bulk of the educational system, and virtually all of the schools operating in the regional languages, do not articulate with the top sector of the higher education system. Thus, mobility is limited for the graduates of this sector of the educational system. There are gross inequalities in expenditure per pupil, in facilities, and in the quality of teachers among the segments of the education system.

While there has been much clamour for access to education by all segments of the Indian population, there has been remarkably little protest against the inequalities within the educational system or against the 'dead end' of much of the system in terms of employment. Most Indians seem satisfied, at least at present with the fact of access. That the schooling does not lead directly to the elite does not seem to be a source of discontent—education does have a payoff in incremental social mobility in many cases and even where this does not occur, it retains a significant measure of prestige, particularly in the rural areas.

Religious Traditions in Educational Policy

Katherine Young, referring to Arvind Sharma's paper on religion and education, raised the question of whether comparative religion should be taught in Indian schools. She said in part:

> Presumably Sharma agrees that the model of India as a secular state is here, and with good reason, to remain. Hence the presupposition of religious *neutrality* is the starting point for any discussion of religious education. Yet Dr. Sharma has shown on historical and logical grounds that religious neutrality has three possible definitions—*no*, *all*, and *general*. He has ruled out *no* religious education. Though he himself has not stated why, we may abstract reasons from the historical treatment that are pertinent—the need to foster tolerance given the dangers of communalism, the importance of values for a society, and the questions of identity and contribution to development, nationally and globally. His rejection of the view that each religion teaches students of its own persuasion no doubt was eliminated, as it was in the past, because it is not practically feasible. The remaining possibility is 'general religion'. While Dr. Sharma does not tell us why he prefers education in comparative religion to 'universal religion,' we may assume that he has heeded the warning that 'universal religion' may appear to be 'neo-Vedanta' to some, therefore an imposition of the religion akin to the majority (i.e., Hinduism) on the minorities or that it is syncretistic by definition and consequently not representative of any religion. The outcome is a decision to support the study of comparative religion in state-run educatioal institutions.

It should be pointed out, however, that the study of comparative religion does not *necessarily* foster tolerance, cultivate values, or preserve and 'progress' identity.

To the degree that the methodology of comparative religion as a discipline stresses *empathy* as a starting point and exercises *epoche* (bracketing out truth claims) as a way to understand each religion in its *own* terms, it is assumed that tolerance is an effect of such education. Yet it can be argued that if *epoche* itself is absolutized (i.e., if there is a failure to come to terms with the fact that religions do make truth claims, that such truth claims are usually central to the religion and provide the fulcrum by which the religious personality anchors faith in absolute/extra-historical realities to govern thought or confidence, action and emotion), then it does injustice to the religions and perhaps even denies the spiritual dynamic itself. This issue is particularly sensitive: Religion A claims that there is only *one* true path and the goal has certain features; religion B may acknowledge differences at the lower stage but argue that there is only a true path/goal at the higher stage; religion C may argue that there are many paths but one is preferred for some reason (accessibility, values, identity, etc.) while the goal is common to all. Obviously religion C appears to be the most tolerant but if this tolerance is not recognized there is a sense of betrayal: 'I accept you but you do not accept me.' Such a sense of betrayal, in turn, may breed intolerance. The latter model may also conceal in the language of tolerance and preference the very same religious dynamic that posits an absolute for ultimate meaning. In short, *empathy* and *epoche* are extremely valuable starting points for understanding and appreciating the world religions but failure to recognize the existence and dynamic of competing truth claims may obscure the very real differences that exist. Indeed, this is the greatest challenge to the study of religion today: to find a perspective that does justice to this inevitable tension and which is not reductionistic nor absolutistic. Location of such an intersection would allow one to dwell metaphorically *between* the historical and the absolute and to incorporate the positive aspects of both. And, as a corollary, one would dwell metaphorically *between* unity and difference, which means to live in freedom and responsibility, between the oneness and common values of humanity and the difference of world religions or, for that matter, today's many ideologies and worldviews. In short, *empathy* and *epoche* are useful tools but there are underlying issues that cannot be ignored if religious education is to foster a harmony where difference is acknowledged and the spiritual dynamic has its source and goal in the extra-historical or at least the superhuman. We need the best minds thinking about such issues so that comparative religion can play a true mediating role. In the meantime it is important not to obscure the complexity of the situation.

A second serious question is: How can the study of comparative religion help to cultivate moral and spiritual values, especially when one of the criticisms against comparative religion is that the methodology of *epoche* leads to a relativism of values, and one of the criticisms against 'universal religion' is that it leads to syncretism. Utmost care must be used to find ethical values that are truly universal to the religions of India and supportive of the values of modern India. This is not an impossible task but there are many pitfalls (e.g., if *ahimsa* is viewed as a universal value and not just common to Hinduism, Jainism and Buddhism and that too within certain limitations and with different interpretations). When it is not possible to establish exact correspondences, then it is necessary to locate where values have a common ground and build from there or to argue that new values are necessary for the modern age despite the tradition. Perhaps emphasis should be placed on the process rather than the content of ethical decision-making.

The question of identity and religious education is, perhaps, the most delicate of all. While a study of comparative religion may help one to become *informed* about one's tradition and how the various religions contributed to Indian history, identity ultimately has to be posed in 'Indic' terms rather than a specifically religious frame of reference. Like values, shared idioms are difficult to locate and minorities may quickly complain if they do not perceive identity in the same way. At the same time, it is a legitimate activity to discover as many common points of identity as possible. Shared space and history are the obvious starting points as are leaders from various religious groups who speak to the issue of a common past and a cooperation towards national unity.

Then, too, a study of comparative religion must always be in the context of a dialogue with the humanities and sciences which may describe and explain in purely human and physical terms. Too easy syncretistic solutions between religious and secular world-views may obscure the real insights that all have to offer or even prevent adequate use of the methodologies that lead to new knowledge. Bridges between the different intellectual domains must be built but at the same time there may be a need to recognize degrees of autonomy. This, too, belongs to the modern agenda of unity and difference where one must think metaphorically between nature and religion without allowing polarities to create insurmountable impasses in understanding and communication. At the same time, it is important not to develop such unity of thought that tensions are denied or ignored and with them the creative thrust to evolve is deadened.

In sum, comparative religion is probably the best starting point for religious education but, as the discipline now stands, it may not meet the hidden agendas of tolerance, values and identity and the larger agenda of models for understanding and living in 'unity and difference'. Theories and strategies need to be worked out and then adapted to the stages of child development (is there an Indian equivalent to Piaget and Kohlberg?) so that a student is gradually informed, cultivates important values, and matures in understanding the complexities of the issue of unity and difference. While recognition of spirituality may be a bonding factor in the Indian context, there should not be short thrift of other views.

Just as there are some problems involved in expecting the study of comparative religion to meet the various agendas of previous policy committees, so there is a problem with Sharma's suggestion that state-aided schools be allowed to impart 'religious education specific to a particular religion so that the cause of religious freedom be furthered and religious fanaticism eliminated'. There is no guarantee, however, that such a measure will eliminate religious fanaticism, given the fact that there are no controls on what is taught in the name of religious freedom. If it is argued that comparative religion be taught in state-run schools to foster tolerance, cultivate values and preserve and progress identity, then it could be argued that such a curriculum is also important for students in state-aided schools and that if, for the sake of religious freedom, religious education of their choice is to be allowed, that it should be *in addition* to the study of comparative religion.

Several years ago, I saw a cartoon in *The New Yorker* that cleverly depicted the alienation that can become habitual in one's line of work. The time was the mid-1960s when all America was, or seemed, abuzz with programs to build 'The Great Society'. Many departments had been created in the federal bureaucracy to eliminate poverty in America. In the cartoon, one tall, obviously overfed, well-dressed, high level federal civil servant at an opulent Washington party was responding to the question of another equally wealthy civil servant: 'I am with *Poverty* now,' he said with nary a facial expression that might reveal discomfort at the obvious contradiction. Academics organize and present papers at conferences and publish their articles, as we have done here. They are, no doubt, worthwhile activities. But academics interested in education have an obligation, it seems to me, to do more, i.e., to engage in praxis. Such engagement would help us develop theories that shape humane policies and which, in turn, can lead to real improvement in the lives of the people. True praxis, of course, also holds out the promise of better theory development. We hope that this book will make a significant, albeit small, contribution to the development of praxis.

Reference

MAKHIJA, INDRA. 1985. *High-Yielding Varieties of Wheat and Rice, Fertility and Schooling: Rural India.* Illinois: Institute of Technology (mimeo).

About the Contributors

Poromesh Acharya is Senior Research Staff at the Indian Institute of Management, Calcutta. He has published several papers and his research interests include education and agrarian relations.

Suma Chitnis is at present Professor and Head of the Unit for Research in the Sociology of Education, Tata Institute of Social Sciences, Bombay. She has written extensively on education, change and development. Books co-authored by her include *Papers in the Sociology of Education* (1967); *Field Studies in the Sociology of Education* (1970); and *The Indian Academic Profession: Crisis and Change in the Teaching Community* (1979). She has also written *A Long Way to Go....* (1980).

Joseph Di Bona is at present Associate Professor of Education, Duke University and Chairman of the Committee for the Program in Perspectives on Marxism and Society. His research interests vary widely from film criticism to the education of terrorists and racial segregation in the United States. His publications include *Change and Conflict in the Indian University* (1969); *One Teacher One School* (1983); and *Language Change and Modernization* (1970).

Ratna Ghosh is Associate Professor in the Department of Administration and Policy Studies in Education, McGill University, Montreal. She has previously served as Resident Director of the Shastri Indo-Canadian Institute, Delhi and is currently on its board of directors and a member of its Executive. Her publications are in

ABOUT THE CONTRIBUTORS

the areas of women's studies, multiculturalism, human rights and development education. At present she is doing research in Latin America.

Anrudh K Jain is Senior Associate and Deputy Director, International Programs of the Population Council, USA. He has had extensive experience in working with professionals and institutions in developing countries; in assessing the fertility impacts of development projects; in the analysis of and evaluation of family planning programmes; and in the demographic analysis of census and sample survey data. Books co-edited by him include *Fertility in Asia* and *Determinants of Infant Mortality in India*.

Krishna Kumar is Reader in the Department of Education, Delhi University, and also Fellow of the Nehru Museum and Library, Delhi. His publications include *Raj Samaj aur Shiksha* (1978); and *The Child's Language and the Teacher* (1986). He has also co-edited an anthology *Sociological Perspective in Education* (1985).

Vina Mazumdar is at present Member Secretary and Director of the Centre for Women's Development Studies, Delhi. She was formerly Director, Programme of Women's Studies, Indian Council of Social Science Research, Delhi and Member Secretary, Committee on the Status of Women in India. Her publications include *Education and Social Change: Studies in 19th Century Bengal*; and *Changing Status of Women in Contemporary and Recent History (since 1973)*.

Dinesh Mohan holds the State Bank Chair for Biomedical Engineering at the Indian Institute of Technology, Delhi. He completed his Master's in Bioengineering from the University of Michigan and has specialised in epidemiology and the biomechanics of injury. At present, he is doing research on road and agricultural injuries in India.

Moni Nag is at present Senior Associate of the Population Council's Centre for Policy Studies and Adjunct Professor of Anthropology at Columbia University. He has served as a consultant to the World Bank, WHO and other United Nations agencies. He has published numerous papers on the social and cultural aspects of human fertility and mortality. Books written by him include *Factors Affecting Fertility in Nonindustrial Societies* (1961).

Usha S Naidu is at present Professor and Head of the Unit for Child and Youth Research, Tata Institute of Social Sciences, Bombay. She has previously served as a consultant to the WHO. Dr Naidu has published several books and papers on problems and issues related to children, youth and social change, and has edited *Child Labour and Health: Problems and Prospects*.

A M Nalla Gounden is Professor of Economics, University of Madras. He was formerly Associate Professor at Jawaharlal Nehru University, New Delhi and has also been a consultant to the Planning Commission. His pioneering work in the area of economics of education has been widely quoted.

Iqbal Narain is Member-Secretary, Indian Council of Social Science Research, New Delhi. Among the various posts he has held during his career was that of Vice-Chancellor of Rajasthan and Banaras Hindu Universities. His research interests include Indian government and politics, state politics, rural politics and development administration. He has published numerous articles and books and is currently working on a book on Educational Administration in India.

Arvind Sharma is at present at the Department of Religious Studies, University of Sydney, Australia. His publications include *The Hindu Scriptural Value System and India's Economic Development* (1980); and has co-authored *Religious Ferment in Modern India* (1981). He obtained his doctoral degree from Harvard University in 1978.

R P Singh is Professor of Education, NCERT, New Delhi. Among the various posts he has held during his career was that of Joint Secretary in the Ministry of Education. He has published several books and papers on education; and was a Fulbright Fellow on Higher Education (1980).

Rajesh Tandon is Coordinator, Society for Participatory Research in Asia, New Delhi. He has worked in several educational and research institutions in India. He has also published numerous articles and books, and has written extensively on various issues including participatory research and training, rural development, social change, trade unions, and organising rural and urban poor.

ABOUT THE CONTRIBUTORS

Mathew Zachariah teaches comparative education and sociology of education in the Department of Educational Policy and Administrative Studies, University of Calgary, Canada. He was formerly president of the Comparative and International Education Society (USA) and was on the board of directors of the Shastri Indo-Canadian Institute, Delhi. At present he is on the advisory editorial board of *Comparative Education Review*. His publications include several papers and a book *Revolution Through Reform* (1986).